Paul Cropper has been researching animal mysteries [since] the age of fourteen, he became fascinated by [the] phenomenon.

Tony Healy's involvement began in 1969 at the age of 24, when he became obsessed with the sasquatch mystery while working in the forests of British Columbia.

Between them the authors have searched for water monsters, hairy giants, alien big cats and other semi-legendary animals in Fiji, North America, the Bahamas, Iceland, Scotland, Ireland, Nepal, Malaysia and every Australian state. They have also spent hundreds of hours sifting through newspaper archives and libraries for relevant historical material.

Since meeting while on the trail of the Kangaroo Valley panther in 1981, they have combined their files and shared all new information.

AUTHORS' NOTE:

The authors are always interested to hear of further mystery animal sightings. They can be contacted through Post Office Box 13, Croydon Park, NSW 2133.

OUT OF THE SHADOWS
MYSTERY ANIMALS OF AUSTRALIA

By Tony Healy and Paul Cropper

Line drawings by David Rowe and Gary Travis
Maps by Gordon Anderson

IRONBARK

Dedicated with great affection to
Eddie and Coralie Cropper and to Phil and Betty Healy

First published 1994 in Ironbark by Pan Macmillan Australia Pty Limited
63-71 Balfour Street, Chippendale

Copyright © Tony Healy and Paul Cropper 1994

All rights reserved. No part of this book may be reproduced or transmitted
in any form or by any means, electronic or mechanical, including
photocopying, recording or by any information storage and retrieval
system, without prior permission in writing from the publisher

National Library of Australia
cataloguing-in-publication data

Healy, Tony, 1945-
Out of the Shadows: Mystery Animals of Australia

ISBN 0 330 27499 6

1. Animals – Folklore – Australia. 2. Exotic animals – Australia. 3. Extinct animals – Australia. 4. Animals, Mythological – Australia. I. Cropper, Paul. II. Title.

001.9440994

Typeset and design by Brevier Design
Cover illustration by Barry Olive
Printed in Australia by McPherson's Printing Group

CONTENTS

INTRODUCTION

THE TASMANIAN TIGER   1

MAINLAND THYLACINES   21

ALIEN BIG CATS   55

THE QUEENSLAND MARSUPIAL TIGER   99

THE YOWIE   111

THE BUNYIP   159

A GLIMPSE INTO THE SHADOWS   181

INDEX   194

ACKNOWLEDGEMENTS

A great many people assisted us in our research and the preparation of this book. In particular, we would like to thank the following: Doris Blinman, the Bruem family, Bill Chalker, George Chaloupka, Peter Chapple, John Conn, Kevin Farley, Jason Follett, Linda Gibson, Lyall Gillespie, John Green, Colin Groves, Eric Guiler, Geoff Healy, Sue Healy, John Higgins, Olga Howell, Graham Joyner, Les Lewis, Bernie Mace, Peter Makeig, Nick Mooney, Barry Morris, Geoff and Vicki Nelson, Garth Nix, Henry Nix, Ray Noakes, Gary Opit, Kay Plunkett, Steve Rushton, Sid Slee, Christy Smith, Malcolm Smith, Percy Trezise, Bryan Walters, Merrilee Webb, Russ Wenholtz, Sharon West, Keith Zeinert.

We have attempted to contact all copyright owners of material used in the book, but this has not proved possible in every case. The publishers would be pleased to hear from any copyright holders who have not been acknowledged.

INTRODUCTION

Most Australians are familiar with the monster tradition of Loch Ness and with the bigfoot and yeti legends of North America and the Himalayas. It is not generally recognised, however, that Australia has produced six separate, distinct – and very well documented – animal mysteries of its own:

- **The thylacine (or Tasmanian tiger):** Did the 'tigers' really become extinct in 1936 or do they – as many eyewitnesses insist – continue to roam certain areas of the Tasmanian bush?
- **Mainland thylacines:** Thylacines are supposed to have become extinct on the mainland thousands of years ago. Do they – as much testimonial and some forensic evidence suggests – still exist in several remote areas?
- **Alien big cats:** Huge cat-like creatures have been reported from various corners of the country for over a hundred years. They have cut a bloody swathe through the flocks of many a grazier. Have feral cougars and leopards become established in the Australian bush or are the 'big cats' something else; perhaps the descendants of the prehistoric marsupial 'lion', *Thylacoleo*?
- **The Queensland marsupial tiger:** Were the North Queensland Aborigines and pioneers right: does a type of striped marsupial 'cat', the size of a hefty dog, lurk in the steamy jungles of Cape York?
- **The yowie:** Could these yeti-like ape-men – widespread in Aboriginal tradition and reported by hundreds of Europeans from the 1840s to the present day – possibly exist?
- **The bunyip:** These large, elusive, swamp and river dwelling creatures were believed in by all the Aborigines of southeastern Australia. They were allegedly seen by hundreds of white pioneers and are still occasionally reported today. Is the bunyip more than a legend?

In this book we examine all of these mysteries. We spell out the Aboriginal tradition, retell the stories handed down by the pioneers, examine chronological and geographical patterns, discuss photographic and forensic evidence, and present for your consideration dozens of sighting reports by modern eyewitnesses.

All of these creatures *might* be real but some, perhaps, are more likely to exist than others.

The Tasmanian tiger, though surrounded by mystery today, could be seen as the least 'far-out' of our semi-legendary beasts. The creature did, after all, undeniably exist up to at least 1936. Skulls, skins, skeletons and old movie film testify to that. At the other end of the scale the bunyip seems the most improbable of our mystery animals. Although eyewitness testimony was fascinating and in many ways quite consistent, and although the search for the bunyip has an interesting place in Australian history, it would be very difficult at this late stage to prove the creatures ever really existed.

This book, then, covers a range of mysteries: from the all-but-real Tasmanian tiger to the semi-mythical bunyip.

Between these two extremes lie the Queensland marsupial 'tiger', a creature so well documented that naturalists once listed it in standard works on Australian wildlife; the equally well documented 'cougars' and 'panthers'; the mainland thylacine, whose continued existence is hinted at by bones and other evidence, and the yowie, the existence of which is supported by a great deal of fascinating testimonial evidence.

If even one of these shadowy creatures

is proven to exist it would be seen as the zoological find of the century. If *none* of them exist the phenomenon of their being reported so consistently, in so many areas, over such a long period, should still be of great interest to historians, sociologists and psychologists.

Whether they be fact or fantasy, the ancient legends and modern reports discussed in this book are an important part of Australia's cultural heritage. At the very least they represent an area of Australian folklore – and folklore in the making – which has been sorely neglected and is deserving of serious study.

Out of the Shadows is the result of twenty years of joint research. Between us we have spent hundreds of hours in libraries, interviewed scores of witnesses and visited the reputed hunting grounds of many and various semi-legendary creatures in every state and territory.

We have devoted a good part of our lives to these mysteries and consider it time well spent. Our investigations have taken us into many strange and little-known corners of the country, we have met many interesting people and have gained many new perspectives on Australian history, on Australian natural history and on the Australian character.

Best of all, perhaps, the hunt has been a lot of fun!

We hope this book will inspire others to begin their own fieldwork or historical research. To assist them we have provided several maps plus comprehensive lists of source material.

In cryptozoology (the study of hidden animals) it is very important, of course, to keep an open mind and also, hopefully, a healthy scepticism. We believe, however, that in this strange business it is even more important to have a good sense of humour.

Over the years we have entertained several different theories about whether or not these creatures really exist, where they might come from and what they might be. We have had a lot of fun during our research and hunting forays, bouncing those ideas around, but in the tradition of Charles Fort – a pioneer in this field – we have always avoided coming to any rock-solid conclusions. We see ourselves primarily as collectors of data and as chroniclers of the mystery animals saga.

As the title suggests, our aim in writing this book is to bring all the ancient tradition and modern data relating to the Australian mystery animal phenomenon out of the shadows and into the light.

Some readers may conclude that the creatures in question are real, flesh and blood animals; some may decide the phenomenon is largely psychological in origin; others may come to even stranger conclusions.

We believe, however, that anyone who reads this book thoroughly must at least acknowledge that – whether or not the creatures themselves are real – the phenomenon of their being reported by sincere people from antiquity down to the present day definitely *is* genuine.

Something funny is going on – and has been for a long, long time.

Out of the Shadows is twenty years of research put into as coherent a form as we can manage. These are the facts as we know them. Please make up your own minds.

Chapter One

THE TASMANIAN TIGER

THE TASMANIAN TIGER

The island of Tasmania is one of the world's more pleasant places. It is fertile, scenic, peaceful, uncrowded, unhurried; it has a cool climate, an historic, marvellously sited capital and many picturesque villages. It has orchards, trout-filled lakes, snow-capped mountains, hundreds of miles of green rural land, and, in the southwest, one of the world's last great wildernesses.

In the troubled late twentieth century world the island state is, with its natural beauty and friendly, easygoing people, a great place to visit and a nice place to live. This, however, was not always the case. In fact, when one reads of the crimes which were committed there against man and nature in the nineteenth and early twentieth centuries it seems almost unbelievable that a place with such an horrific past could have evolved into the pleasant haven it is today.

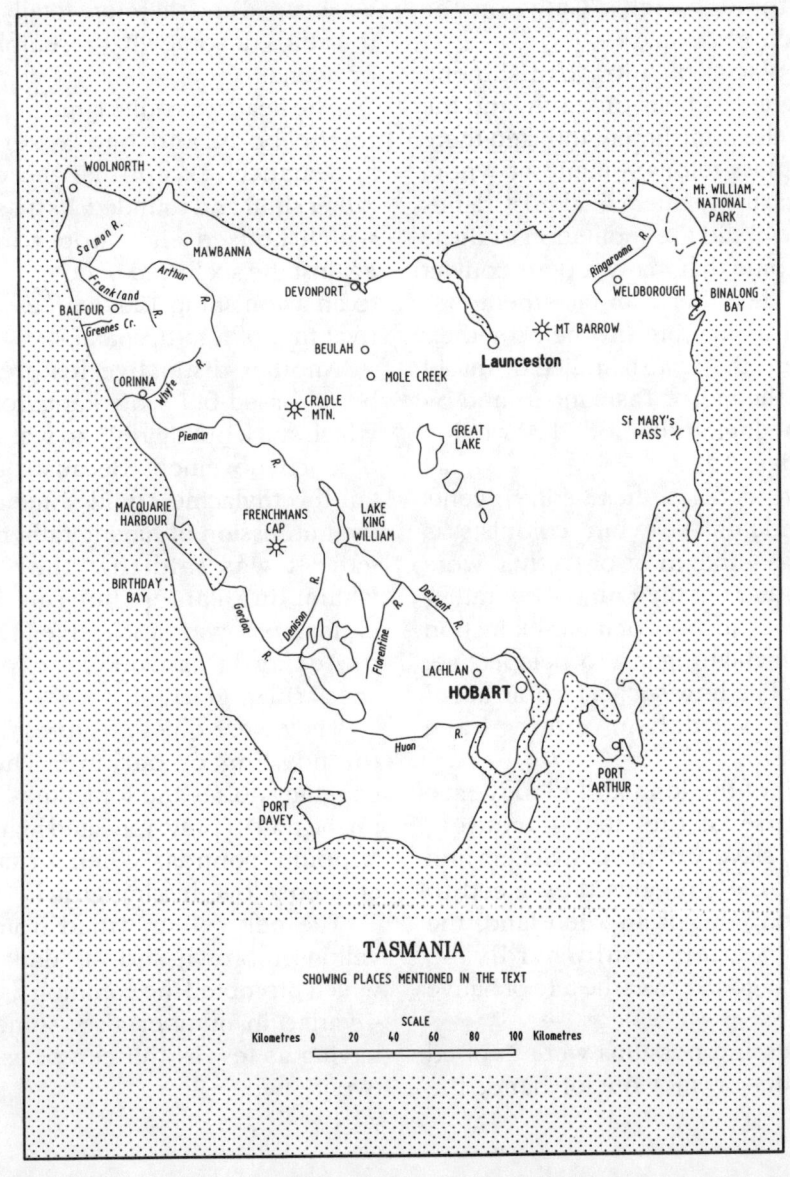

TASMANIA
SHOWING PLACES MENTIONED IN THE TEXT

From 1642, when it was discovered by Dutch mariners, until 1854, Tasmania was known as Van Diemen's Land, but between the time of the first British settlement in 1803 and the end of the convict era it might well have been called 'Demons Land'.

Life was nasty, brutal, and often short, in all of Britain's antipodean gulags, but bad as things were for convicts on the Australian mainland conditions in Van Diemen's Land were generally worse. Worse still were the places set aside for secondary punishment: Port Arthur on the east coast and infamous Macquarie Harbour, through Hell's Gates on the godforsaken west.

These places of 'ultra banishment' were designed as hells-on-earth, and the severity of the punishment inflicted there on the hapless felons – many of whom were political prisoners – almost defies belief. So evil did the reputation of these places become that many a poor convict chose suicide rather than face them.

As well as making life hell for their countrymen, the British inflicted untold misery on the native Tasmanians and by 1876 not a single fullblooded Aborigine was left alive.

We have detailed these sorry events not to condemn the white colonists as brutal thugs – like most of us they were simply products of their time – but rather to put the extinction or near-extinction of the Tasmanian tiger into perspective: to help explain how such a terrible act of ecological vandalism could have occurred.

Because of the long and bloody race war, because of the near-starvation, sadism and slavery of the convict era and because of the struggles they faced to carve a living out of an alien land, the European settlers could hardly be expected to agonise over the fate of native animals.

Wallabies and possums were trapped for their furs or shot out of hand; the hundreds of thousands of elephant seals which lived along the coast were almost annihilated; by 1865 the last Tasmanian emu was slain and by about the same time the Tasmanian tiger was well on the road to extinction.

The Tasmanian tiger *(Thylacinus cynocephalus)* was the world's largest carnivorous marsupial. The animal measured up to two metres in length, 60 centimetres (2 feet) in height and could weigh up to 35 kilograms (77 lbs). The skin of one exceptional individual was recorded as measuring seven feet nine inches (2.36 m) from nose to tail. Although a marsupial and therefore totally unrelated to canids, it somewhat resembled a wolf or hyena.

The head was quite large in proportion to the body and had a very canine appearance, except that the ears were rather short and rounded. Its massive jaws, which housed eight upper incisors as against the six found in dogs, could open to an astonishing 120 degrees: a gape to rival that of a rattlesnake.

Another distinctive feature was the broad-based but long, kangaroo-like tail which stuck out rigidly and was incapable of much movement. Because of this rigid tail the thylacine could sometimes give the impression of having rather a clumsy gait. It was said that they ran in a 'shambling canter' but this apparent clumsiness was deceptive; they were quite agile animals, capable of spectacular, graceful leaps.

They were quiet creatures, not noted for howling or barking. They made coughing noises and sometimes, when hot on the trail of prey, repeated high-pitched, 'yipping' sounds. When irritated they emitted a low, hissing growl.

The pelt colour varied from grey to yellowish-brown and the dark stripes – which prompted the common name 'tiger' – varied in number also: some animals having as few as thirteen or as many as twenty-two.

THE TASMANIAN TIGER

The first stripe was usually in the vicinity of the shoulder and others crossed the back and rump right down to the base of the tail. Faint rings could sometimes be seen further down the tail. Females carried up to four newborn cubs in a pouch which – presumably to prevent snagging on undergrowth – opened to the rear.

The tiger's feet were fairly distinctive. Unlike the narrow triangular 'palm' of a dog's foot, the thylacine's 'palms' were broad, well-upholstered and creased by three deep grooves. There were five clawed toes on the front feet, but because the innermost one was slightly raised it was observed by trackers only in very soft ground.

The rear feet were also quite unusual: in addition to four toes and the creased 'palm' they had a long heel which sometimes showed up in tracks. These heel imprints sometimes occurred because the angle between the heel and the rest of the foot was very acute in the tiger's hind legs – much more than in those of a dog. Film of the last captive thylacine shows the creatures could use their long heels and powerful tails to stand erect like their relative the kangaroo.

During the colonial era it was often said the creatures could, when cornered by dogs, not only rear up but also jump around like kangaroos. Experts are now divided on this point.

Because few people bothered to study the thylacines while they were relatively plentiful, little is known today of their behaviour in the wild.

Most old trappers agreed that the creatures were not particularly fleet of foot. Some said they lay in wait for their prey but most said they tracked their quarry by scent and, travelling at a steady trot, relentlessly ran it down. Once locked on to a scent they were very hard to shake: they would plunge right into the icy waters of lakes in pursuit of their victims.

Having analysed its brain structure, Dr

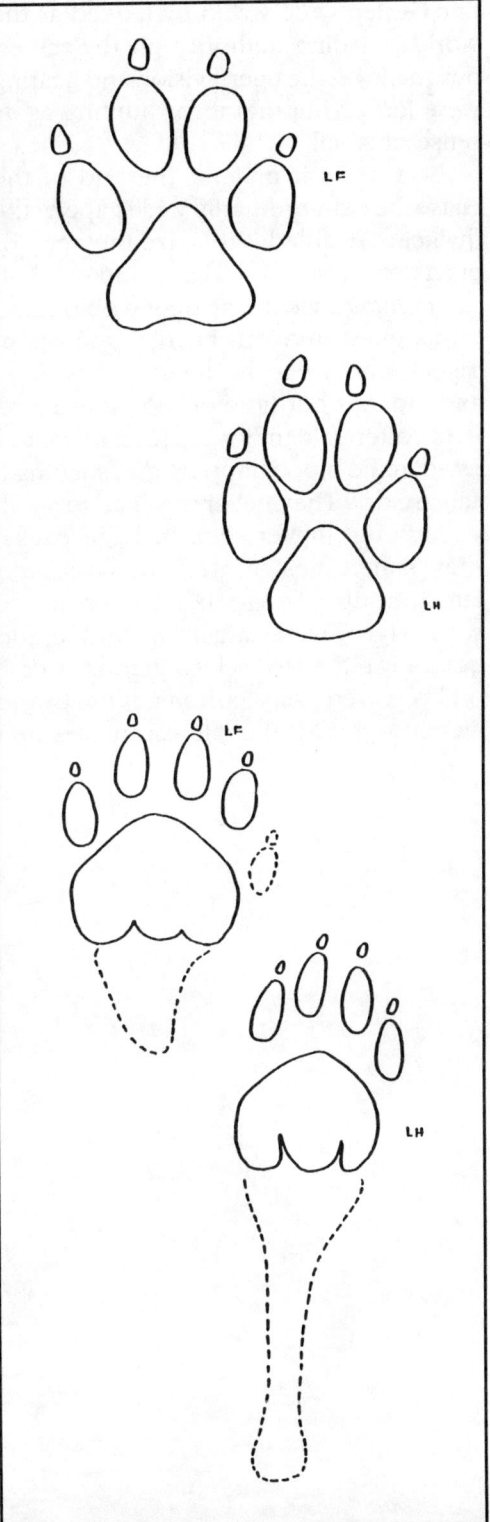

Thylacine tracks (above) compared to those of a domestic dog (top).

Eric Guiler, widely acknowledged as the world's leading authority on thylacines, now believes the tiger's vision and hearing were just as important for hunting as its sense of smell.

Be that as it may, at the end of the chase the extraordinarily wide gape of the thylacine enabled it to seize the neck or even the chest of a wallaby and crush it. After felling a victim the tiger would stand on its chest and rip the rib cage open. Tigers would eat the heart, lungs, liver and kidneys but little of the other meat. It was often said they were primarily interested in the blood, lapping and sucking a carcase dry. They never returned to a kill.

Although never seen in large packs, they sometimes hunted in pairs, and family groups of up to six were sometimes seen. Tigers were largely nocturnal and generally retired to rocky outcrops by day.

They were very curious animals and were often said to circle camp sites and to trail bushmen for miles through the scrub.

There are a very small number of accounts of unprovoked attacks on humans. Thylacines were generally not aggressive at all and would usually fight dogs only when cornered. Even when trapped in snares or pits they were remarkably passive.

Thylacines inhabited virtually every part of Tasmania in precolonial times, but the fact that only four were caught in the first seventeen years of European settlement indicates they were never particularly numerous.

Although the tiger (also known in those days as the 'zebra-wolf', 'zebra-opossum', 'hyena' and 'tiger-wolf') was at first perceived as a harmless curiosity it soon became, in the eyes of the Europeans, a terrible menace: a threat to the colony's shaky economy. This came about because of the explosive growth

The thylacine could use its long heels and powerful tail to stand erect, like its relative the kangaroo.

of the Tasmanian wool industry during the 1820s and 1830s, when the number of sheep in the colony swelled from 200,000 to over one million and sheep farming spread towards the centre of the island. The tigers found mutton very much to their taste and apparently increased in numbers in response to the new abundance of prey.

Dr Guiler now believes most of the stock predation was actually the work of feral dogs, but the great majority of nineteenth century graziers were certain thylacines were responsible.

By the 1820s the creatures were being shot on sight and in 1830 the slaughter became organised when a large pastoral firm, the Van Diemen's Land Company, offered a bounty for each tiger scalp brought in. In 1888, after much pressure from graziers who claimed tigers were killing 30–40,000 sheep annually, the Tasmanian government offered its own bounty of one pound per adult tiger.

During the next 21 years 2898 bounties were paid by the government and the Van Diemen's Land Company. There is also evidence that considerable numbers of pelts and live animals were sold to foreign animal traders during that period.

The relentless attrition had the desired effect and by 1909, when the government bounty scheme was terminated, the thylacine had become a very rare animal indeed.

Tigers continued to be caught occasionally in snares set for wallabies or possums and no thylacine snared accidentally was ever released. A grotesque, superstitious custom among bush dwellers of nailing tiger skulls to barn doors reflected the callous attitudes which prevailed.

Another factor may have combined with shooting and trapping to decimate the thylacines. Wildlife authority Dr Bob Brown, MP and others have suggested an illness related to distemper, which apparently killed a great many quolls and Tasmanian devils at the turn of the century, may have delivered a crushing blow to the already hard-pressed tiger population.

Evidence that Australian and foreign zoologists were conscious of the thylacines' rarity after 1909 can be seen in the prices paid for live specimens. In 1910 one was bought locally for eight pounds, in 1917 the price had risen to twenty pounds and in 1926 London Zoo paid 150 pounds for a female.

Incredible as it seems today, the Tasmanian government, in spite of the obvious rarity of the animals, allowed their continued slaughter and by 1930 the hapless marsupials had practically disappeared. The last confirmed shooting of a tiger – by farmer Wilf Batty – occurred at Mawbanna in May 1930, and in 1933 in the Florentine Valley, Elias Churchill trapped what may have been the island's last wild tiger.

On 14 July 1936 the Tasmanian government finally outlawed the trapping or shooting of tigers. The timing was almost perfect: just two months later, on 7 September, 'Benjamin', the animal trapped by Mr Churchill three years earlier – and quite possibly the last thylacine on planet Earth – died a lonely death at the Hobart Domain Zoo.

After the horse – not to mention the elephant seals, emus and thylacines – had bolted, the government decided to close the barn door. In 1937 it was proposed a wide area of southwestern Tasmania should be set aside as a wildlife refuge. In that year and in 1938 expeditions were sent out to make a general assessment of the area and to search for traces of tigers.

During both trips expedition members, including the noted bushman Trooper Arthur Fleming, reported the discovery of many clear thylacine tracks. They made a cast of one 'exceptionally good' track, which is now lodged in the Tasmanian Museum and Art Gallery. On the basis of the evidence Tasmanian naturalist Michael

Members of the 1937-38 expeditions reported the discovery of many clear thylacine tracks.

Sharland decided the creatures were at that time, though greatly reduced in numbers, 'fairly well distributed over the western and southwestern parts of Tasmania ...'.

Despite the promising signs found by the experts in 1937 and 1938 and despite a few claims of tiger sightings by laymen during the late 1930s, no concrete evidence of the creature's continued existence emerged. Because of this the Victorian naturalist David Fleay obtained, in 1945 and 1946, permission to set traps at various places on the west coast.

Although they tried every kind of snare and baited their traps with live sheep, wallabies, possums and other toothsome delights, the 1945–46 expeditioners didn't so much as glimpse a tiger. Like the previous searchers, however, they claimed to have found fresh, unmistakable tiger tracks.

Despite the track finds, a few sighting reports by bushmen and the possible cry of a thylacine which he heard along the Old Frenchman's Track, Fleay was not optimistic about the tiger's chances of surviving much longer. The cause of his concern was the wholesale trapping of possums and wallabies which had begun in the southwest in 1941.

Although the trappers were not actually hunting thylacines their activities posed a serious threat to the tigers' food supply. Worse than this was their quite legal practice of laying poison baits for Tasmanian devils, quolls, feral cats and any other carnivores which might damage the skins of the trapped animals.

Although trapping for furs and the associated baiting was eventually banned, any tigers which may have continued to eke out a living into the 1950s were confronted with yet another threat to their existence. Throughout the 1950s, 1960s and into the 1980s the use of 1080 poison was allowed for rabbit control and, although they normally ate only freshly-killed meat, the surviving tigers would have been at some risk during that time of ingesting poison at second-hand.

The late Adye Jordan, a veteran

bushman, suspected Tasmanian devils of playing a part in the tigers' decline.

Though much smaller than the thylacine, the devil would be quite capable of preying on tiger pups left alone while the mother was hunting. Mr Jordan saw evidence of this in the 1920s when the devils were quite rare, and he pointed out that in recent decades the fierce little creatures seem to have experienced a population explosion.

It occurs to us, also, that in recent times thylacines must have been under considerable pressure from feral dogs which, after 190 years of European settlement, now roam almost every part of the island.

Despite the wholesale shooting in earlier days, the trapping and poisoning, the flooding of large areas of bushland for hydro-electric projects and the absence of any concrete proof, many scientists and laymen are still convinced of the thylacines' continued existence.

Given the absence of hard evidence such as a fresh carcase, live specimen or clear photograph, the optimism of the believers seems to many sceptics to be misplaced. Essentially, all they have to back their belief in the tigers' existence is 'soft' evidence: the testimony of people who claim to have seen live tigers since 1936.

While eyewitness testimony may be viewed as low-quality evidence, the *quantity* of such evidence is quite impressive. In his excellent research report *The Tasmanian Tiger – 1980*, National Parks and Wildlife Service (NPWS) scientist Steven Smith listed 315 claims of tiger sightings between 1936 and 1980. The total number of reports now exceeds 400.

Surprisingly, Europeans never successfully introduced the fox to Tasmania. However, since many thousands of domestic dogs have gone feral since 1803 it seems likely that at least some tiger reports have been the result of misidentification.

Bull terriers, greyhounds, great danes and other medium to large dogs sometimes have a brindle pattern which can give the impression of faint stripes and this has confused some witnesses. Researcher Jeremy Griffith once rushed to the Launceston tip where an old man claimed to have trapped a tiger – it turned out to be a greyhound.

Other reports may have been the result of hallucinations caused by driver fatigue and some, of course, have been hoaxes.

The Tasmanian devil

The Tasmanian devil (*Sarcophilus harrisi*) is a small, stocky, bear-like marsupial scavenger. Its common name derives from its widely gaping jaws, large teeth and feisty temperament.

The body is black with a single white band across the chest and sometimes a white patch near the rump. The animal grows to about the size of a fox-terrier, the head and body being a maximum of 70 centimetres [28 inches] in length, plus a 30 centimetre [12-inch] tail.

The creature looks nothing like a thylacine. Confusion does sometimes arise, however, simply because the common names 'Tasmanian devil' and 'Tasmanian tiger' are rather similar.

Also, as mentioned elsewhere, the footprints of large devils have sometimes been taken for those of young thylacines.

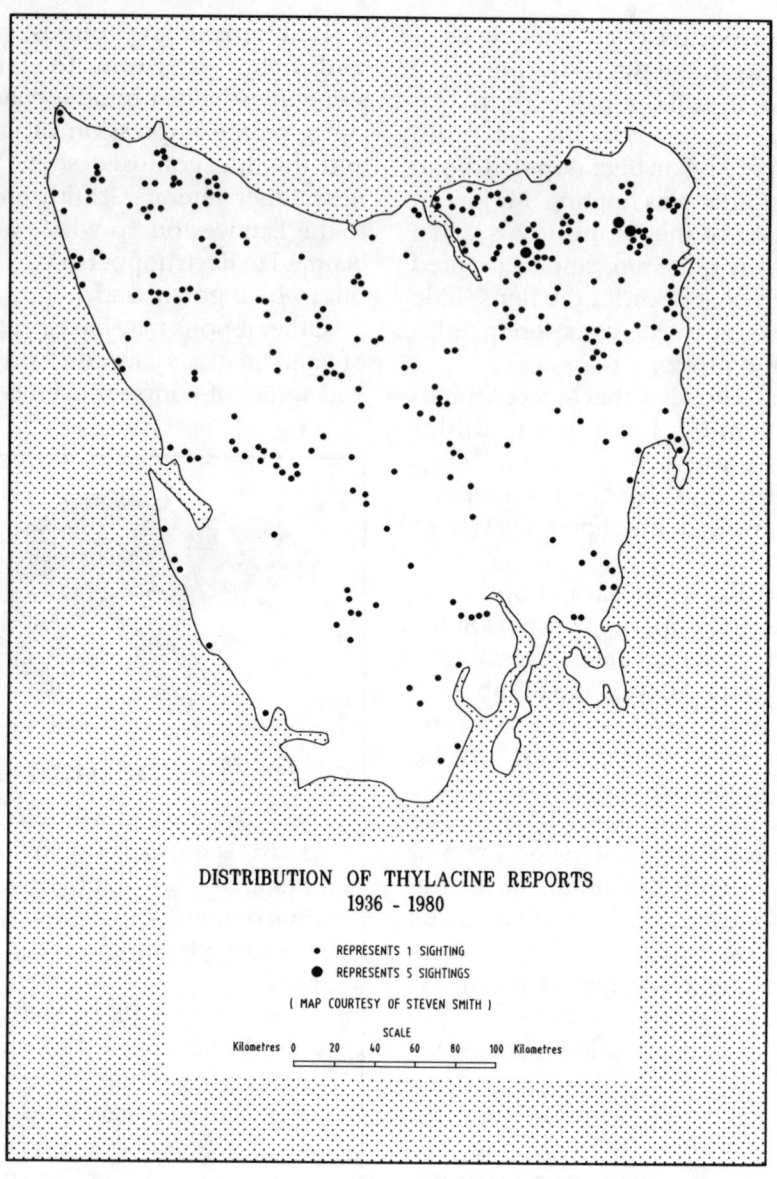

DISTRIBUTION OF THYLACINE REPORTS
1936 - 1980

• REPRESENTS 1 SIGHTING
● REPRESENTS 5 SIGHTINGS

(MAP COURTESY OF STEVEN SMITH)

One tiger story, which appeared at first to be quite substantial and which attracted a great deal of media attention, later became clouded with confusion and uncertainty. The incident allegedly occurred at Sandy Cape on the west coast.

One night in August 1961 two fisherman, Bill Morrison and Laurie Thompson, were awakened in their isolated camp by an animal which was rummaging in their bait bucket. Reports varied somewhat, but the general drift was that Thompson clubbed it to death with a piece of wood. Morrison described the creature as '... about the size of a kelpie dog, standing about 18 inches to 20 inches high, and about 2ft 6in long, excluding the tail. The tail was rigid. The animal's coat was dark and I could discern only one stripe behind the shoulders and extending around the chest'. The two men claimed the carcase later mysteriously disappeared from their camp.

Although the carcase could not be

produced, the Sandy Cape incident was often put forward – even by respected scientists such as Desmond Morris – as 'proof' of the thylacine's continued existence. Morrison was always quite adamant that the creature was a thylacine, but some years later Thompson admitted the unfortunate creature had been a home-and-garden variety Tasmanian devil.

Because hoaxes and cases of mistaken identity have certainly occurred, we feel it would be a little rash to declare absolute belief in the thylacine's survival. However, after reading through all the recorded reports and ruthlessly discarding any which seem in any way dubious, all but the most sceptical of researchers have been left with a hard core of reports which seem almost impossible to explain away.

Steven Smith concluded that 103 of the 315 sightings reported between 1936 and 1980 could be classified as 'good'.

It is often assumed that most alleged tiger sightings have been of a fleeting nature, taken place at night and involved people of low credibility. Smith's data suggests otherwise. He found that 44 per cent of sightings lasted for more than one minute and that in 36 per cent of cases the observer was within ten metres of the animal.

As one would expect with a nocturnal animal, most sightings were made at night when the creatures were caught in headlight beams. Almost one third, however, occurred in broad daylight. In just under 50 per cent of reports more than one witness was involved. In seven instances the witnesses were policemen.

Ninety-five per cent of reports mention a single animal but up to five tigers have been seen together in family groups. One report involved an adult with four cubs and another two adults with three cubs.

To an outsider, it would seem logical to expect that thylacine sightings would occur most frequently in or on the fringes of the great southwestern wilderness. The statistics, however, show a different pattern. While some reports have come from the southwest, most have come from the north and in particular the northeast of the island. This unexpected distribution of sightings can be fairly easily explained: the southwest wilderness, though vast, is mainly very poor, unproductive sedgeland and forest, incapable of sustaining great numbers of the animals thylacines used to prey on.

Another consideration is this: whereas the southwest of the state is practically uninhabited, almost 50 per cent of the state's population lives close to the north coast. Where there are no witnesses there can be no reports. It seems likely, in fact, that thylacines and rural people just happen to prefer the same kind of habitat. The thylacine was never really a forest animal. While it liked to retreat to the forested hills, it preferred to hunt in reasonably open, productive country.

It is important to point out that the mere presence of potential witnesses does not automatically produce a greater number of sighting claims: the southeastern area, which includes Hobart and about half of the state's population, has produced only a handful of reports.

Although the major national parks and wilderness areas are in the southwest, large areas of bushland occur over much of Tasmania. Thylacine enthusiasts, pointing out that in the nineteenth century the tiger was common through the north and northeast, believe small but viable populations exist in several different areas of its old range. The two greatest concentrations of post-1936 reports are around Weldborough, near the headwaters of the Ringarooma River to the southwest of Mt William National Park, and in an area roughly centred on Mt Barrow, only 25 kilometres east of Launceston.

As mentioned earlier, eyewitness reports were collected by David Fleay and others in the years immediately following the demise of the last captive tiger in 1936.

These reports are interesting because in the 1930s and 1940s the tiger had not yet achieved the semi-legendary status which may have affected the judgement of more recent witnesses.

In an article in Australia's *Wild Life* magazine in June 1946, David Fleay gave a vivid account of an incident which occurred two years earlier:

Mick Tiffin, road patrolman for the Cardigan River ... took me to the scene ... a great fallen tree butt with a sheltered cavity at its base. Mr Tiffin had been crosscutting this fallen warrior for firewood and as the last section fell he was frightened out of his wits by a 'tiger' which jumped out from the cavity ... uttered a husky cry and bounded into the scrub. The scare was mutual. From the description of size, this thylacine was undoubtedly a young specimen.

In December 1947, B. Thorpe and A. Woolley of Huonville had a close encounter with what appeared to be a tiger near the Denison River in the southwest. The creature, which appeared to be in pursuit of a wallaby, passed within twenty yards of the bushmen. Woolley described it as '... a sort of grizzled, grey colour, with stripes on the lower part of its back'. The sighting occurred in broad daylight – at 7 am – and in lightly timbered country.

In February 1949 Mr Lovell, a Huon Valley farmer, nearly trod on a large striped animal which '... turned quickly, making a growling noise and leapt over the gate. What convinced me at the time that it was a tiger was that my dog, which had never been bluffed before, would not tackle it'.

In all, Steven Smith documented 36 sightings between 1936 and 1950.

One of Tasmania's best-known bushmen, Charles Abel, who had seen many tigers along the Gordon River in his youth, reported seeing an adult and two cubs in 1955. 'I couldn't mistake them,' he said. 'They shambled off into the bush.'

Two rather interesting air-to-ground sightings occurred in 1957. In January of that year, Australian National Airlines (ANA) pilot Jim Ferguson and two passengers spotted from their helicopter a tawny, striped, German shepherd-sized animal trotting along Birthday Bay beach on the west coast. Ferguson particularly noted the animal's long tail which stuck straight out in classic thylacine style.

Because he often flew over the same area, Captain Max Holyman, another ANA pilot, decided to pack a camera in his helicopter. About a week later he spotted what he assumed was the same animal and swooped his machine down to seven metres. As he chased the animal around a sand dune his passenger, helicopter chief I. Grabowsky, took several photographs.

Predictably, perhaps, the quality of the pictures is not good. The creature they show *might* be a thylacine but it looks somewhat too shaggy. It is probably a feral dog.

Encouraged by the eyewitness reports, by sheep and wallabies killed in a way reminiscent of tiger predation and by supposedly thylacine-like tracks found in 1957, some experts, including Dr Guiler, remained convinced in the late 1950s that the thylacine was not yet extinct.

In one of the ironies of the thylacine saga it was the Sandy Cape fiasco of 1961 which finally persuaded the state government to finance a serious search for proof of the animal's continued existence. Between October 1963 and May 1964, using a one thousand pound grant, a team led by Dr Guiler set thousands of leg snares at Greenes Creek near Sandy Cape, around Woolnorth in the far northwest and around Balfour. The expedition caught no thylacines but they found 'probable' tiger tracks and Dr Guiler remained convinced that small numbers of the animals survived.

Since 1964 more than a dozen privately sponsored groups have set out in search of thylacines. Between 1968 and 1972 Trowutta dairy farmer James Malley and Sydney zoology student Jeremy Griffith, assisted by corporate sponsors and the Australian Conservation Foundation, drove thousands of miles of back roads, trod many mountain trails and combed remote beaches all up and down the wild west coast. They also deployed several homemade camera monitors in apparent tiger hot-spots in the northwest.

The herculean efforts of Malley and Griffith – and of Dr Bob Brown, who provided a great deal of assistance – surely deserved success.

To their immense frustration, however, the thylacines managed to elude them completely. Their automatic cameras, when they functioned at all, photographed only more common animals and they were not lucky enough to happen across a single tiger in the flesh.

Their efforts did, however, achieve limited success in two important areas: Malley found paw prints near the northwestern settlement of Beulah in May 1971 which, though not perfectly clear, were similar to old illustrations of tiger tracks, and through appeals for information he and Griffith gathered about 120 previously unrecorded sighting reports.

By late 1972, despite the testimony of so many eyewitnesses (who he reluctantly decided must all have been mistaken) the badly disillusioned Griffith concluded the thylacine could no longer exist. Bob Brown concurred, but Malley, his hopes buoyed by photographs of thylacine-like tracks taken on the west coast in January 1973, remained optimistic.

Other impressive efforts were made in 1979–80 by a Tasmanian NPWS team partly financed by the World Wildlife Fund, and in the winter of 1984 by wildlife park operator Peter Wright who conducted, by helicopter, a search of the state's remote snow fields.

A sustained effort was also made by David Watts, a professional wildlife photographer who, in the late 1980s, scoured the back blocks setting camera traps and interviewing witnesses. Still active after several years is 60-year-old grazier Ned Terry who, recognising that a big percentage of all sightings have been made from vehicles, patrols bush tracks at night with a permanently operating video camera bolted to the bull-bar of his four-wheel drive.

He is now too old to go on long expeditions, but veteran hunter Dr Eric Guiler still occasionally ventures into the bush. Although recognised as the world's leading thylacine authority, the feisty Irish-Australian has had to endure, over the years, considerable ridicule from certain colleagues on the mainland. He remains undaunted: 'Bugger them,' he says. On that great day when someone finally gets a tiger photograph he will take it to those sceptics and gleefully 'shove it up their arses'.

Despite the mighty efforts of Dr Guiler and the other tiger hunters, it cannot be denied that, as Bob Brown says, there has been no indisputable evidence of the creature's existence since 1936. It might therefore be a good idea at this point to break down what evidence there is – both positive and negative – into categories and attempt to assess its worth.

Tiger tracks

As mentioned earlier, the tiger's feet were in many ways rather unique. But while their footprints, when clearly reproduced on paper, seem markedly different from those of other animals, in the bush things are not so simple.

The Tasmanian devil's feet are rather large for the animal's small size. The forefoot of a large devil on hard ground, where the thumb and rear of the pad may not show, can leave a decidedly thylacine-like print.

Dog tracks (which can vary greatly

from breed to breed) cause many false alarms and even the forefeet of small wombats on hard ground have fooled experienced bushmen.

Even after taking these difficulties into account, several reports of footprint finds since 1936 sound fairly convincing.

Because Trooper Fleming and Michael Sharland had, presumably, both seen and tracked the creatures prior to 1936, it would seem likely the paw prints they identified as tiger tracks in 1937 and 1938 really were made by thylacines. Since David Fleay was, in his day, one of the most highly-regarded naturalists in Australia, it would also seem likely that the tracks he found in 1946 were real.

It may be worth noting that although Fleay spent much more time in the field than the 1937–38 expeditioners, he found fewer tracks than they did. This suggests the tiger population may have dramatically declined in the intervening decade. Since 1946, tracks have become, it seems, increasingly harder to find and those which are discovered are never quite clear enough to convince sceptics of the creatures' existence.

We have not seen photos or plaster casts of the tracks found by James Malley at Beulah in 1971, or of the January 1973 tracks which he found so encouraging, but since his own long-time partner Jeremy Griffith found them unconvincing it seems they could not have been particularly clear.

Other supposed tiger tracks have been reported by very highly qualified people. Alan Fox, chief wildlife officer with the Tasmanian NPWS, was certain he found thylacine tracks in 1950. In 1970 John Simmons, one of Tasmania's leading naturalists, photographed twenty metres of 'fresh and clear' tracks in the damp sand of Swimcart Beach near Binalong Bay. 'They were unmistakable,' he insisted.

Peter Wright, owner of the Tasmanian Wildlife Park at Mole Creek, made what was said by some to be the best modern footprint find on a high button-grass plain near Cradle Mountain in February 1981. While trying to free their bogged vehicle, Peter and his wife Judy stumbled across a long line of tracks and made a cast of the best imprint. It looks rather non-canine, but while it resembles illustrations of thylacine tracks it seems more 'fleshy' and therefore does not appear a perfect match.

Although it was declared thylacine-like by Dr Bob Green of Launceston's Queen Victoria Museum, Peter Wright's paw print – and all the other tracks found since 1936 – have done little to win over the more stubborn sceptics.

Nick Mooney is the government research officer whose duty it is to document and investigate new thylacine reports. He attempts to check out the scene of each new sighting and has spent many months combing the bush in the vicinity of particularly interesting reports. Although he would like above anything else to see proof of the tiger's survival, he has never seen tracks which he feels are definitely the real thing.

To his eye the 'exceptionally good' track cast by Fleming and Sharland in 1937 is '*very* wombat-like'. He also feels that the cast made by James Malley in 1971 and those made by Dr Guiler at Woolnorth are not terribly convincing. The 1981 Peter Wright cast, he declares flatly, 'is *not* thylacine'.

Photographic evidence

Apart from Mr Grabowsky, whose 1957 picture was too unclear to be of any value, no one has photographed a tiger in Tasmania since 1936. Given the number of camera traps which have been set up over the years, the absence of thylacine photographs could be seen as strong evidence that they are now extinct. Up to 1933 the tigers were, after all, not noted for their skill in avoiding traps.

Wildlife photographer Dave Watts pointed out, however, that since it took him eighteen months to get a picture of a feral cat, which are common, it is not remarkable that no one has obtained pictures of tigers. It is also worth noting that while the seventeen cameras Steven Smith's team deployed in 1980 photographed 364 Tasmanian devils and many other native animals, feral dogs – the creatures whose lifestyle is presumably most similar to thylacines – managed to completely avoid the cameras.

The absence of road kills

Since a large percentage of all reported tiger sightings have been made from motor vehicles, and since cars have killed thousands of other native animals, it does seem a bit unreasonable that not a single tiger has been run over and killed since 1936. Dr Guiler has been expecting such an occurrence for years but, so far, it has never happened. Steven Smith, however, mentions several near misses and one case in which a tiger supposedly hobbled into the bush after being bowled over by a car.

In 1978 tiger hunter Chris Tangey claimed that, seven years earlier, a motorist ran over and killed a thylacine on St Mary's Pass but hid the body for fear of being prosecuted. The driver supposedly changed his mind a month later and reported the matter to the Tasmanian NPWS, which then recovered the remains.

The department has denied the claim and it is, indeed, difficult to imagine why the agency would want to cover up such an incident, even if it could.

In fact, if a tiger was lying dead beside the road for a month there would be virtually no remains, short of devil dung, to recover. Devils are the vacuum cleaners of the Tasmanian bush. Thanks to them few carcases, no matter how large, are recognisable after one night in the open – let alone thirty.

Quite apart from the alleged St Mary's Pass incident, the devil's appetite for carrion could well explain why thylacine carcases are never found anywhere else in the Tasmanian bush.

Tigers shot or trapped since 1936

In early 1949 veteran tiger hunter Adye Jordan was employed by the eminent naturalist Sir Edward Hallstrom to trap a pair of tigers in the hope of starting a breeding program at Sydney's Taronga Park Zoo. The brief expedition ended in February 1949 when the Tasmanian Fauna Board abruptly cancelled the trapping permit.

Many years later, however, Mr Jordan claimed that six days after the permit was cancelled he caught a young female thylacine. Angry at the bureaucracy and uncertain of his legal position, he released the animal. Four days later he found what was apparently the same thylacine in another of his pits – and released her again.

Since spotlight shooting of rabbits, possums and other creatures is a widespread practice in Tasmania it would seem reasonable to expect that if they still roam the bush someone would sooner or later shoot a tiger, if only by accident.

Like most other investigators, we have received second-hand reports of tigers being shot more recently than 1936. These stories, which usually involve the supposed destruction of the carcase by a farmer who fears prosecution, have so far proved impossible to verify. It is usually difficult even to establish the name of the person involved.

In his definitive work *Thylacine: The Tragedy of the Tasmanian Tiger*, Eric Guiler remarks that he has reason to 'strongly suspect' that Mr H. Pearce of Derwent Bridge killed a female tiger and three pups near the present site of Lake King William in 1948.

In 1989 another supposed tiger killer went public with his story. The man, 61 year-old Bert Maher, a retired trapper, said he had captured and killed a thylacine in the foothills of Mt Scott in 1953. He added, rather unconvincingly, that the incident had been hushed up by a Fauna Board inspector who feared 'all the lunatics in the state' would descend on the area.

Interesting as these stories are, at this late date they prove nothing.

Hair analysis

Analysis of animal hair is a far from exact science and so far examination of hair found in the vicinity of claimed tiger sightings has proved nothing. What was thought to be a recently occupied thylacine lair was discovered in a disused boiler near the Whyte River in 1966. Dr Guiler said hairs collected from the site possessed an external scale pattern which indicated they were tiger hair but other scientists were not so sure. Hans Brunner of the Keith Turnbull Research Institute declared that other hairs taken from the same location were not from a thylacine.

Analysis of the distribution of sighting reports

In early 1990, Dr Henry Nix of the Australian National University announced that a computer program called BIOCLIM had cast some new light on the question of the thylacine's possible survival.

First, he fed all the available data on the thylacine's original habitat and diet into a computer. Second, he added data relating to the change in Tasmania's vegetation and demographic patterns since 1936. Finally, he used the BIOCLIM program to generate a map predicting where the thylacine, if it still existed, was most likely to occur.

When a sheet marked with the locations of all alleged post-1936 sightings was overlaid on the BIOCLIM map he found there was a near-perfect overlap. Dr Nix believes the correlation is too good to be a mere chance result and that in undisturbed regions of their former range the creatures may be no rarer than prior to the European invasion.

Eyewitness testimony

Whenever possible Nick Mooney, the main NPWS 'tiger man', visits the location of each new sighting and tries to reconstruct what occurred. Through these investigations, he has concluded that most witnesses underestimate the distance involved by 100–150 per cent. 'That is, if they say it was 100 metres away it was probably twice that or more.'

In the light of what he says, several of what might once have been considered good sightings now seem more questionable.

Many sightings have occurred at such very close range, however, that it is difficult to see how the witnesses could possibly have been mistaken. As Nick himself acknowledges, 'There are always those stubborn few that I just can't throw away.'

As we have already looked at examples of eyewitness testimony from the period 1936–61 it would, perhaps, be useful to examine some more recent examples.

Viv Kelly, Lachlan, 1968

One September evening, while checking fences on his farm at Lachlan near New Norfolk, Mr Kelly saw a tiger follow a rabbit onto a game trail. Standing about seven metres above the animal, he watched it make a loping, easy leap onto a log. It was not in a hurry and he watched for some minutes as it stopped and looked around three times. It had a yellowish coat and 'outstanding stripes'.

As a young man Mr Kelly had seen many tigers and had believed for some years that they were moving back into the Lachlan–Huon area.

Gavin How and friends Mole Creek, 1980

Three hunters, Gavin How, Peter Webb and Kim Aylett, claimed a very close encounter with a thylacine near Mole Creek on 15 July 1980.

While driving along in their utility, they picked up a set of eyes about 100 metres

THE TASMANIAN TIGER

'It stood absolutely still and every part was clearly visible...'

ahead. As they got closer they realised it was something 'a little funny'. In the beam of their spotlight, they had a clear view for about ten seconds. It didn't seem at all bothered and walked to within ten metres of the vehicle – so close, they said, that they could have caught it.

They estimated it to be about 45 centimetres high, 76 centimetres long, with a long, straight tail, a dark orange-gold coat with black stripes and a head like an Alsatian dog. It 'waddled a bit like a wombat'.

Gavin How worked at the Mole Creek Wildlife Park, specialising in the care of nocturnal animals. He was also a very experienced bushman, so it is hard to believe he could have been mistaken.

Jack Talbot, Port Davey, 1982

Mr Talbot spent most of his life as a diamond driller on the west coast and claims to have seen several tigers over the years in the region's almost impenetrable forests.

His most recent sighting occurred near Port Davey in about 1982:

One evening I was camped near a swampy area where there were a lot of water hens. I heard a strange noise and went out to investigate – there was a Tasmanian tiger quite close to the tent, investigating the scraps from the camp fire.

The thylacine looked like a female and this was confirmed when it reappeared the next evening with a young cub.

I tracked it to its lair, which was under a waterfall. A day or two later I noticed a log had been washed over the entrance trapping the animals, so I cut it away with a chain saw. They were back again near the camp later that day.

Hans Naarding, Togari/Arthur River, 1982

In 1984, after keeping it a secret for two years, the Tasmanian NPWS released details of what appeared to be one of the best sightings since 1936. The report was exciting not only because of the close proximity of the beast and the duration of the event (about three minutes) but also because it involved a witness whose judgement and credibility seemed beyond reproach: a highly respected, extremely experienced wildlife researcher working on contract with the service.

Hans Naarding, a recognised authority on the biology of a unique little bird known as Latham's Snipe, was 51 years old at the time of the thylacine incident and had already devoted several decades to the study of wildlife in both Africa and Australia. As his boss remarked later, '[Mr Naarding] is a good bushman, he knows all the animals of the bush and is a reliable observer. His views are respected, his opinions are credible and his work is first class.'

On the rainy night of 9 March 1982, he had gone to sleep in the back of his Landcruiser at a remote road junction in a forested area of the northwest, near the headwaters of the Salmon River. Waking at 2 am, he shone his spotlight around and got the surprise of his life: '... it came to rest on a large thylacine, standing side-on some six or seven metres distant.' Since his camera was out of reach he examined the creature carefully before moving.

I saw the animal for three minutes, which is one hell of a long time. It stood absolutely still and every part of him was clearly visible. It was a fully-grown male wearing a fine (sandy-coloured) coat which was in good condition. I counted twelve black stripes over its back. It had a massive angular head with small rounded ears. The tail was very slender, but very thick at the butt, quite unlike the tail implant of a dog ...

It just stood there, staring into the distance – he didn't seem to notice me or the driving rain.

Its eyes reflected a pale yellow and it moved only once: an enormous yawn in the best thylacine tradition. Finally, when Mr Naarding attempted to reach his camera bag, he disturbed the tiger, which moved away into the scrub. Walking to the spot where it had stood, the naturalist could find no tracks, but noticed a strong, musky scent.

'The interesting thing,' he remarked later, 'was that I recognised the smell. We lived in Africa for a long time, and if hyena were about, there was always no mistake because you could smell them. It was the same characteristic sort of smell.'

Because Mr Naarding was alone at the time and was asleep immediately before the event, sceptical readers may suggest that he experienced not a real sighting but rather a hypnagogic episode – a waking dream.

This certainly *could* have been the case; the incident does have a faintly dreamlike quality about it. The camera which was just out of arm's reach – a detail so familiar to us from Loch Ness and other 'monster' locales – also makes us wonder a little.

It seems slightly odd, too, that a carnivore which relies to a large extent on scent to track its prey, should be venturing forth in the pouring rain. Then again, in northwest Tasmania, where it often rains for days on end, perhaps a hungry tiger has no choice in the matter.

No doubt partly because he was one of their own, the wildlife service considered Mr Naarding's report the most convincing since 1936. As a result, a team of officers rushed to the site, conducted all-night vigils, searched for tracks and set up ten automatic camera traps.

After a month the search was scaled down but a smaller team continued to monitor a larger, 250 square kilometre area. Nick Mooney, who was in charge of the effort, spent a total of fourteen months in the locality.

Although no hard evidence was discovered, the officers collected seven other recent sighting reports, some of them judged to be 'excellent', from the immediate area.

Although he is now a little more sceptical, Nick Mooney concluded in 1984, in an internal report, 'that the search area was used at least irregularly by thylacines up until autumn 1982.'

Turk Porteus, Frankland River, 1986
Mr Porteus lives with his wife Midge in a tiny beach shack at Arthur River in the northwestern corner of the state. One day, as he was clearing a walking track near the Frankland River, he heard an unusual rustling in the scrub and turned to find himself eyeball to eyeball with a female thylacine.

'She was very close to me, maybe twenty yards,' he said later. 'She stopped and had a look at me for quite a few seconds then slowly moved back into the scrub'. The tiger was a sleek blue-grey and displayed sixteen well-defined stripes. Her pouch was hanging loosely, indicating it had recently accommodated large cubs. 'I know she had cubs with her,' he said, 'because she took so long to move off. If she'd been alone she would have cleared off at the sight of me.' Later he followed her tracks and found the footprints of two juveniles.

Mr Porteus's report is interesting for several reasons, not the least being that, unlike almost all modern witnesses, the old bushman was quite familiar with tigers before their supposed extinction in 1936. The fact that as a boy he often saw their tracks lends credence to his claim that the 1986 tracks were those of thylacines: 'You can't mistake a tiger's footprints because they walk right up on their toes.'

In about 1929, Mr Porteus's brother caught a female thylacine and three cubs, which were kept in a cage at their home for some weeks. The tigers were eventually sold to the Hobart Zoo. Although the eleven pounds they brought was sorely needed in those days of the Great Depression, Mr Porteus has long regretted the incident and was very pleased to have it confirmed – to his own satisfaction at least – that the creatures still survive.

Sceptics might argue that Mr Porteus's subconscious conjured up the whole incident as a way of exorcising the remorse he felt for his family's part in the tiger's demise. Such arguments are worth keeping in mind, but Mr Porteus's subsequent discovery of tracks indicates the incident was not just an hallucination.

Reports such as those of Turk Porteus and Hans Naarding keep the hopes of tiger hunters such as ourselves alive, but, when you get right down to it, eyewitness reports are virtually the *only* evidence for the tiger's survival. None of the many recent track finds has been good enough to convince more than a minority of scientists.

We sometimes feel, in our more sceptical moments, that the Tasmanian tiger can be put in virtually the same category as the Loch Ness monster and the yeti. The only element which appears to make the tiger more 'real' than the others is that up to 1936 it did indisputably exist.

Since then, however, considerably *less* evidence has been found for the tiger's existence than there has been for, say, the bigfoot/sasquatch (thousands of eyewitnesses, a film, plus hundreds of footprint casts) or, as we will show, the Australian mystery big cats (hundreds of witnesses, scores of footprint casts, some pictures). An even greater irony is that, as we will see in the following chapter, there is as much evidence to suggest thylacines presently exist *on the Australian mainland* as there is in Tasmania.

Despite all this, we find the Tasmanian testimony fascinating and feel there is still a slim chance tigers continue to roam the quieter corners of the island state.

As the awareness of past and ongoing ecological disasters and species extinctions press upon our collective imagination and as reports of striped dog-like animals continue to trickle in, the thylacine has come to be seen by many conservationists, searchers and believers as a kind of walking, breathing Holy Grail of zoology.

In an article in *Australian Mythological Sites*, author Rob Horne refers to the search for the tiger as a quest, and makes the interesting point that because of 'the cultural context within which it is articulated' the tiger has become a mythical creature *whether it exists or not*. Among other things, he feels that in the minds of many Australians the tiger, with 'its indeterminate status between reality (biological specimen) and fantasy (missing signified)', has been fused with the immense but perpetually threatened wilderness of southwestern Tasmania 'into a sort of mythological unity ... an extraordinary symbol of mystery ... the last zoological mystery – in the last place on earth'.

Although some of Horne's concepts and much of his academic jargon are difficult for we mere mortals to wrestle with, there is probably much in what he says. The tiger certainly does possess considerable symbolic significance. Although many would vehemently deny it and many others are unaware of it consciously, most white Australians feel some degree of shame and regret for what their forefathers did to the Aboriginal people, to many of the forests and rivers, and to the native animals. Part of the tiger's mystique may be that it is seen as a chance – if only we can find it and ensure its survival – to begin to make amends, to set things right.

References

Advertiser (Adelaide), 24 February 1990
Age, 21 and 22 February 1990
Australasian Post, 4 October 1984; 21 September 1991
Beresford, Q. and Bailey, G., *The Search for the Tasmanian Tiger*, Hobart, Blubber Head Press, 1981
Canberra Times, 12 May 1984; 29 July 1989
Daily Mirror, 21 May 1991
Denis, A., 'They Hunt Tigers, Don't They?', *Good Weekend*, 5 May 1990
Fleay, D., 'On the Trail of the Marsupial Wolf', *Victorian Naturalist*, no. 63; and 'Tasmanian Tiger Hunt', *Wild Life*, June 1946
Guiler, E., *Thylacine: The Tragedy of the Tasmanian Tiger*, Oxford University Press, 1985
Herald (Melbourne), 22 August 1975
Hobart Mercury, 12 September 1968; 6 April 1972; 3 February 1978; 28 December 1979; 31 July 1980; 1 August 1980; 10 February 1981; 21 January 1984
Horne, R., 'The Quest for the Tasmanian Tiger', *Australian Mythological Sights, Sites, Cites*, Third Degree Publication, Sydney, 1986
Jordan, A., *The Tiger Man*, Wordswork Express, Hobart, 1987

Launceston Examiner, 26 April 1968; 7 August 1980; 11 October 1987
Mooney, N., National Parks and Wildlife Service, Tasmania, Technical Report, 1984
Morgan, G., 'The Tasmanian Tiger Comes Out of the Shadows', *Leatherwood*, Vol. 1, No. 4, 1992
The News (Adelaide), 20 February 1990
People, 17 August 1960; 9 May 1962
Ride, W., *A Guide to the Native Animals of Australia*, Oxford University Press, 1970
Scott, R., 'Tasmanian Tiger – Extinct or Merely Elusive', *Australian Geographic*, September 1986
Sharland, M., 'Tracking the Thylacine', *Wild Life*, June 1939
Smith, S., *The Tasmanian Tiger – 1980*, National Parks and Wildlife Service, Tasmania, Technical Report, 1981
Sun Herald (Sydney), 22 October 1989
Sun (Sydney), 15 June 1968; 28 May 1980; 10 February 1981
Troughton, E., *Furred Animals of Australia*, Angus and Robertson, Sydney, 1946.
Walkabout, August 1973
Woman's Day, 24 December 1973

Chapter Two

MAINLAND THYLACINES

MAINLAND THYLACINES

Over the past 150 years or so, the vast, desolate, unforgiving Nullarbor Plain, so alien to Europeans, has been the death of many a traveller, many a stockman and untold thousands of cattle, most of whose bones have long since been ground to dust and scattered by the wind.

One day in 1966, however, as two scientists were groping their way through a limestone cavern deep beneath the plain, their torch light fell upon the remains of a creature which, though it had died long before Europeans even dreamed of Australia, was almost perfectly preserved: the 4600-year-old body of a thylacine – a Tasmanian tiger. Naturally mummified by the cave's cool, dry atmosphere, the carcase was so well preserved that its bones, teeth and skin were all intact: amazingly, even its stripes were perfectly discernible.

From that day on, the cave, on Mundrabilla Station near Eucla, WA, has been known as 'Thylacine Hole'. Its remarkable contents dramatised what the scientific community had long known from more fragmentary evidence: that in ancient times thylacines were not confined to Tasmania but roamed all over the Australian mainland and also New Guinea.

Because the most recent mainland tiger remains are roughly 3000 years old, and because no thylacine has been shot or trapped on the mainland since the Europeans arrived, it is generally assumed the creatures disappeared from the mainland between, say, 1000 BC and 1788 AD. Because dingoes were introduced to Australia – either by a late wave of Aborigines or by Malay fishermen – about 7000 years ago, it is thought the mainland thylacines died out after having their zoological niche gradually usurped by the more efficient newcomers. Dingoes, unlike tigers, are capable of hunting in packs.

According to this theory, thylacines managed to survive in Tasmania only because that land mass was cut off from the mainland by rising sea levels about 12,000 years ago – just before the dingo arrived on the continent. Ancient cave paintings of thylacines in Western Australia's Pilbara and in Arnhem Land provide clear evidence that mainland Aborigines were quite familiar with the animals.

The mainland tiger, then, is officially as dead as the dodo. Like the parrot in the well-known Monty Python skit, it is 'deceased, defunct, gone to its heavenly reward, turned up its toes ... become stone-cold motherless dead. Carked it, mate!'

There is only one slight problem: like the Tasmanian thylacines, the mainland tigers, though dead, refuse to lie down. For the last 40 years at least – and possibly for over a hundred – people have reported occasional encounters, on the sunny side of Bass Strait, with animals which seem to bear an uncanny resemblance to the thylacine.

In all, we know of approximately 500 mainland tiger reports. Consider the following examples:

Near Inverell, NSW, 1937

In 1965, Jim Ramage of Mount Pritchard, NSW, told Bill James of *Australian Outdoors* magazine that he had seen three thylacines – two dead, one alive – while working, at the age of sixteen, with his father and brother in the rugged, heavily-forested Staggy Creek area, about 50 kilometres southwest of Inverell, in the New England ranges.

First sighting:
Not far from where we were working there was a small creek in a gully. One day my brother told me: 'There is the body of a very funny animal down there. I don't know what it is!'. The animal appeared to

have been dead several weeks and we did not examine it too closely. At first sight it looked like a large dingo. The head was like a dog's only larger, and the fur a dusty brown colour. It appeared to be striped towards the back legs. The thing I particularly noticed was the unusual shape of the back legs. The foot appeared to be about four inches [10 centimetres] long. The animal also had a long thick tail.

The hindquarters reminded him of a kangaroo's: 'There was a similarity in both the back legs and the tail.' He thought the creature may have taken one of the many poison baits which had recently been laid for foxes.

Second sighting:

There were some other chaps camped in the area catching rabbits and about this time one of these men shot another animal like the one I had seen. He was going round the traps with a kerosene lantern when he saw the animal's eyes in the bush. It circled around and followed him back to camp, so the man got his rifle and shot it.

Mr Ramage said the skin of the animal had been exhibited in two stores at Inverell and hundreds of people must have seen it:

I saw the skin myself. It was hanging on a board. The stripes were very distinct, starting about three-quarters of the way towards what you might call the shoulders and fading out on the underpart.

Third sighting:

One afternoon, near sundown, he was walking back to camp along the edge of a bushy hillside. Over his shoulder was a sugar bag containing the weekly meat ration. Suddenly he saw a large striped animal:

It stood there with its head towards me. He was quite a big bloke, about 5 ft [1.5 metres] from nose to tail. He looked higher in front than at the back and the tail came down in a sweep, nearly to the ground ... [it] took off into the scrub ... it was more like pictures I have seen of hyenas than anything else.'

Mr Ramage claimed that in 1964, when he first saw an illustration of a thylacine, recognition was immediate: '... this was the animal I saw'.

Near Bourke, NSW, November 1949

In 1968, after reading of the mummified thylacine found under the Nullarbor Plain, S.J. Paramanov of Canberra wrote to the *Western Australian Naturalist* to describe an animal he encountered nineteen years earlier:

During the CSIRO Entomological Expedition, November 1949, I had the good fortune of seeing the animal on the route from Bourke to Wanaaring, in an uninhabited area a few miles past the Warrego River, where I was collecting on the right-hand side of the road, only a few yards from the road. It was 11 am, and I observed the animal for 1–2 minutes from a distance of about 15–20 metres; it ran along the sand which was covered with some very small bushes, the rest of the area being sandy.

I saw the animal from a somewhat oblique angle, and the head was not clearly visible. Its size was that of a medium-sized dog, and the body proportions were also dog-like; it was uniformly grey-brown, with short hair; the strange tail, extremely wide at the base, seemed to be a continuation of the hindquarters; the hind leg was strongly marked with almost black horizontal stripes.

Generally, although dog-like, it was not a Canid, because of the structure of the hind part of the body. The most remarkable feature was the strange manner of running: although the animal was swinging regularly sideways, the hind part of the body made a kind of bobbing, up and down movement; the impression was as if the animal was drunk, as I had never seen anything like it. I hoped to find some specific characteristics from the footprints, but the sandy soil did not show them up; they were of the size of a medium-sized dog's imprint.

I made all the observations with great care, hoping to discuss the animal with my colleagues, but they unfortunately had been collecting on the opposite side of the road, and had not seen it. Later, back in Canberra, I came across an illustration of the Tasmanian Tiger, and immediately recognised it as the animal I had observed on my trip.

The discovery of the carcase in the area of Eucla, and my observation of the live specimen, convinces me that the animal still exists on the mainland of Australia.

Warrumbungle Mountains, NSW, January 1971

One afternoon in January 1971 young Philomena Haylock got off her horse beside a big hollow log on the side of a scrubby hill just west of Mt Naman and was suddenly confronted with a 'very ugly striped animal'. It had big jaws and was only twelve feet [3.6 metres] away. She stood frozen to the spot until it turned and awkwardly loped off.

The next day Philomena and her aunt, Mrs Kath Haylock, were riding in open country just downhill from the site of the first incident when they came upon the same or a very similar animal. They followed it up the hill and noted its striped brindle coat and small, round ears. Its stiff, low set tail was thick at the base and thin at the end. The hind legs were very ugly and bent but the animal was healthy looking and covered the ground much faster than its clumsy, leisurely lope suggested.

Mrs Haylock, a skilled artist, later made a careful sketch of the animal.

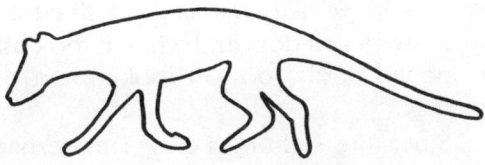

There had been overnight rain and the animal left many very clear footprints. Mrs Haylock and a friend, Mrs Janet Finch, who later contacted the Australian Museum in Sydney, took plaster casts, photographs, careful sketches and measurements of the tracks.

Curiously, all the prints from fore and hind feet showed only three toes and no claw impressions, totally unlike those of a thylacine, or for that matter any other Australian animal.

Although they measured only 2 ½ inches by 2 ¼ inches [55 by 50 milimetres] – no bigger than those of a blue heeler – the tracks were pressed very deeply into the ground compared with those of the family's dogs. Mrs Finch estimated that the animal must have weighed about 60 pounds [27 kilos].

Near Corin Dam, ACT, 1982

For seven years, from the mid-1970s, National Parks ranger Peter Simon patrolled the mountainous, heavily-forested area around Corin Dam in Namadgi National Park, about 25 kilometres southwest of Canberra.

In 1984, eighteen months after the event, he told us of seeing a striped animal as it moved across a clearing near Gibraltar Creek, about seven kilometres east of the dam. Mr Simon had seen many illustrations of Tasmanian tigers and was adamant this creature, which he observed at a range of 30 metres, in daylight, for several seconds, could have been nothing but a thylacine.

After nightfall he returned to the spot and heard, coming from the bush, a very strange, harsh panting. His dogs, which had been in at the death of over 300 wild pigs, absolutely refused to get out of the truck. Over the following twelve months two separate groups of tourists approached the ranger to report Tasmanian tiger sightings in virtually the same spot.

The well-known cryptozoologist Rex Gilroy has made reference to sightings at

Tidbinbilla, just five kilometres to the north of Gibraltar Creek, and the Rare Fauna Research Society (a group of energetic amateur naturalists based in Victoria) has one report from the same area.

Near Pambula, NSW, August 1984

In early August 1984, John Chevalier and his sister Sharon were camped with a small party of bushwalkers near Hart's Creek, about three kilometres south of Lake Pambula on the NSW south coast. At about 6.30 am they heard a 'low, coughing sound' just outside their tent:

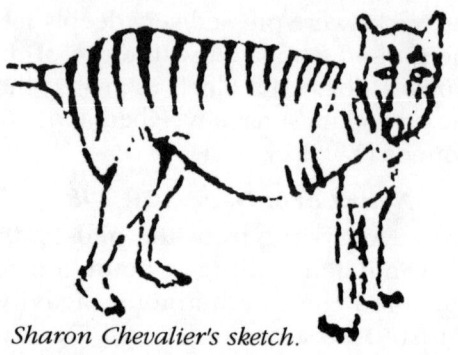

Sharon Chevalier's sketch.

We opened the flyscreen and first of all noticed that half a loaf of bread from the night before had gone. We went outside and there we saw this large animal munching on something, probably our bread. It stood like a monument side on to us for about 30 seconds. It was as large as a Great Dane dog. Its head was like a wolf and its hindquarters were larger than its front quarters. It was a dark ginger colour and had vertical stripes across its back which became lighter in colour towards its neck. There were three stripes under its chest and it had foot claws like a dog.

We were flabbergasted. We thought, first of all, that some animal must have escaped from a zoo. Sharon screamed, I was a bit scared myself. We picked up a wooden stake just in case, but the animal bounded off into the bush. We followed it and caught another sight of it before it disappeared in an easterly direction into the scrub.

Jowalbinna, Queensland, 1993

Percy Trezise, the well-known bush pilot, artist, writer and rock art expert maintains a bush retreat at remote Jowalbinna, in the wilderness beside the Little Laura River about 200 km west of Cooktown.

For some years the Trezise family had been aware of occasional reports of thylacine-like animals in northern Queensland. These reports seemed to come mainly from the Daintree wilderness many kilometres to the southeast. Suddenly, however, in mid-1993, they realised such creatures might be lurking quite literally in their own backyard.

One dark night in July of that year as Mr Trezise's sister, Olive Anger, and her husband Neville approached Jowalbinna homestead a strange, alien-looking animal stepped straight into the lights of their Landcruiser.

The creature was walking straight down the track towards them and they initially assumed it was one of the many dingoes which frequent the area. When it stopped, turned side-on and headed for the bush, however, they realised it was something very much stranger.

The animal was only 20 metres away, starkly illuminated by the powerful driving lights. 'There is no way in the world we could have been mistaken', Neville insisted. 'We know all the ordinary wildlife and have seen dingoes dozens of times. Percy even raised one right there at Jowalbinna.'

The creature had a large odd-shaped head and well-defined vertical stripes running down its haunches. Another striking feature was the shape of the hindquarters. 'Its rear end looked really odd,' said Neville, 'it was more like that of a 'roo than a dog, and when it took off it moved oddly too – it looked sort of clumsy.'

Since the sighting Percy Trezise has

regularly set out food around Jowalbinna and has collected plaster casts of several interesting footprints. The tracks, found in raked sandy areas near the food lures and on nearby muddy tracks, are much larger and deeper than those left in the same ground by adult dingoes.

As well as the large tracks, Mr Trezise, a noted bushman and skilled tracker, has found imprints of the creature's distinctive rigid tail and small tracks of juvenile animals. He is now convinced at least two or three adult thylacines – one with a litter of pups – have moved into the area.

Although he has maintained many nocturnal vigils since his sister's sighting, the creatures have so far evaded his efforts to photograph them. Soon, however, he hopes to physically trap one of the creatures and obtain comprehensive video evidence of its existence before releasing it unharmed.

It is difficult to say with certainty when Europeans first started reporting tiger sightings on the mainland but in Australian *Wild Life* magazine, November 1947, a journalist named Morrison referred to 'persistent reports' in earlier years.

Although sightings have been reported from many parts of the country the great majority have come from the relatively well-watered, forested areas in the east and southeast of the continent, within a couple of hundred kilometres of the sea. Within this zone there are several smaller and fairly well-defined areas which have produced so many reports of strange, striped animals over so many years that they have come to be talked of as 'hot-spots': prime 'tiger' country.

Sometimes so many reports emanate from a particular locality that the press or public coin nicknames which give the animals a sort of regional identity. Probably the best way of showing the scale and ongoing nature of the mainland tiger mystery would be to examine two or three of these hot-spots in some detail.

The Wonthaggi monster
— Southern Victoria, 1955-1994

(Seen mainly in the area bounded by Cape Patterson, Cape Liptrap and Wilsons Promontory to the south and to the north by Wonthaggi, Leongatha and Foster.)

At first blush, it seems totally outrageous to suggest that thylacines (or unclassified animals closely resembling them) could be roaming wild in this coastal area only about 60 kilometres from Melbourne, Australia's second largest city. Although most of Wilsons Promontory is covered with bush (and is a declared national park) and although Cape Liptrap and other parts of the region are also quite well forested, a great part of the Wonthaggi monster's supposed range is fairly open country. It is also, by the standards of rural Australia, rather densely settled.

Despite this, almost a hundred people have, over the last four decades, reported close encounters with thylacine-like animals in the area. The exact number of reports is impossible to pin down but the best known authority on Australian folklore, Bill Wannan, said there were 70 sightings between Wonthaggi and Inverloch in the period 1951–72. A local journalist, Tom Gannon, told us he recorded 25 reports in a very limited area from three to six kilometres east of Wonthaggi between 1955 and 1965 and the *South Gippsland Sentinel Press* (Wonthaggi) of 11 March 1987 referred to over 80 sightings since 1955.

When you consider that all of Tasmania has produced on average only seven thylacine reports per year since 1936, the scale of the Wonthaggi monster phenomenon becomes more apparent.

The Wonthaggi saga began in 1955 when stock began to be killed in alarmingly large numbers and in ways that seemed different from ordinary dog or fox predation. 'The appetites of half a dozen foxes wouldn't run to eating a sheep

'It popped out of the scrub in front of us and ran alongside the road. It was brown striped, had a sleek coat and got along with a peculiar bound ...'

overnight,' said grazier Peter Atkinson, referring to an incident on his Outtrim Road property. 'Neither would their combined strength enable them to drag a sheep 200 yards.'

In December, people began reporting glimpses of a large, unidentifiable animal and someone coined the name 'Wonthaggi monster', a term the Victorian press eagerly pounced upon. Newspaper coverage of the early sightings was generally slightly hysterical and very sloppy and some reporters seemed to allow themselves a great deal of journalistic licence. At first the press seemed intent on categorising the beast as a huge, striped, tree-climbing felid but gradually thylacine-like descriptions began to predominate.

At 10.15 am on 6 December 1955, Ern Featherstone, a car salesman, was demonstrating a vehicle to Mr and Mrs T. J. Schmedje only one and a half kilometres out of Wonthaggi when the 'monster' appeared.

'We had been talking about the animal when it popped out of the scrub in front of us,' said Mr Featherstone. 'It ran along the side of the road and disappeared into some scrub and when we stopped [there] it was looking at us. I've never seen anything like it. It was brown striped, had a sleek coat and got along with a peculiar bound. It was about two feet six inches [76 centimetres] high, five feet [1.5 metres] long and had a tail as long as its body.'

Mr Schmedje said it reminded him of a hyena with a tail. 'It moved like a wallaby does when running on all fours. It had a fox-like head and a long nose.'

In January 1963, after ewes and calves had been killed and eaten on neighbouring properties, George Slater and Mr and Mrs J. Caldwell saw the 'monster'.

'It was about 3½ feet [1 metre] high and about four feet [1.2 metres] long,' said Mr Slater. 'It had a big, round head like a calf, and big broad, round ears. Its head was dark and it had fawn stripes around its ribs.'

A dramatic incident which occurred in 1965 made it seem, for a short time, that the 'monster' saga had come to an end.

On 15 September of that year, just one and a half kilometres from Wonthaggi, Albert Sharp shot and wounded a rabbit, which rolled into a burrow. He was trying to reach the screaming animal 'when a strange feeling came over me and I looked around ... there, 25 yards away, was this amazing looking animal'.

I realised it was the monster. It did a back flip when the first 2 ¾ inch number three shot hit it. It also let out a cry I cannot describe. My second shot bowled it sideways. In my haste to reload, I dropped two cartridges. The monster disappeared into scrub. Its right front leg was dangling, and it staggered.

In the days that followed, the trigger-happy Mr Sharp received several blasts himself – from conservationists.

'As regards the animal and the individual who maimed it,' said R. Staub of the Victorian Fauna Protection Council, 'nature lovers differ as to which is the "monster".'

In any case, it soon became apparent that if he really wanted to kill the creature Mr Sharp should have used silver bullets: sightings of the apparently quite healthy 'monster' continued through the late 1960s.

By the 1970s most of the eyewitness descriptions seemed to agree fairly well with what we know of the thylacine.

At 2.30 pm on 5 November 1979 Mr and Mrs Charlie Thorpe of North Balwyn were driving in the Promontory's National Park when a strange creature emerged from the bush about a kilometre north of the aerodrome. It hesitated and then, without any apparent fear crossed the road in front of their car.

We ... were not moving fast, probably about 40 km/h, and got a good look at the animal. It was taller than my Labrador but was lower in the hindquarters. It moved with a peculiar hopping gait. The tail was very thick at the base and longer than a dog's, tapering to a point. It appeared to be a dark to light grey in colour and had distinct darker bands around its hindquarters. The stripes did not appear to be black but were a darker grey than the rest of the body.

When shown a picture of a Tasmanian tiger, Mrs Thorpe said it was definitely the same kind of animal.

In late 1979 the Wonthaggi beast appeared to extend its range a little to the northwest – bringing it to within 30 kilometres of Melbourne itself. Unlikely as this may sound, the witnesses were again quite adamant they had seen thylacines.

Two sightings involving the same group of witnesses occurred within three days in late December near the General Motors-Holden proving ground at Lang Lang. Both happened around 5.40 am when the witnesses, Ian Garry, Ernie Hade and Slim Holland were driving to work, and on both occasions the creature, moving with a loping gait, crossed the road 50 metres ahead of the car.

'We looked at each other with disbelief,' said Mr Garry. 'It had a long tail. Its back sloped away to its hindquarters. It was thick-set with stripes and it had a square head like a pig's snout.' Apart from the detail of the strangely-shaped head, which seems jarringly out of whack, Mr Garry's description tallies well with what we know of the thylacine. The creature showed no great fear of motor vehicles: 'It just looked at the car without being disturbed and kept crossing at its own pace.'

When the men discussed their experiences later, a workmate, Les Doak, admitted he had seen the same thing ten kilometres south at The Gurdies eighteen months earlier. He had said nothing at the time for fear of ridicule. Local journalist Tom Gannon, leading chronicler

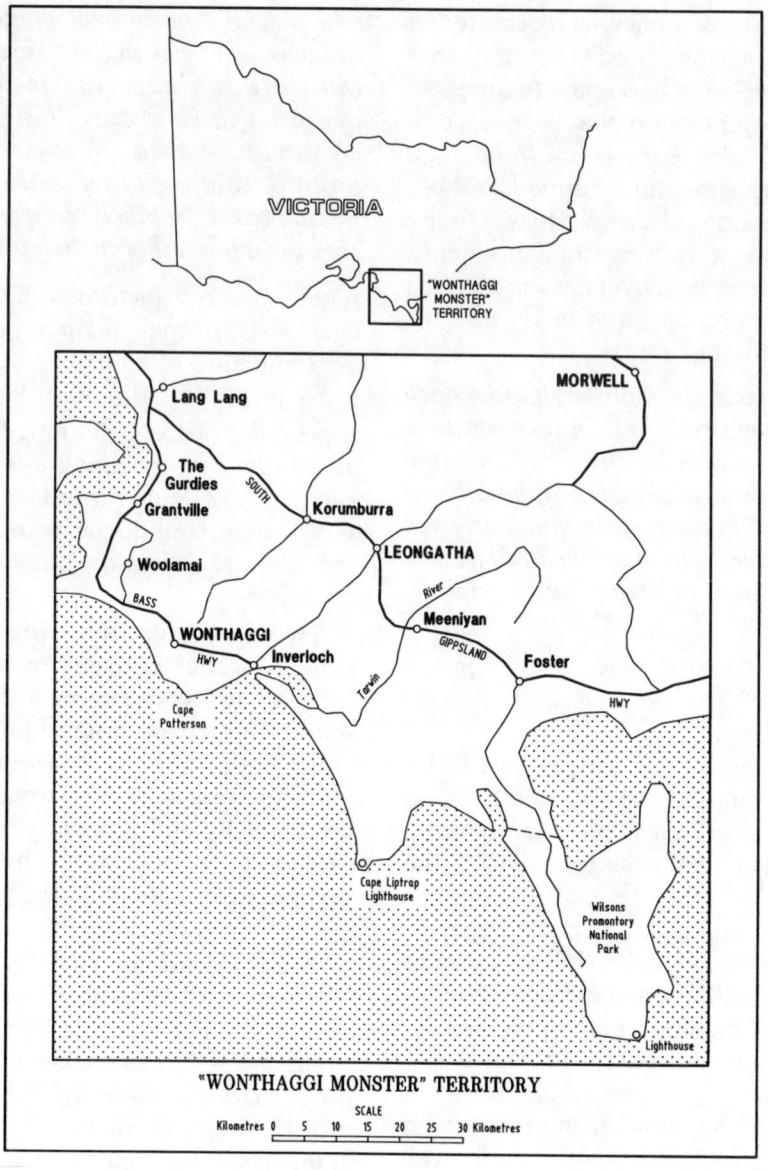

"WONTHAGGI MONSTER" TERRITORY

of the Wonthaggi beasts, commented that sporadic reports had been coming in from around The Gurdies and from nearby Grantville since about 1968. Subsequently, in late 1980 or early 1981 a Mrs Pateman, her husband and a Miss Davis told the Victorian National Parks and Wildlife Service of seeing a similar animal in their car's headlight beams near Lang Lang.

Although the 1979 Lang Lang witnesses were sure they saw Tasmanian tigers, Ian Garry's insistence that the creature had 'a square head like a pig's snout' is, to put it mildly, a little disconcerting.

More definitely thylacine-like was the animal seen by mail contractor Rose Bristow near Woolmai, only ten kilometres northwest of Wonthaggi in March 1987. In broad daylight (11 am) Mrs Bristow watched the animal for 2 ½ minutes from a range of only 10 metres after it crossed Trews Road ahead of her car. Although she stopped close by, the creature did not immediately move away:

'... its ears were erect and it was sniffing the air. After watching it for a while I got out of the car. It got scent of me and hurried back to the scrub. It was in excellent condition, and young. I did not notice whether it was a dog or a bitch.

Because the 'sandy, sable-coloured' animal was so unusual, she took great care to note its characteristics. It was too big for a fox and smaller than a kelpie, with a 'peculiar' head, dark stripes from shoulder to loin and a thick, heavy, un-furred tail. When Mrs Bristow, who has bred and shown dogs for 40 years, was shown a photograph of a Tasmanian tiger she did not hesitate: 'That's what it was.'

The only detail of Mrs Bristow's report which is not entirely suggestive of a thylacine is this: although the animal had a dog-like appearance, its movements were 'feline'.

The witnesses involved in a more recent Wonthaggi monster sighting, reported in the *Leongatha Star* 20 November 1990, also seem to be clearly referring to thylacines:

Mr Sjoerd Reitsma told us that his wife and father-in-law had seen what they were sure was a thylacine on Hillgroves Road, about 100 metres from the intersection with the Inverloch–Leongatha Road in broad daylight last Thursday. The two rushed back home and grabbed a copy of last week's Star *which featured a drawing of the Tasmanian Tiger and Mrs Reitsma told her husband that it was definitely what the two had seen.*

'My father-in-law knows animals and it definitely wasn't a fox, dog or regular animal, it was definitely a thylacine,' said Mr Reitsma. He said his wife and father-in-law had commented particularly on the unusual shape of the animal and the striped back.

The Reitsma incident was just one of a series of seven sightings documented by the Rare Fauna Research Society in the two months to 16 January 1991.

Despite being shot by Albert Sharp and the passage of nearly 40 years since it was first reported, the Wonthaggi monster certainly appears to be alive and well in the mid-1990s.

Obviously, if the 'monster' is flesh and blood, there must be more than one creature; there must be a breeding colony of them in south Gippsland. As far as we know, however, there have been no definite reports of more than one creature seen at a time.

Crazy as the notion of thylacines running loose in southern Victoria may seem, there is a certain logic to it, in geographical terms at least. If the theory that the thylacines were wiped out by the southward movement of the dingoes is correct, then the Wonthaggi–Wilsons Promontory area – the most southerly tip of the continent – could well have been one of their last mainland refuges.

Despite the large number of sightings which have come in over the last four decades, however, not a skerrick of tangible evidence has been produced to support the physical reality of the 'Wonthaggi monster'. None of the creatures has been shot dead or trapped. None of them has been photographed and, as far as we know, few casts have ever been made of their tracks.

The Ozenkadnook tiger, 1885–1994

Somewhat more tangible evidence has come from another mainland tiger hotspot: the border area of southwestern Victoria and southeastern South Australia, roughly bounded by Kingston, Bordertown, Horsham and Hamilton in the west, north and east, and by Bass Strait to the south. This was, and is, the reputed haunt of the 'Tantanoola tiger' and the 'Ozenkadnook tiger'.

Although researchers now know thylacine-like creatures have been reported on both sides of the border since at least 1960 – and probably for many years before that – it was not until 1962 that the phenomenon received widespread publicity.

In that year strange stories emanating from the immediate vicinity of Ozenkadnook, a hamlet in Victoria's Wimmera district, began to attract the interest of regional newspaper editors. The Ozenkadnook reports involved strange, striped dog-like animals and finally became so numerous that a Horsham newspaper, the *Wimmera Mail Times,* sent reporter Ken Hooper to investigate. After interviewing several witnesses he rode into the bush with them and was shown large dog-like tracks which convinced him of the reality of the beasts.

Soon big city papers took notice and quickly christened the anomalous creature or creatures the 'Ozenkadnook tiger'. The 'tiger' had been sighted mainly in, or on the fringes of, a 1200-hectare patch of dense bush and marshy swamp which is part of a great scrub-belt running right through the Wimmera. Eyewitness testimony suggested the creatures were thylacines even though some physical details and some sounds attributed to the animals did not seem quite right.

Typical of the early stories was that told by local farmer Cyril Tucker, who, armed with a .22 rifle, tracked one animal until he came within 20 yards of it. When it gave forth an 'unearthly scream' he ventured no further. It was larger than a German shepherd and had a kangaroo-like face with a pig-like muzzle. It was grey with black stripes on the rump. The body was low-slung and the tail kangaroo-like: thick at the butt and tapering towards the end. It appeared rather high in the withers. The gait was a peculiar 'loping' movement – the hind legs appearing to move in unison.

Subsequently, Mr Tucker encountered the creature again and set his dogs onto it. The animal reared up as it rushed away and seemed to cover several yards before its front paws regained contact with the ground.

On a third occasion, Mr Tucker and his wife saw the same or a similar animal while driving to Edenhope. 'I will never forget the strange red glow of its eyes as it walked into the beam of the car lights,' he said.

While the Tasmanian tiger, judging from pre-1936 photographs, did not have what most people would call a pig-like muzzle, it must be admitted that this detail matches the description of the Wonthaggi monster's head given by Ian Garry at Lang Lang in 1979. As far as we know, 'unearthly screams' were never attributed to thylacines in Tasmania and the supposed 'strange red glow' of the eyes is at variance with the pale yellow reflection noted by Hans Naarding in Tasmania.

It soon became apparent to investigators that the 'Ozenkadnook tiger' (or the 'OK tiger' as it was sometimes called for convenience) was not a solitary beast. Cyril Tucker's sixteen-year-old son Stewart saw an animal similar to the one seen by his parents but somewhat smaller, and a yellow-grey colour beneath its stripes. Mrs V. Burns of Ozenkadnook also reported seeing a smaller animal. *Wimmera Mail Times* reporters estab-lished that throughout 1962 dozens of other people had seen creatures resembling those seen by the Tuckers.

On 20 August, nine members of the Edenhope Hunt Club chased one of the animals through the scrub at Ozenkadnook and Stewart Tucker, who was along for the ride, experienced his second sighting. Miss Lee Lightburn, who also saw the animal clearly, agreed it was 'amazingly like the Tasmanian tiger'.

A photograph was taken but at such long range that the moving animal could not be distinguished from the scrub.

Although the 'OK tiger' reached the peak of its notoriety in 1962 it had, according to locals, been seen on and off for many years prior to that.

Howard Hinch, a former rabbit trapper and grazier, said he had caught glimpses of the animal as early as 1956, had often seen its huge dog-like tracks and heard its 'eerie cry'. He had lost full-grown sheep in the scrub and later found them torn to pieces. Trapped rabbits – and the traps themselves – had been dragged off.

Although they provided no documentation, the *Wimmera Mail Times* reporters stated more than once that reports of strange animals living in the dense forest of Patyah, near Ozenkadnook, had been made for 80 years or so. The phenomenon would therefore date from the mid-1880s.

The tracks examined by reporter Ken Hooper were said to be 'almost the size of a man's hand' but to judge from the photo were about the size of a man's clenched fist: no larger than the track of any big dog. No mention was made of the number of toes and the photo is not clear enough to help in that regard.

After the chase on 20 August, members of the Edenhope Gun Club found where an animal appeared to have stopped sharply, making a deep impression resembling the elongated hind paw of a dog. They made a cast of the track, which measured 20 by 8 centimetres, and because they had by then researched the Tasmanian tiger and become aware that its 20 centimetre-long heel was sometimes visible in prints, they were quite excited by the find.

When the cast was sent to the National Museum in Melbourne, however, the official verdict was disappointing: the imprint was said to have been made by the leg of a large dog – either domestic or a dingo.

The wave of tiger sightings continued in the area through 1963 but no further tracks were photographed or cast. In 1964 however, a more dramatic piece of evidence appeared. It was a photograph of the 'tiger' supposedly taken by a Melbourne woman, Rilla Martin, while holidaying with relatives at Goroke, near Ozenkadnook.

The incident allegedly occurred while she was driving alone from Goroke to the neighbouring town of Apsley. It was a bright, sunny day and because she had plenty of time, she chose not to take the most direct route. Around midday she reached a belt of scrub in the vicinity of Ozenkadnook and turned off on a dirt track which passes the local rubbish tip before rejoining the bitumen after a kilometre. Because she had been using it to photograph relations at Goroke, her small box camera was beside her on the front seat. Suddenly, in the bush to the side of the track, something strange caught her eye.

Eyewitness sketches of thylacine-like animals sighted in southeastern South Australia.

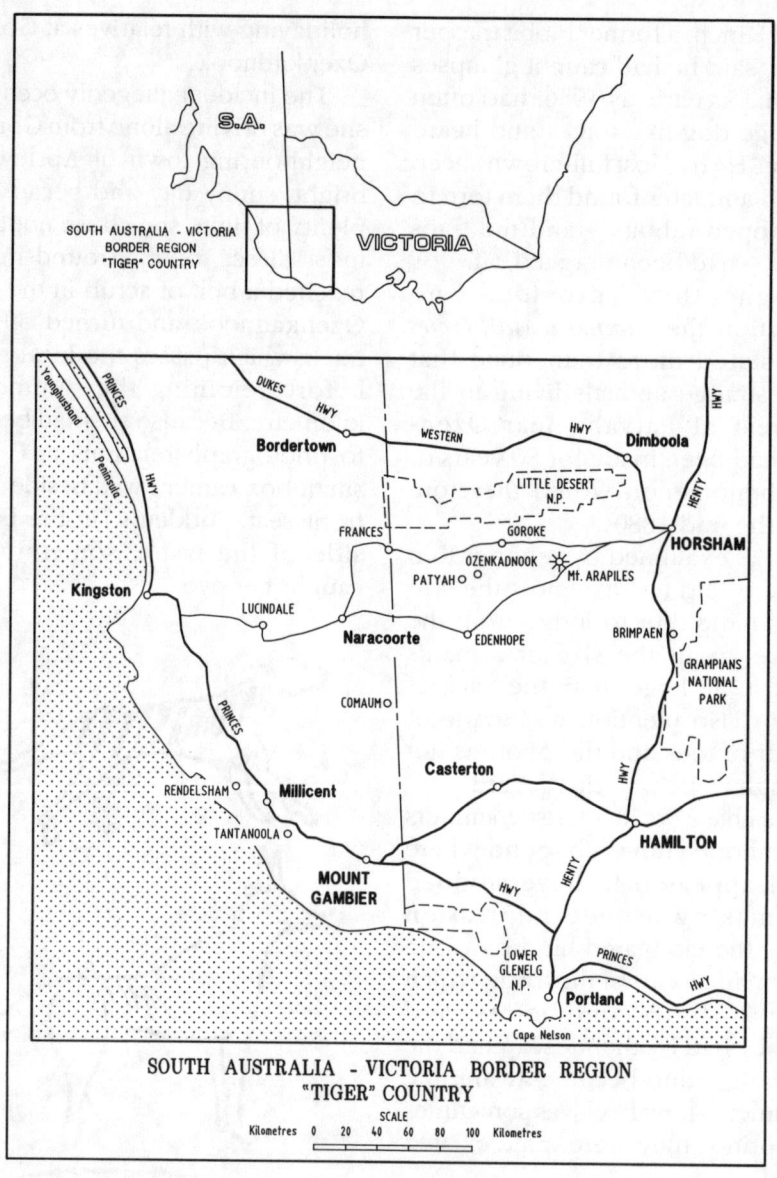

SOUTH AUSTRALIA - VICTORIA BORDER REGION
"TIGER" COUNTRY

'I noticed this peculiar animal', she said later, 'and took a quick photo. The sound of the car engine made it alert ... within a flash it was gone over the log.'

Like the many 'not quite near enough, not quite clear enough' photos from Loch Ness and from the stamping grounds of America's bigfoot, the Rilla Martin photo is just clear enough to intrigue cryptozoologists and people already inclined to believe in the mainland tigers, but not clear enough to convince sceptics or to reveal the shape of the animal's entire body.

There is no way of knowing for sure whether the picture is genuine, but it appears to show a striped quadruped partly obscured by shadows and foliage. Although, with broad bands covering its neck and shoulders as well as its hindquarters, it appears to be more heavily striped than the Tasmanian tiger and although the stripes appear to be white on a black background, it *could* be a variety of thylacine or something related to them.

The body, forequarters, hindquarters and tail, though partly obscured, conform generally to those of a thylacine. The head is difficult to make out but although it is seemingly more canine than feline in shape and is held high in the manner of a Tasmanian tiger, it does not really look like that of a thylacine.

Miss Martin always stressed the fleeting nature of the incident, but she was left with the impression that the animal was about the size of a Labrador dog and that it had a large head with a snout rather like that of a pig. It had, she thought, 'a very thickset front, stripes on it which I didn't notice much at the time because of the shadows' and hindquarters which seemed 'very light in structure'.

Because her photo was given a hostile reception by the zoological establishment – which simply could not identify the creature it showed – Miss Martin has since refused to comment on the matter.

After Miss Martin's experience the tiger sightings continued unabated in the Patyah–Ozenkadnook area for another year. In early 1966, however, residents remarked that the animal's 'plaintive' cry, which had been heard in the district every July, had not been noticed that year, and that sighting reports had fallen away almost to zero. Mrs Cyril Tucker thought the creatures may have moved away because her husband and other farmers had recently cleared large areas of scrub.

Though it was absent for a while, at least, from the place which gave it its name, the 'OK tiger' or similar animals soon popped up elsewhere in the general area. Sightings were claimed at Goroke, Dimboola, Mt Arapiles and Casterton. In October 1967 at Brimpaen near the western edge of the Grampians, two men pursued a striped creature for some distance in their truck.

The incident began at noon on 2 October, when Bob and Wendy Rethus saw a strange animal eating a sheep carcase about 180 metres from their farmhouse. At first they thought it was a dog but when they observed it through binoculars they saw it was something entirely unfamiliar.

As they watched, the animal chased away two wedge-tailed eagles which were also interested in the sheep: 'He went for them and when they took off, the animal jumped in the air, trying to pull them down. Its hindquarters were almost three feet [one metre] off the ground when it jumped.'

After lunch Mr Rethus and a shearer, Des Marra, took a utility and drove down to some low bushes where the creature was last seen:

We hunted it out and chased it across open country. I was doing about 30 miles [48 kilometres] an hour but the animal kept about 15–20 yards [14–18 metres] in front of us.

I had a clear view of it and Des watched it more closely while I drove. It was very dark brown and had distinct, almost black stripes running around its rib cage. Its fur was short and thick, similar to some dogs. The tail was long, stiff and smooth and curled back at the end. It had a big head with small ears. The head sat up almost vertical to its body as it ran, something like a horse when it arches its neck.

After a chase of about 300 metres it disappeared into the scrub. Later, after consulting a book on Australian wildlife, Mr Rethus said the animal was similar in some ways to the Tasmanian tiger.

South Australian thylacines

In August 1967, after a group of children reported seeing a strange striped animal running along in front of their school bus between Naracoorte and Lucindale, the *Wimmera Mail Times* asked 'Has the Ozenkadnook tiger migrated into South Australia?' and suggested half-seriously that hunters and tourists tramping through the bush around Ozenkadnook in search of thylacines had driven the creatures west.

South Australia, which is largely desert, is not a place you would normally associate with large, unknown animals. The southeast corner of the state, however, is different: well-watered by the Roaring Forties blowing across the Great Australian Bight, it is a mixture of good farming country and forest, and is really a continuation, geographically and climatically, of southern Victoria. Its numerous areas of thick scrub and swamp might be just extensive enough to provide a safe retreat for a small population of large predators.

After the school bus incident, Mrs Dawn Anderson, the mother of one of the young witnesses, began to collect other reports from the area and was surprised to find how numerous they were.

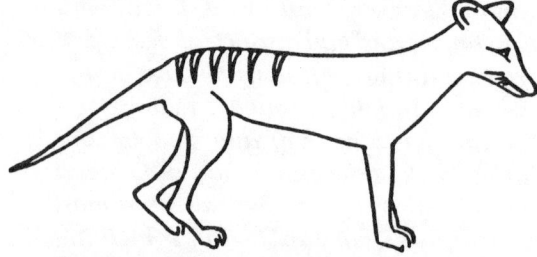

Dawn Anderson's sketch of the animal sighted from the Lucindale school bus.

'I think', she said, '[the creatures] exist in numbers. I have had reports ... of two seen at once, and of animals with varying size and colouring which would indicate different ages. These reports have come from highly respectable and responsible citizens.'

In addition to actual sightings, sounds – 'weird and sinister, like a woman screaming' – were heard and attributed to thylacines. Tracks were found in the vicinity of some sightings and Mrs Anderson made a sketch of one which appears to have the four toes and long heel suggestive of a thylacine's rear foot.

To explain the apparent absence of thylacine reports on the mainland in colonial times, she came up with an interesting theory. She suggested that the mainland tigers were actually the descendants of thylacines brought over from Tasmania and released prior to 1936.

As new reports came to hand, Mrs Anderson visited the locations involved and in the course of two and a half years experienced three sightings herself. In mid-1967 she and her son observed a thylacine-like animal for fifteen minutes as it moved along a ditch in a swamp. In February 1968, with fifteen other people in three cars, she tried to corner one in a reed bed, and in March she glimpsed one crossing a paddock.

Two months later she made plaster casts of tracks and collected hair at a spot on the Lucindale–Naracoorte road where a stock agent, Trevor Taylor, reported a sighting. She claimed the casts showed that the creature's toes, like those of a thylacine, were comparatively small compared with its large 'palm' pad. Since no mention was made of five toes, it seems there were four and that Mrs Anderson assumed the tracks were of the thylacine's hind foot.

She sent the hair and casts to the South Australian Museum but instead of congratulations received a stinging rebuff: the Curator of Mammals dismissed the tracks as those of 'a medium-sized dog of a broad-footed breed, perhaps a beagle or small Labrador...' No further mention is made of the hair sample.

Although, as it was subsequently discovered, thylacine-like creatures had been reported intermittently in southeast South Australia since at least 1960 and possibly for a decade before that, 1967 and early 1968 produced a veritable flood of reports. A local journalist, Samela Harris of the *Naracoorte News*, joined Mrs Anderson in her investigations and between them they collected statements from over a hundred witnesses. Some reports were rather sketchy but some, such as that given by Parks Commission employee, Jack Victory, were quite impressive.

Mr Victory's sighting occurred at a property fronting the Coorong, a long, thin finger of salt water behind Younghusband Peninsula:

I was about 400 yards [365 metres] away, looking at birds through a telescope. I just didn't know what he was ... he was a large animal, a bit like a fox and a bit like a kangaroo. But he was neither. He started to run with a long, loping gait. He had a dog's head and a large tapering, rather stiff-looking tail. His torso was striped in grey. The rest of his body was brown.

When we got to the spot where we had seen him, we found his paw marks in the clay. They were about the size of my fist and looked quite similar when I stuck my fist into the clay beside his imprint. We estimated his weight as about 120 to 150 pounds [54-68 kilos]. The animal's appearance fits only that of the thylacine.

Millicent tourist officer, John Pocock, claimed a sighting in a private wildlife sanctuary near Grey, just outside of Rendlesham: 'It was a weird looking thing, with canine features in the upper part of the body and marsupial features, like a kangaroo, at the rear. It was striped like a tiger.'

Mr Pocock was rounding up emus in long, tussocky grass when he spotted the animal, which was sitting up, watching the proceedings with some interest. After getting over his initial shock he remembered a commonwealth film unit was in the sanctuary at the time, filming wildlife, but by the time he located the cameraman the creature had gone.

Mr Pocock said his sighting was just one of many from the area which is very rugged, with patches of dense scrub interspersed with water soaks and largely a declared wildlife sanctuary.

Naracoorte engine driver, Don Gilette,

Naracoorte train driver Don Gilette sighted this animal twice from his train near Lucindale, South Australia.

told of sighting thylacines twice from his train near Lucindale and provided the *News* with a rather well-executed sketch of what he saw. Interestingly, the creature it depicts appears very similar in shape and bearing to the animal in Rilla Martin's 'Ozenkadnook tiger' photo, although the stripe pattern is somewhat different.

Thylacine sightings continued to be reported in the southeast throughout the 1970s and two local residents, Kath Alcock and Mrs Dorothy Parker assisted Dawn Anderson in documenting them. The animals seen were usually thought to be full grown or near full grown but on the night of 1 November 1974 Barbara Adams of Frances and her children had a close encounter with some much younger animals.

The night was brilliantly moonlit and at 9.45 pm, as they drove past the Frances Gun Club, they saw two small animals ahead of them playing on the edge of the dirt road. The pups were so preoccupied with their scuffling that they did not run away until the car approached to within just a few feet.

'We could have touched them,' Mrs Adams claimed. She and her four children agreed the animals were 'about 12 inches [30 centimetres] tall, sandy in colour with dark markings on the flank, too heavy in the hindquarters to be foxes, heads like lion cubs with small ears; tails smooth and hanging in a downward curve or ellipse'. After checking a book on Australian marsupials they were satisfied the pups resembled Tasmanian tigers.

At 5 pm on 26 December Peter Knight almost ran over a somewhat larger animal in almost the same spot. He said it was golden with dark stripes, round ears, and a bit smaller than a whippet. Four years earlier, after reports of strange animals in the same area, Mrs Parker had found, in soft sand, an 'absolutely perfect' track showing the five toes typical of a thylacine's front foot.

In June 1975 a thylacine was sighted near a flock of sheep at Comaum. Kath Alcock investigated and found that several sheep and lambs had been killed in the district at about the same time. They had been fed upon in a way reminiscent of the thylacine: the blood had been sucked from their bodies.

Reports of thylacine-like animals continued to come in from southeastern South Australia and eventually the phenomenon came to be taken seriously by some government officers such as Dr Tony Robinson of the National Parks and Wildlife Service, who accumulated quite a dossier of reports in the late 1980s.

Sad to say, despite the often excellent eyewitness testimony dating back so many years and despite the efforts of all the investigators, both government and private, very little in the way of tangible evidence has ever been produced to support the existence of thylacines in South Australia.

Flashback: The Tantanoola tiger
1895

When the South Australian thylacine reports began to receive wide publicity in 1967 local historians were quick to retell the legend of the 'Tantanoola tiger', a creature which cut a bloody swathe through the sheep population of the southeast for two or three years up to 1895, when it was supposedly shot.

The Tantanoola saga, however, is a frustrating hodge-podge of fact and folklore, journalistic licence and outright fabrication.

The 'tiger's' depredations appear to have begun in about 1893 and at the height of its reign of terror it was held responsible for killing up to 50 sheep a night. Large tracks were found and it seems many settlers really thought a Bengal tiger was loose in the area. Women and children were kept inside as parties of armed men scoured the district.

Several people apparently sighted the creature, but names are not supplied and details are a bit sketchy. One man described it, rather melodramatically, as 'grinning, yellow and gleaming with satin stripes', and a youth riding home from a dance was said to have seen a great beast leap a high fence with a sheep gripped in its jaws.

A local schoolteacher supposedly reported that one night during a storm he heard noises in his kitchen. Jumping from bed to investigate, he saw a huge animal leap through the open doorway. 'It was a tiger,' he declared.

The mystery was supposedly solved on 21 August 1895 when Tom 'Foss' Donovan dropped the tiger with his .44 Winchester at Mt Salt, 30 kilometres from Tantanoola.

The dead animal, however, was no Bengal tiger. It was a dog, albeit a rather unusual looking one. It is often said that it was identified as an 'Assyrian' or simply 'Syrian' wolf, but the expert who supposedly made this identification is never named. The wolf was believed to have swum ashore from the ship *Helena* which foundered about 32 kilometres from Tantanoola.

Whatever its true ancestry, the animal was stuffed and has been on display ever since in a glass case at the Tiger Hotel in Tantanoola. Whether it is a Syrian or any other kind of wolf we cannot say, but it is certainly not a remarkably large animal – only about the size of an average

German shepherd – and its coat is not in the least striped.

Apart from Foss Donovan's insistence that it was the mysterious predator and the apparent tapering-off of sheep deaths about the time it was killed, there is little to suggest the dog in the glass case is in fact the dreaded 'tiger'. In fact, several witnesses vehemently denied that the creature shot by Donovan was in any way similar to the fearsome animal they saw in the wild.

That the animal is in any way exotic is, in fact, quite doubtful. In 1957 a 90-year-old pioneer, Alf Warman of Adelaide, happened to visit the Tiger Hotel and as soon as he laid eyes on the animal in the glass case he shouted: 'That's my dog!' He claimed that when he was a young man his brother Ted gave him a puppy which was the offspring of a European deerhound and a bloodhound. The dog soon grew too large and expensive to feed, so Alf sent it to some acquaintances in the southeast who intended to use it, ironically enough, to help in the tracking and killing of wild dogs. The 'tiger' reports began soon afterwards.

Mr Warman's story sounds good, but like everything else to do with the 'tiger' is not entirely satisfactory: to our eyes, the not particularly huge creature in the glass case looks nothing like a bloodhound and nothing like a deerhound.

As if the Tantanoola saga was not already convoluted enough, it also transpires that a pair of stock thieves later used the 'tiger's' reign of terror as a cover for their nefarious activities.

Beginning in 1895, just after Tom Donovan shot the 'Syrian wolf', Robert Edmondson and David Bald of Tantanoola began stealing large numbers of sheep from surrounding properties. Sometimes they left pools of blood at the scene to implicate the 'tiger'.

Regardless of how many graziers were actually fooled by the traces of blood, the thieves got away with their racket until December 1910 when a group of hunters stumbled across several sheep yards hidden within a virtual jungle of ti-tree near Lake Bonney. Edmondson was later arrested by a detective disguised as a swagman and sent to gaol for six years.

Given the confusion which surrounded the episode and the number of years which have gone by, it is probably impossible now, in the case of the 'Tantanoola tiger', to separate myth from reality.

Perhaps a pack of wild dogs killed the sheep and moved on after the leader was killed; perhaps thylacines *were* involved and for some reason kept a low profile between 1895 and 1961. The term 'tiger' may have been prompted by a fleeting glimpse of a thylacine's striped back but may also have been used simply because it sounds well with 'Tantanoola'. Had the 1890s outbreak occurred near, say, Lucindale, the phantom creature may well have been christened the 'Lucindale leopard'.

One person who is familiar with the dog in the glass case and who also claims sightings of thylacine-like animals in recent times has made a direct comparison between them. J.B. Pascoe, who glimpsed strange quadrupeds three times near Port MacDonnell between 1950 and 1960 stated that 'It was nothing like the notorious Tantanoola tiger. It was quite a bit bigger, had a stiff tail and seemed weak in the back legs. It seemed to be more like the Tasmanian tiger'.

Cape Nelson, Victoria, 1971–1974

Although few reports have come in recent years from the 'tiger's' old hunting grounds in the immediate vicinity of Ozenkadnook, thylacine sightings have continued to be reported from various other parts of southeastern Victoria throughout the 1970s, 1980s and into the 1990s.

One particularly intense outbreak

occurred at Cape Nelson, just south of Portland in the early 1970s, when farmers and road crews told of repeated close encounters with large, striped quadrupeds. A description given by a piggery owner, Bob Herbertson – who claimed six separate sightings in early 1971 – was, though rather colourful, not entirely inconsistent with what we know of the thylacine. It was, he said, 'strange, grey and furry', with stripes running around its rib-cage and was about a metre high. It had the muzzle of a dog, the head and forequarters of a cat, with powerful hindquarters and tail almost like those of a kangaroo. It covered the ground in tremendous bounds.

A similar animal was examined through binoculars by Andrew and Dora Murrell at their farm three kilometres from the Cape Nelson lighthouse. It was half as big again as a fox, tall, long and thin, with a tail almost as long as the body. It was dark brown with 'lines or bands' around the body.

The jaw 'was like that of a dog but it had ears like a fox. It was about a hundred metres from the house and we watched it for about five minutes before it ambled off back towards the lighthouse'.

At least one organised party, which included a Fisheries and Wildlife officer, attempted to search the area but were thwarted time and again by the thickness of the scrub and the roughness of the terrain.

Sightings became so numerous at one time that at least one roadworker, Graham Mibus, began to take a camera to work with him. Predictably, perhaps, Murphy's Law immediately came into operation: Mr Mibus, who had seen the creature at close range on two previous occasions, never so much as glimpsed it again.

Sightings of thylacine-like creatures continue to be reported from the South Australia–Victoria border region up to the present day. Exciting as the eyewitness testimony is, and intriguing as nineteenth century stories about the 'Tantanoola tiger' certainly are, it has to be admitted that apart from several intriguing sketches by eyewitnesses and some footprint casts the only evidence which could be described as tangible is the 1964 Rilla Martin photo.

We believe the Martin photo *could* be genuine. Also on the positive side, we feel there are, in the South Australian and Victorian eyewitness testimony, certain distinct patterns which indicate the mainland tiger phenomenon is more than a protracted series of hoaxes or hallucinations.

West Australian thylacines

Any readers who have had trouble accepting stories of Tasmanian tiger sightings in southern Victoria and southeast South Australia will find the location of the next mainland thylacine 'hot-spot' even harder to accept.

Southwest Western Australia could hardly be further from Tasmania – Perth is almost as far from Hobart as Darwin is, and the suggestion that thylacines could still exist there seems, at first blush, to be utterly absurd.

When the following factors are taken into consideration, however, the possibility begins to seem a little less remote.

First, southeast Western Australia is, unlike most of the state, well-watered and quite heavily forested.

Second, 'Thylacine Hole' – the cave in which the 4500-year-old tiger carcase mentioned earlier was discovered – is in Western Australia, albeit in the southeastern rather than the southwestern corner of that huge state. Furthermore, thylacine bones have been found at six other West Australian locations.

Third, ancient Aboriginal pictographs of thylacines have been found at various sites in the state.

Finally, in a paper which, surprisingly, received almost no attention from the

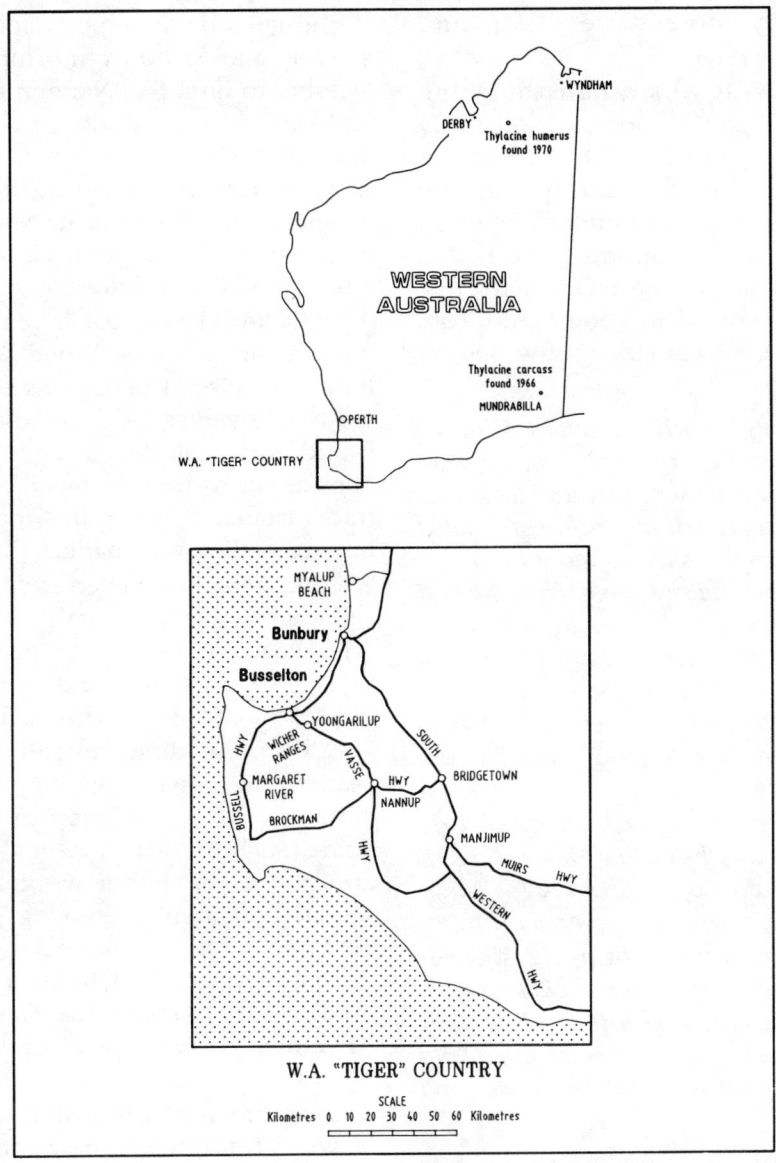

popular press, zoologist Dr Michael Archer of the University of NSW said that bones found in a deposit which included a thylacine humerus (shoulder bone) in the Kimberleys in 1970 had been carbon dated at *less than 80 years old* (more about this startling discovery later).

The West Australian thylacine phenomenon came to the attention of the general public in a way quite similar to the emergence of the South Australian and Victorian tiger stories.

It seemed to begin about 1969, when reports of 'tiger' sightings started to appear intermittently in regional newspapers. Next, a handful of interested local people began collecting reports and footprint casts. They also did research which uncovered references to Western Australian thylacine sightings and slayings in earlier decades.

The story began to feature in national newspapers and reached a climax when photographs of what may or may not have been a thylacine were taken and displayed in 1984.

When West Australian thylacine sightings began to be reported fairly regularly in the early 1970s the location mentioned most frequently was the Nannup district, a forested area between Busselton and Manjimup, about 290 kilometres south of Perth. One of the first sightings occurred in 1966 when Tom Longbottom, a local farmer, saw one on his property:

I had the lights all on when I heard something in the calf yard. When I went to look, there it was. I stood and looked at it for two to three minutes before it ambled out of the yard. I was no more than 15–20 feet [4.5–6 metres] away from him. It was about the size of a roo dog with a big head, long body, heavy shoulders, long tail with brush on the last 12–14 inches [30–36 centimetres] or so. Some dark bands went around the body as well. Its eyes were not like dogs' eyes.

I have been in the bush all my life and never seen anything like this before. It came back quite often for milk I left in a dish. I made a trap but never got him.

The tracks were not dog tracks. We hear funny sounds at night like a choking or a soft barking which I'd say was him. Our dog ... had a big fight in the roadway but he won't go out there any more. I don't blame him.

There were only one or two other sightings in the 1960s, but in the Spring of 1970 several other people reported seeing striped dog-like animals around Nannup, mainly in a large pine plantation ten kilometres north of town.

Although some of the newspaper reports are frustratingly vague it seems most witnesses said the animals were '... dark, striped, with a long tail, fast-moving and about the size of a big dog', and it seems some locals, quite early in the piece, suspected the creatures were related to the thylacine.

Intrigued by the reports, forty people set out one Saturday morning in late October to hunt the 'Nannup tiger'. The highlight, or perhaps low point, of the day came when the searchers fell victim to a practical joke: a sheep, shorn to the shoulders, painted with stripes and with long hair tied to its tail, had been put where it would be found.

'It looked like the real thing and caused quite a stir,' admitted David Blythe, the hunt's organiser. The day was not entirely wasted, however, as a sizeable lair was found and a plaster cast of what was considered to be an unusual four-toed track, similar to footprints found some months earlier, was made.

Although they never experienced a sighting themselves, Mr Blythe and his wife Pat remained convinced of the thylacine's existence and continued to document all sightings in the area.

When the dust settled after the 'Nannup tiger' safari, sighting reports of varying quality continued to be made. Some, such as that in which Bill Lavis and two other timber workers told of seeing a creature resembling '... a cross between a fox, a dog and a cat' were frustratingly sketchy. Others, such as that made by Freda and Joe Carmody in November 1972 were of considerable interest.

The Carmody incident occurred between Bridgetown and Nannup:

... the animal started to cross the road (it was 6 pm at the end of a very hot day and it had evidently been going down to a nearby pool to drink) and only noticed when our car was almost on it. Then it leapt around in the middle of the road with a most unusual bound, more like a kangaroo than anything and loped off ... in no great hurry, with its head turned towards us, and finally disappeared into a growing crop.

It was a 'grand, upstanding creature'. They particularly noticed the broad head, neck and shoulders, all much heavier and stronger than any familiar animal and were scornful of the 'mangy fox' explanation often used by officialdom. 'Both my husband and I,' said Freda Carmody, 'are pretty keen on the bush and were both raised in the country, seeing enough dingoes and foxes to know what *they* look like.'

The couple were within 10 metres of the animal and said it looked exactly like photographs of Tasmanian thylacines.

Their sighting so impressed the Carmodys that it literally changed their lives, inspiring them to set out on a quest through Western Australia, South Australia, Victoria, New South Wales and Tasmania for proof of the thylacine's survival. Although tangible evidence eluded them, the energetic couple, in collaboration with Pat and David Blythe, collected a great deal of testimonial and archival material to add to the mainland tiger file.

Because their claims were modest and their approach low-key, the activities of the Blythes and the Carmodys attracted rather sympathetic but minimal press coverage. Then, in the early 1980s, the media discovered Sid Slee, of 'Hillside' farm, Yoongarillup, who made for much more exciting reading.

Although Mr Slee's claims put those of previous tiger researchers in the shade and may appear preposterous to some, the West Australian newspapers gave him a fair hearing. We intend to do the same – because what he says about the colouration of the beasts, if correct, may be an important clue to the real identity of the mainland 'tigers'.

Mr Slee insists he has seen the animals 'many, many times' since about 1940 and that on two occasions has examined the carcases of dead thylacines. He has discovered kangaroos with their heads chewed right off and has found the thylacines' distinctive tracks on many occasions. All this has allegedly occurred within the confines of his own boundary fence.

In the mid-1970s, tiring of his neighbours' scepticism and ridicule, he hung a defiant sign on his front verandah: 'HILLSIDE – The Haunt of the Marsupial Wolf'.

According to Mr Slee the thylacines have lived at 'Hillside' on and off for many years and take refuge in two large, virtually impenetrable thickets. Throughout the 1940s he glimpsed thylacines near these thickets on many occasions and thought them responsible for the mauling of seven young heifers and many kangaroos found dead on the property during the war years.

His best sighting of a live animal did not occur until 1972, when as he was doing his morning rounds, a large thylacine appeared right in front of him. It was tall, thin but muscular, light yellow with a chocolate stripe down the spine and six or seven stripes on the hindquarters; the tail was dark and apparently hairless. From nose to tail it measured about seven feet [2.1 metres]. The animal was so close that when it turned to run it kicked gravel over his shoes.

As it ran, the farmer noted several interesting features: it moved both back legs in unison like a rabbit or kangaroo, and, when it glanced back at him over its right shoulder, '... its tail moved to the left to keep perfect balance'.

Although Mr Slee's encounters with live animals are interesting enough, the most remarkable elements of his story relate to his supposed discovery of dead thylacines. The first such incident occurred one day in 1940 when he set out to search an area where a shooter claimed to have wounded a fox. To his amazement, he found not a fox, but the body of a creature '... longer and thinner than a fox with light-yellow biscuit-coloured hair one inch [2.5 centimetres] long covering its body and a stiff, almost hairless tail which was darker in colour'.

Although it was not striped he knew it was not merely a feral dog because it had the form of a '... part dog, part cat and part kangaroo'.

The most interesting aspect of this report is the absence of stripes on the animal. This would indicate, fairly clearly, that the mainland thylacines are not the descendants of Tasmanian tigers brought over from the island state and released prior to 1936, but an entirely separate species.

The second dead thylacine Mr Slee examined in 1943 when he was 12 years old, also lacked stripes but was different from the first in that it was *jet-black*. The young farmer found this animal dead in one of the many snares he set for kangaroos. It was 'large, sleek and shiny' and was black all over apart from a few flecks of white which he assumed had grown over old scars.

Not knowing what to do with them, Mr Slee simply left both carcases to rot in the bush. This may seem an odd thing to do, but perhaps back in the early 1940s, when it was generally assumed the thylacine still existed in Tasmania, finding thylacine-like animals on the mainland may not have seemed so strange as it would today. That these discoveries occurred during the momentous early years of the Second World War also may have tended to make them seem less important to Mr Slee, who was, after all, only a boy at the time.

Mr Slee believes the thylacines have been building up in numbers since about the early 1970s and thinks they are responsible for the disappearance of the grey brush wallabies which previously thrived in the area. The animals also apparently prey on kangaroos. Over the years Mr Slee has found several killed and mutilated in a most distinctive manner: their heads had been torn off and completely devoured.

His dogs, he says, can sense when the creatures are on the prowl: though they are not normally allowed indoors, on some nights they scurry inside, apparently scared witless.

Because Mr Slee claims such a large number of thylacine sightings and because he can produce no absolutely indisputable physical evidence, it is tempting to dismiss his stories altogether. To do so, however, would be foolish and unfair, because much of what he has said about the West Australian thylacines – even the most improbable details – has been verified by other witnesses.

When describing the animals, several other eyewitnesses, such as June Maughan, who saw one near the mouth of the Margaret River, insisted the creatures, though thylacine-like in every other detail, were definitely *not striped*.

Others, like Mrs N.F. Hemery of West Pingelly, have supported what Mr Slee says about the animal's gait. During a lengthy and very close encounter with a large and possibly quite old animal, Mrs Hemery and her two children noticed that 'the tail was shaped like a kangaroo and the hind legs moved like a kangaroo, the front legs like a galloping horse'.

Even what Mr Slee says about the thylacines' predilection for head-hunting has also been backed up by other witnesses. Tom Longbottom of Nannup, for instance, said thylacines sometimes appear on his property and that '... now and again we find a lamb with its head eaten off. Just the head. Then we find 'roos with their heads gone as well'.

His claims about the behaviour of his dogs are also borne out by the testimony of several other people, including the Holland family of Busselton. After a series of thylacine sightings around their farm they heard 'a blood-curdling scream' one night. 'Our dog,' said Garry Holland, 'which is not allowed in the house, came grovelling in on his stomach. He seemed petrified with fright'.

Throughout the late 1970s thylacine sightings continued to be reported throughout the southwest of the state, but the story did not develop in any significant way until, in the early 1980s, Kevin Cameron became involved in the mystery.

Mr Cameron, now in his late forties, was employed for many years as a feral pig hunter by the Agriculture Protection Board (APB) and is, by all accounts, an exceptionally good, highly experienced bushman and tracker. He was called upon frequently by police and emergency services to assist in the search for drugs and lost people, and on one occasion saved the life of nine-year-old Edward Davies, missing for two days in cold, rainy conditions.

During his career with the APB he killed more than 1300 wild pigs. Proud of his Aboriginal ancestry, he often set aside his rifle and did the job with a spear. In 1981 a badly injured right leg left him temporarily unemployed, and led him, inadvertently, into the hunt for the thylacine.

Late in that year, for something to do, he checked out reports of thylacine-like animals near Myalup. After finding blurred tracks, and some duck and kangaroo carcases, he became badly infected with the 'tiger bug'.

Thereafter, he visited the locations of many sightings. Sometimes, using a steel spear to support his injured knee, he scoured the bush alone; more often he directed operations from a vehicle, leaving the bush-bashing to his sons Kevin and Shane and to his tracker dogs, Sam and Lobo.

On 18 October 1983 they experienced their first clear sighting when they surprised a thylacine and drove to within ten metres of it on a remote forest track near Nannup.

'It reared up on its back legs', said Mr Cameron 'and leapt forward to cross the road.' It had a large head, rounded ears, several stripes, and a long rigid tail. He released Lobo who chased it into the bush and bailed it up. As Mr Cameron hobbled after them he could see its head above the underbrush: 'It gave a series of cough-like sounds and seemed to be standing on its hind legs'. The animal made a successful break for freedom when it saw him approach. Mr Cameron and young Kevin later photographed two sets of tracks.

The most extraordinary feature of this incident is, of course, the claim that the thylacine is capable of rearing onto its hind legs and hopping like a kangaroo when hard pressed. As we mentioned in the first chapter, however, several colonial-era Tasmanians said the same thing about the Tasmanian tigers. Mr Cameron's observation is supported, also, by the testimony of at least one other West Australian witness, Garry Holland.

Mr Holland said that at 7.30 one sunny morning he was driving near his Busselton farm when 'I saw this animal resting on its hind legs like a kangaroo about 30 metres ahead of me. It watched me for about a minute before it disappeared into the forest. It had a mottled coat and stood about half a metre high. It had a strange sort of prancing gait'.

In 1982 Mr Cameron met Sid Slee and for several months they worked together in an effort to collect tangible evidence. At 'Hillside', using sand traps and bait, Mr Cameron succeeded in making several very clear plaster casts of footprints. Some of them showed five toes and resembled the forepaws of a thylacine and some showed the four toes and distinctively long heel of the animal's back feet.

Several more headless kangaroos were also found and photographed. However, despite a great deal of spotlighting by night and bush-bashing by day – and one or two apparent near misses when their dogs got on the creatures' scent – the men did not succeed in filming the creatures.

They had no luck, either, with the traps painstakingly built by Mr Slee and his son Ian: they were sprung occasionally, but caught only foxes.

The Cameron photos, 1984

After his efforts with the Slees in the Yoongarillup area, Kevin Cameron soldiered on alone. Finally, in early November 1984, while checking an area he had searched many times before, his luck changed: he spotted a thylacine, and before it became aware of him, began to stalk it, camera in hand.

'I got to within 10 metres of the animal,' he said, 'but it was so well camouflaged that if I hadn't been looking for it I could have passed without seeing it.'

The animal was so involved with digging into the base of a burnt-out jarrah tree, that it wasn't aware of him until he had taken six photographs. Finally, however, 'The click of the camera disturbed it and it stopped digging to look at me squarely before it vanished into the surrounding vegetation'.

The two pictures which we have seen show the animal in two slightly different positions but in both only the hindquarters and the tail are clearly visible. The pelt is dark with broad stripes which extend down the rear legs and a long tail projects stiffly out from the body, ending in what looks like a tuft of hair.

After Mr Cameron showed the photos to Alex Harris of the *West Australian* and the story hit the headlines, there was a sudden surge of interest from previously sceptical scientists, some of whom began to sound like born-again thylacine believers.

Dr Anthony Burbidge, head of the Western Australian Wildlife Research Centre said the pictures were the best evidence yet produced for the existence of the mainland thylacines. 'We are taking the sighting very seriously,' he said. Dr Des Kitchener, Curator of Mammals at the Museum of Western Australia, found them very interesting and thought they 'very much warranted further examination'. The Western Australian Minister for Fisheries and Wildlife, Mr Evans, said this could be one of the wildlife events of the century and that if the creature was proven to be a thylacine his government would immediately declare it an endangered species.

Believing they had great commercial value (he mentioned a figure of $53,000) Mr Cameron did not allow his photos to be used by any Australian newspapers. However, when Athol Douglas, a retired museum official, wrote an account of the WA thylacine phenomenon for the British *New Scientist* magazine, Cameron reluctantly allowed him to use them.

When he examined the negative, Mr Douglas saw the film had been cut and that some frames were missing. He could see that the photographs had been taken from different angles which made it 'impossible for the series to have been taken in 20 or 30 seconds, as Cameron had stated'.

Although Cameron had told him he was alone at the time, one negative appeared to show the shadow of another person pointing what looked like a shotgun.

When the article was published *New Scientist* readers quickly pointed out that shadows in two of the photos suggested they had not been taken at the same time. This idea gained strength when Mr Douglas later subjected the pictures to colour separation tests. From these tests he deduced the photographs had been taken not in 20 or 30 seconds, but over several hours.

Kevin Cameron would never tell Mr Douglas where the photographs were taken and he failed to respond to many other relevant questions.

Despite this, interestingly enough, Mr Douglas still thought the pictures were of a real thylacine. He thought one photograph – the one in which the shadow of the man with the shotgun is visible – was of a live creature. All the others, he believed, were taken several hours later of the same animal in a state of *rigor mortis*.

Mr Douglas hoped that, after a decent interval, the carcase would be found, 'shot by persons unknown'. That was perhaps wishful thinking; the hoped-for carcase has never surfaced.

Perhaps the most frustrating thing about Mr Cameron's story is that he claims that on becoming aware of him, the creature '... stopped digging to look at me squarely before it vanished into the surrounding vegetation'.

Why, then, didn't he photograph its head?

One would also expect that after the event, in order to establish the size of the animal, something of known dimensions – a rifle, a dog, a human being – would have been photographed next to the jarrah tree. If such comparison shots were taken they were not shown to Athol Douglas or to any other scientist.

Mr Cameron's story, as reported, leaves many other questions unanswered (where, for instance, were his ever-present dogs on this occasion?) but one of its oddest elements is what the tiger-hunter says about his clothing. After spotting the animal, he said, 'To cut down the noise I peeled off my clothes and crawled through the undergrowth in my underpants'.

Mr Cameron's disrobing gave some newspaper editors an irresistible headline opportunity. ('HUNTER IN UNDERPANTS SNAPS WHAT MAY BE TASMANIAN TIGER' trumpeted the *Sydney Morning Herald*) but they did not question the logic of it. To us, however, this detail seems strange to say the least.

We detect, as it were, four holes in the 'underpants' story. First, disrobing would have consumed valuable time; second, doing so would result in little if any reduction in noise; third, while Rambo may run through the jungle bare-chested, in real life few hunters who have the option of clothes deliberately crawl through the undergrowth naked. Finally, during his time with the Slees, Mr Cameron often dressed from top to toe in camouflage fatigues. Such an outfit – or any ordinary bush gear – would be, we imagine, much less conspicuous than Mr Cameron's pale skin: despite his Aboriginal ancestry he has the colouration of a European.

There are, on the other hand, some positive aspects to the story.

Mr Cameron, unemployed and short of money, could have sold the pictures to any Australian tabloid. Instead he chose to send them gratis to *New Scientist*, whose sophisticated readers, he knew, would subject them to microscopic examination and sceptical appraisal.

If there really are thylacines in Western Australia, Mr Cameron, by all accounts a courageous and exceptionally gifted hunter and tracker, would be just the kind of man to find them.

Naturally, we would *like* to believe the Cameron photographs are genuine. Since 1985, however, Kevin Cameron has become almost as hard to track down as the thylacine itself.

As the years go by, it seems less and less likely the object in the Cameron photographs is a thylacine, dead or alive, at all. That, however, does not necessarily mean the entire West Australian thylacine phenomenon is an illusion. Since the photos were taken in 1984 people have continued, intermittently and in the same general areas as before, to report encounters with large, striped, dog-like animals: the mystery goes on.

The nearest thing to hard evidence of the mainland tiger's survival is the thylacine humerus (shoulder bone) found in northwest WA in 1970.

This bone was found, by Dr Michael Archer and colleagues, in a cave too small for human habitation and was surrounded by the crushed bones of many smaller animals. Since there was no trace of any other large predator, it seemed logical to assume the thylacine had occupied the shelter for some time and had killed at least some of the smaller animals.

Because the broken thylacine humerus was quite small and would be destroyed in the process, it was not subjected to radiocarbon dating. A sample of the other bones, however, was analysed and the scientists were surprised to find the material tested out at less than 80 years old. The dating of these bones has never been challenged.

Dr Archer is careful to note that 'it is possible the age of the thylacine bone differs from the age of the bone in the sample' but we find it difficult to see how the bone could be 3000 years older than material lying right beside it in a tiny cave.

Dr Archer, in fact, accepts the possibility of the humerus being only 80 years old. He points out that there is reason to suspect thylacines may have lingered on in the Kimberleys longer than in most parts of the mainland. This is because the dingo – the thylacine's great competitor – didn't seem to impact the ecology of the area as heavily or as early as most other parts of the continent. Mr Archer is also aware of numerous eyewitness reports of thylacine-like creatures which have come from the Kimberleys in the modern era.

Although Dr Archer's thylacine humerus represents the closest thing yet to concrete evidence of the mainland thylacine's survival, there is, just possibly, one other piece of hard evidence.

At the beginning of this chapter we used the story of the discovery of the mummified Mundrabilla thylacine carcase to illustrate, in a dramatic way, the fact that thylacines really did inhabit mainland Australia thousands of years ago. Since writing those lines, however, we have become aware of a startling theory put forward by Athol Douglas, the scientist already mentioned in relation to the Cameron photographs.

Mr Douglas, formerly a senior experimental officer at the Western Australian Museum, maintains that far from being 4600 years old when discovered in 1966, the carcase may have been only *one year old*.

On examining the carcase just after it was found, Mr Douglas decided immediately that it was very recent. It was '... fully covered with hair, had a musty odour, and looked like a recent dried-out carcase after the maggots had left but before the hide-and-fur-eating invertebrates had begun their attack. It was *not* a dehydrated carcase with dried intestines and flesh.'

When the carcase was carbon dated at 4600 years, Mr Douglas reluctantly accepted the finding, although he was aware that dry tissues, not bone, were used in the dating. Later he re-examined the carcase and became convinced his initial opinion was correct.

He is adamant that the animal is not dried and mummified as claimed. He points out that Jacoba and David Lowry, who found the carcase, said at the time that 'the soft tissue had decomposed to a tarry substance which coated the exposed bones ... However, the tongue and left eyeball were still recognisable, and a musty odour of decomposition was noticeable ... [rats] ... appeared also to have chewed the abdomen ... [rat] faeces were scattered around the carcase.'

Mr Douglas believes the tarry substance is dried adipocere, 'grave wax', which he has seen many times on recent carcases of other animals found in caves and mine shafts.

During a 1986 visit to 'Thylacine Hole', Mr Douglas established that the rocks on which the carcase was lying were a very recent fall from the cave roof. He also found a dingo carcase, which, since it was not present in 1966, was less than twenty years old. The dingo carcase, hairless, dry and odourless, is in a far worse state of preservation than the supposedly 4600-year-old thylacine.

Mr Douglas points out that although the bulk of modern Western Australian thylacine reports come from the southwest of the state, some have come from Mundrabilla Station and the surrounding area. We also have had a report of a young couple on a motor bike almost colliding with a thylacine on the Nullarbor in the vicinity of Mundrabilla.

The thylacine remains may or may not prove to be recent but there are other pieces of evidence which, though perhaps not rock hard, are nevertheless a bit more tangible than mere eyewitness testimony.

Footprints

Given the large number of sighting reports, remarkably few plaster casts or photographs of tracks have been collected. There could be four reasons for this:

1. A thylacine's footprints do not, to the average person, appear radically different to those of a dog and may not therefore attract the eye. A thylacine's tracks are also not spectacularly huge: no bigger than those of a medium to large dog.
2. In the late twentieth century most city people, and most country folk as well, are very poor trackers.
3. Animal tracks are notoriously difficult to photograph clearly.
4. Plaster of paris is not a substance usually kept close at hand, and for various reasons casts of tracks are not always easy to make.

We have yet to see a photo of alleged thylacine tracks *in situ* which is clear enough to be of any use. Some sketches of tracks are a little better as evidence: the one by Mrs Anderson, for instance, appears to show the long heel characteristic of the thylacine's rear foot, but most are of little real value.

Mrs Anderson and two or three other people in South Australia and Victoria have made plaster casts of tracks over the years. Most of these have apparently not been particularly clear, but some casts displayed recently by the Rare Fauna Research Society do seem very similar to pre-1936 sketches of Tasmanian tiger tracks.

The clearest casts of all are those produced by Kevin Cameron at Sid Slee's 'Hillside' property. These casts are so perfectly well defined that, providing they are genuine, they come near to proving thylacines exist in the west.

If the casts seem a little *too* good, it should be remembered that Mr Cameron was a professional hunter and tracker. He obtained the casts by setting up (in an area where thylacines had often been reported) several areas of raked sand baited with freshly-killed rabbits.

Photographs

As has already been mentioned, the creature in the Cameron photographs closely resembles a thylacine. Unfortunately, however, serious doubts have been raised as to the validity of the pictures. We have some serious doubts, also, about the 1964 Rilla Martin photograph.

The exact type of camera and film she used and the distance between her and the animal are unknown. The absence of comparison shots taken at the same site is frustrating, as is Miss Martin's absolute refusal since the late 1960s to be interviewed.

E.H.M. Ealey of the Monash University Zoology Department, who took a considerable interest in the Ozenkadnook tiger in the 1960s, did not think much of the photograph. In 1969 he wrote to Melbourne researcher Keith Zeinert:

Miss Martin saw something dash away through the scrub, pointed her camera at it and exposed some film. She gave the film to her cousin to develop and it was not returned to her until some seven months later, showing this remarkable beast ... As the cousin ... is known for his practical jokes, it is thought that he constructed a dummy tiger, photographed it, and placed it amongst Miss Martin's negatives in place of the picture she took, which must have only shown a blur anyway.

Although he sounds sure of his facts, much of what Mr Ealey said sharply contradicts the story which accompanied the photograph when it was first published in the *Wimmera Mail Times* in September 1964.

In 1975 Australian film-makers Gordon Glenn and Keith Robertson made a 53-minute documentary 'On the Track of Unknown Animals' which examined Victorian thylacine reports in general and the 'Ozenkadnook tiger' phenomenon in particular.

One of the people they interviewed for the film was Miss Martin's cousin, Graham Martin, who cheerfully admitted to being a bit of a wag but insisted, with apparent sincerity, that the photo was not the result of one of his jokes. Contrary to what Mr Ealey said, Miss Martin had had the photos developed in Melbourne and later sent the print to Graham.

The film-makers also interviewed thylacine witness Cyril Tucker on whose property Mr Ealey had stayed for a week, attempting to catch the 'tiger' in a trap baited with live fowls. It was clear that the affable old bushman had not been overly impressed by the boffin's fruitless efforts.

Also interesting was the film-makers' interview with Peter Basta who was in charge of the ABC TV coverage of the Ozenkadnook events in 1964.

Mr Basta said that the original black and white print of the Rilla Martin shot was only 2¼ inches [5.7 centimetres] square and did not impress him greatly. He obtained the negative, however, and arranged for ABC photographers to examine it. They reported that it was not a touched-up negative, nor did they think it was a re-photograph of a touched-up photograph. They felt the shadows shown in the photo could all have been natural.

A conflicting opinion was given by Ian Ward, photographer with the *Wimmera Mail Times*. He thought it could have been faked – that it might have been a composite picture or a photograph of a cut-out set up in the bush.

In order to test Mr Ward's theory the film-makers went to some trouble constructing a three-ply cut-out, hand-painted to duplicate as far as possible the creature in Miss Martin's picture. Then they photographed it, in bushland close to the original site, with a camera similar to Miss Martin's.

Far from proving Mr Ward's theory, the photos they produced tended to strengthen the credibility of Miss Martin's shot. Their photos of the painted cut-out looked exactly like that: photos of a cut-out.

Although Glenn and Robertson were unable to interview Miss Martin in person, their film contains file footage of an ABC TV interview with her filmed in 1964. On film Miss Martin gives the impression of being a normal, rational, pleasant woman but as we don't have access to a voice-print lie detector, all we can say is that she appears to be telling the truth.

We may never know for sure whether the Rilla Martin picture is genuine. The object in the photograph *might* be a very cleverly constructed cut-out or model, but there are some intriguing things about it which sometimes tempt us to think otherwise.

The 'Ozenkadnook tiger' was widely believed to be a thylacine. If a person was intent on staging a hoax, he or she would surely have made a cut-out or model which closely resembled that animal. Instead, the creature in the photograph, while *thylacine-like* in some respects, is not exactly like a Tasmanian tiger. Its stripe pattern is different, the head and neck do not look quite right and the general bearing of the animal looks somehow different.

However, while the stripes on the Martin animal – which start at the neck rather than the shoulders – do not match those of Tasmanian thylacines, they *do* match some mainland eyewitness testimony and sketches.

As pointed out earlier a sketch done by South Australian eyewitness, Don Gilette, in 1968 shows an animal whose stance and general appearance are strikingly similar to the creature in the photo.

There is a third photograph, in fact an 8 mm movie film, which might show a mainland thylacine. The value of the 'Anderson film', however, depends more on the high quality of the witnesses than on the clarity of the images it shows.

Archie Anderson was a Western Australian police officer and a keen, very experienced wildlife photographer. Wildlife lovers regarded his wife Iris as a virtual patron saint of the state's wildlife. She and Archie kept a sanctuary for injured and neglected animals at their Bicton home.

One day in 1969 Mr and Mrs Anderson, accompanied by Mr and Mrs Moore and their daughter, were driving a few miles south of Carnarvon when they passed a strange-looking animal about 5 metres off the road.

Mr Anderson stopped the car, slowly reversed it, and they all had a clear, if brief, view of the animal. They were nearly certain it had stripes. It looked thin and hungry, its tail was stiff and thick and it had big ears thickly made. It looked, they said, more like a hyena than anything.

As they stopped and reached for their cameras the creature moved. 'All I could do,' said Archie, 'was press the button on my camera as the animal moved off.' The gait had a peculiar cantering motion.

The six-second film clip is not particularly clear. Archie apparently didn't have time to focus properly and when he began shooting, the creature was already about 60 metres away.

As it appears on the film, the animal does not seem to be very large. The tail does not really appear to be as thick as described and is not held out rigidly. The legs appear to be longer in proportion to the body than a thylacine's and the lower rear leg doesn't look quite right. All these features, though, could have been distorted by bad focus and heat shimmer.

On the positive side, the creature's head and the heavy upper hindquarters, out to the butt of the tail, could be those of a thylacine.

Wildlife expert Ian Offer said the film was 'the best recorded evidence that the tiger exists in Western Australia. No normal animal can run in that manner. The way it loped along with its back legs and front legs not coordinated indicated it was a marsupial.'

A West Australian Museum officer, Duncan Merrilees, was not so sure. 'Its gait,' he wrote in an internal report, 'seemed abnormal but not impossible for a dog or fox. Its tail was long and held curved, in length consistent with fox, in curvature with dog. The identity of the animal seemed to me uncertain, with dog, fox or thylacine as possibilities.'

The Anderson film is certainly of interest as a cryptozoological artefact but it doesn't really prove anything. The animal depicted could be a mangy fox. A large fox whose body and tail have been stripped of fur *can* look rather alien. On the other hand, of course, the Andersons, as highly experienced observers of wildlife, had almost certainly seen mangy foxes before.

Animal kills

Several of the kangaroo carcases found in West Australian thylacine hot-spots really do appear to have been killed and mauled in a unique manner: their heads have been torn right off their shoulders and either carried away or eaten whole.

Sceptics, of course, may point out that Tasmanian thylacines were not noted for head-hunting. They might also ask why the supposed mainland thylacines have not engaged in the wholesale slaughter of sheep which was attributed to the Tasmanian variety.

The above constitutes all that could be seen as reasonably 'hard' evidence supporting the existence of the mainland tigers. There are also, however, certain recurring patterns in the testimonial evidence which are worth looking at.

Movement

As we have already discussed, in relation to Mr Slee's evidence, many witnesses have mentioned the way thylacines sometimes move their back legs in unison, as a kangaroo does. Just as interesting are a few reports which refer to vaguely *horse-like* movements by the creatures.

As mentioned earlier, Archie and Iris Anderson said the gait of the creature they filmed had 'a peculiar cantering effect'.

The following excerpts from the statements of other eyewitnesses contain similar details:

1. Mrs Hemery, West Pingelly, Western Australia: '... the hind legs moved like a kangaroo, the front legs like a galloping horse'.
2. Bob Rethus, Brimpaen, Victoria: '... the head sat up almost vertical to its body as it ran, something like a horse when it arches its neck.'

Surely if someone was hoaxing or hallucinating a thylacine sighting, horse-like imagery would not be in the forefront of their mind. However, interestingly enough, such imagery has been used on at least one occasion in Tasmania itself.

In 1970 Mr D. Whayman told Eric Guiler of seeing, on Tasmania's west coast, a thylacine which moved 'like a trotting horse'.

In the light of these statements it is interesting to look again at the creature in the Rilla Martin photo. To our eyes, at least, the carriage of its head does appear rather equine: it *is* held high, rather like that of a trotting horse.

Pelt markings

Most mainland sightings appear to be of animals whose markings more or less match the stripe pattern of the Tasmanian thylacines. As we have seen, however, some mainland witnesses describe thylacines with considerably more stripes than the Tasmanian tigers and others tell of seeing thylacines with no stripes at all.

Attempting to draw conclusions from this may seem foolish but it may be worth pointing out the following:

1. The number and distribution of stripes varied a little on the Tasmanian tigers themselves: some had as few as thirteen stripes and others as many as twenty-two. Beneath the stripes, the basic colour of Tasmanian tigers also varied somewhat: from grey to golden brown.
2. A 6000-year-old rock painting of a thylacine in Arnhem Land, Northern Territory, shows the stripes starting at the neck and covering the entire body – similar to the markings on the animal in the Rilla Martin photo. (On the other hand, the stripe pattern on 'Old Hairy', the supposedly mummified thylacine found near Eucla, Western Australia, is not noticeably different to that of 'ordinary' Tasmanian tigers).

Behaviour

In the early days in Tasmania it was established that the thylacines hunted alone, occasionally in pairs but never in packs. Since very few Australians have any knowledge of the Tasmanian tigers' habits, we feel it is quite significant that among mainland thylacine witnesses exactly the same pattern has emerged. Almost all reports are of single animals, a small number refer to pairs and reports of three or more animals are extremely rare.

Although many of the preceding considerations give us hope that thylacines may exist on the mainland the fact remains that (with the possible exceptions of the bone discovered by Dr Archer and the Mundrabilla carcase) not a single piece of hard evidence has been brought in for examination.

The next most powerful single argument against the existence of mainland thylacines is this: there is no tradition concerning these creatures among mainland Aborigines. Since the collective folk memory of some Aboriginal groups has been shown to extend as far back as 3000 years, the mainland thylacines, however rare, should have rated at least a few casual references in folktales.

The absence of Aboriginal thylacine stories could, of course, be explained by Dawn Anderson's theory. The mainland thylacines might, as she suggests, be the descendants of thylacines brought from Tasmania and released prior to 1936. This scenario is possibly the best single explanation for the mainland thylacine reports.

But while the 'feral Tassie tiger' theory answers many questions it raises several others.

The offspring of a pair of thylacines released in southern Victoria in say, 1880, might possibly have spread throughout southeastern Australia, but what about Western Australia, isolated from the east by thousands of kilometres of desert? Was another pair released there? And what of the stripeless and all-black thylacines? Were the witnesses who reported these variations mistaken or lying?

Three odd incidents which occurred in Victoria *could* be seen as support, of a kind, for the Tasmanian tigers released-on-the-mainland theory: on three separate occasions Tasmanian devils – which are also supposed to have become extinct on the mainland thousands of years ago – have been discovered in Victoria. One was trapped at Tooborac in 1912, another captured by Ian Tantau near Dereel in 1971 and two others were run over in April 1991 near Harcourt.

The existence of a few Tasmanian devils in Victoria, while interesting, does not, of course, *prove* anything about mainland thylacines. First, unlike the thylacine, the devil is not thought to be extinct in Tasmania – it is in fact thriving there. A few individuals could therefore have been brought to the mainland by private individuals at any time from 1803 to the present. Second, devils, only about the size of fox terriers, would have been a great deal easier to catch and transport than thylacines.

While the true age of the Mundrabilla carcase and the Kimberleys thylacine humerus remain in doubt, it would be very rash to state unequivocally that mainland thylacines still exist. On the other hand the testimonial evidence is so plentiful and so consistent that it would be equally rash to declare absolutely that they do not. The evidence is so strong, in fact, that thylacine hunters might be better off concentrating their efforts on the mainland rather than in Tasmania.

References

Advertiser (Adelaide), 22 November 1960; 8 January 1968; 30 April 1968

Age, 7 December 1955; 21 August 1962; 21 September 1965

Archer, M., 'New Information About the Quaternary Distribution of the Thylacine (*Marsupialia thylacinidae*) in Australia', *Journal of the Royal Society of Western Australia*, 57(2). 1974

Australian, 2 November 1971

Ballarat Courier, 25 May 1971

Border Watch (Mt Gambier), 31 July 1971

Carmody, Freda, letter to Mrs Dawn Anderson, 20 November 1973

Daily News (Perth), 11 November 1970

Douglas, A., 'The Thylacine: A Case for Current Existence on Mainland Australia', *Cryptozoology*, 1990

Ealey, E., letter to Keith Zeinert, 3 June 1969

Finch, J., letter to B. Marlow, curator of mammals, The Australian Museum, 15 January 1982

Herald (Melbourne), 6 February 1991

Herald Sun (Melbourne), 16 September 1965; 11 June 1986

Leongatha Star, 20 November 1990; 22 January 1991

Lowry, J. and Merrilees, D., 'Age of the Desiccated Carcase of a Thylacine (*Marsupialia dasyuroidea*) from Thylacine Hole, Nullarbor Region, Western Australia', *Helictite*, January 1969

Merilees, D., Western Australia Museum, file note, 2 October 1972

Naracoorte Herald, 3 July 1967; 7 June 1974; 7 November 1974

Naracoorte News, 17 January 1968

New Scientist, 24 April 1985

News of the North (Western Australia), 18 November 1970

On the Track of Unknown Animals, produced by Gordon Glenn and Keith Robertson, Acme Film Productions, 16 mm film, 1975

Portland Observer, July 1971; 27 December 1974

Slee, S., *The Haunt of the Marsupial Wolf*, South West Printing and Publishing Company, Bunbury, 1987

Standard (Warnambool), 3 February 1988

Sun, 3 May 1965; 26 October 1970; 16 November 1984; 5 May 1986

Sunday Times (Perth), 6 December 1970; 29 October 1972; 3 December 1972

Sydney Morning Herald, 8 December 1962; 17 November 1984

Walkabout, June 1968

Walsh, G., *Australia's Greatest Rock Art*, E.J.Brill-Robert Brown and Associates (Australia)

West Australian, 19 and 26 October 1970; 12 November 1970; 1 August 1979; 16 and 23 January 1984; 28 May 1984; 16 and 17 November 1984

Wild Life, November 1947

Wimmera Mail Times, 6 and 9 August 1962; 18 September 1964; 7 February 1966; 29 July 1966; 5 August 1966; 1 February 1967; 9 August 1967; 15 September 1967; 6 October 1967; 26 January 1972

Women's Weekly, 25 February 1970

Chapter Three

ALIEN BIG CATS

ALIEN BIG CATS

In ancient times Australia was the home of an arboreal, leopard-sized marsupial which is now referred to as *Thylacoleo carnifex*, or more commonly, the marsupial 'lion'.

After examining its subfossilised remains, the British anatomist Professor Richard Owen declared in 1859 that the animal must have been '... one of the fellest and most destructive of predatory beasts'.

The Aborigines, who co-existed with *Thylacoleo* for many thousands of years, must have slept a little easier after the 'lions' finally became extinct – probably with their assistance – about 10,000 years ago. Nowadays, as far as most Australian naturalists are concerned, the nearest true big cats – tigers – are in Java, 1200 kilometres away.

There is, however, one small problem: for the last century or so, hundreds of apparently sane, sober individuals have reported close encounters with big, sometimes *very* big – up to African lion size – cats in the Australian bush.

Of the six major Australian animal mysteries the big cat phenomenon is the most widespread, the most persistent and by far the best documented. We have, at present, more than 1000 reports dating from 1885 to 1994 on file, and every mainland state is involved.

It would be nice to report that the

Thylacoleo carnifex – the prehistoric marsupial 'lion'.

descriptions given by eyewitnesses are consistent in every detail, but that, unfortunately, is not the case. While most witnesses say the animals resemble American mountain lions or big black panthers, a smaller number of people say they look like leopards, African lions or even tigers.

This great variety of colours and markings may not be the crazy hodge-podge it seems. In fact, it is possible to see a rough geographical consistency – and other patterns – in the distribution of the various types of big cat reports.

Although encounters with large, unidentified felids have been reported from many different parts of Australia, some areas – like the New England region of northern NSW, the Southern Highlands of southeast NSW, the Grampians Range of Victoria, and the southwest of Western Australia – have become quite notorious for big cat activity.

The Young Witness – 10 February, 1933

Left: Shoalhaven and Nowra News – 31 March, 1976

Below: The Cootamundra Herald – 25 November, 1954

LION AT LARGE

Seen Near Barwang

BOY GETS FRIGHT

A report comes from Harden to-day of the appearance of what is supposed to be an escaped lion, which has been seen in the vicinity of Blind Creek and Barwang by several people.

A boy named Thomas Blanchwood, 15, went to bring in the cows when he heard a snarl. Looking towards the creek, not many yards ahead of him, he sighted a lion on a heap of old mining tailings. It snarled at him again—this time a bit louder and more menacing than before. The youth was terrified. He couldn't move for some time, and stood gazing at the unexpected sight. The only time he had ever seen a lion before was at Taronga Park some months ago. Then he took to his heels and did not stop running until he reached his parents' home. The household were a little alarmed, and the father got a gun, but by this time the lion had gone away. At night strange noises were heard about the place, but despite [unreadable] watching in the last few [unreadable] sight it again.

EATING [unreadable]

Yesterday, a la[unreadable] in a car via the B[unreadable] having seen a st[unreadable] a rabbit just off [unreadable] or six miles out [unreadable] of the Blanchar[unreadable] rang up and [unreadable] animal tallied.

Mr. Len Bro[unreadable] this locality, [unreadable] sheep huddled [unreadable] almost on th[unreadable] vous breakdo[unreadable] lion had cha[unreadable] caught wha[unreadable] and then le[unreadable]

The Tiver[unreadable] vicinity, an[unreadable] her handfu[unreadable] anxious ti[unreadable] bark of a [unreadable] friendly [unreadable] their hai[unreadable] been car[unreadable] of the [unreadable] children[unreadable]

The [unreadable] sheep [unreadable] settler[unreadable] duri[unreadable] lio[unreadable]

Move to trap panther

A Wollongong car salesman has set himself the task of capturing panther-like animal which he claim he has seen twice in wild bus country near Nerriga.

Nerriga is on the road linking Nowra and Braidwood.

The man, Tony Sernandes (27) contacted "The Shoalhaven & Nowra News" to say that he first saw the beast about 10 weeks ago.

He and some other men were 10 miles north of Nerriga trying their luck at gold panning.

Mr. Serandes said he saw the animal just before dusk.

He said it moved across the road just near where they were camped.

It was definitely not a dog, but resembled all the features of a panther.

BIG PRINTS

It had a round head, and a thick, heavy neck.

He and his friends later found huge prints, as big as the palm of a man's hand on the ground nearby.

Mr. Ferandes said the first incident brought back vivid memories of something he had seen near Griffith in the Riverina four years before.

He was sitting on some high rocks when he saw a jet black cat, of enormous proportions, amble into scrub near the cliff face.

He said the beast was at least 6ft. long.

He investigated and found large prints, similar to those described in reports in this newspaper about sightings on Cambewarra range.

He had not told many people about what he had seen as he had been on his own and would believe him, said.

WANTS PROOF

Mr. Fernandes, aft seeing the animal ne Nerriga, has dedicate himself to trapping it, c at least photographing i to prove his claims.

Recently he returned to the Nerriga district and claims to have sighted the big cat again.

He said it had something dragging from its front left paw, but could not say whether it was a rope or chain.

It obviously wasn't wounded as it was spreading its weight on all four paws.

Mr. Fernandes says he is confident he has narrowed the whereabouts of the animal to a six miles radius.

LEOPARD AT LARGE: Mr. Milton Duncan reported this morning sighting a leopard on h s property at Muttama yesterday afternoon and is prepared to swear to his report on a stack of bibles. He sighted it feeding off a dead sheep and put his field glasses on it. It was larger than a big kelpie dog and was yellow with black spots and had a long tail. Mrs. Duncan also had the field glasses on the animal as Mr. Duncan stalked it with a rifle. It gave him the slip, however, and is still at large. He said it might have escaped from a circus and been wandering around in the hills for some time. What with an elephant at large last month and a leopard this month our district is becoming a regular jungle. Incidentally, Mr. Duncan assures us that he had not been drinking.

Perhaps the best way to find a coherent pattern in the mystery moggie reports would be to examine each of these 'hot-spots' in turn. We will start with the apparently panther-infested New England area of northern NSW, home of the legendary 'Emmaville panther'.

The Emmaville panther

During the late 1950s graziers around Tenterfield, Moree and Tamworth in the rugged New England area began losing sheep to a large, mysterious cat-like creature or creatures. The animal, described by eyewitnesses as 'larger than a greyhound', reached the peak of its notoriety between 1958 and 1962, when it appeared frequently near the village of Emmaville (pop. 500) cutting a bloody swathe through local stock.

Because it killed so often, and in a way which set it apart from feral dogs and dingoes, few local residents doubted the 'Emmaville panther's' flesh and blood reality. During 1956–57 at least 340 sheep were mysteriously slain on one single property, 'Pretty Gully' near Uralla, owned by grazier Clive Berry. Mr Berry said:

'Dogs and dingoes grab a sheep anywhere, often at the kidneys, and they don't mind roughing up the wool a bit.

'This animal seems to avoid touching the wool, and its habit of cleaning the meat from the neck bones is similar to the domestic cat's habit. It takes a big animal to clean the sheep right out as mine have been.'

Massive depredations near Kingstown earned the creature another local name: 'The Kingstown Killer'.

One of the earliest sighting reports came from fifteen-year-old Donald Clifford, who told of seeing 'a giant black cat' prowling around his father's Emmaville property.

'I spotted it coming over a fallen gum tree about 30 paces ahead of me,' he said. On seeing him, it sprang noiselessly into dense scrub.

Although it soon became obvious more than one animal was involved, the press, for journalistic reasons, continued to refer to 'the panther' in the singular. Although the period of their greatest notoriety was 1958–62 the New England cats have made several return appearances, notably in 1969 and 1973.

During the 1958–62 outbreak, Sir Edward Hallstrom was so impressed by eyewitness testimony and by the animals' footprint casts – one was said to be equal in size to that of a Bengal tiger – that he offered what was in those days a huge reward for its capture dead or alive: 500 pounds if it proved to be an escaped leopard or tiger and double that amount if it was a previously unclassified Australian animal.

Sir Edward apparently hoped the Emmaville panther would turn out to be *Thylacoleo* or at least a close relation of that supposedly extinct beast. Even in recent years some observers have suggested that most, if not all, Australian big cat reports are the result of encounters with not-so-extinct marsupial 'lions'.

There are, however, a couple of big problems with the *Thylacoleo* theory. Firstly, although it was cat-like in some ways, the animal also had several features which were definitely not cat-like.

Its hand-like paws, for instance, were designed for grasping tree limbs and would leave nothing like the cat tracks found at Emmaville and elsewhere. *Thylacoleo*'s jaws housed massive tusk-like incisors which protruded from its jaws and gave the creature's face a very distinctive appearance. It is doubtful any close observer would confuse a surviving *Thylacoleo* with a panther or any known big cat. The animal, in fact, may have looked more like a huge, murderous possum than a lion.

The second problem with the *Thylacoleo* theory is that, unless we are badly mistaken, there is no Aboriginal tradition concerning large cat-like animals in any of the big cat 'hot-spots' which we are examining in this chapter. The only area where such a tradition *does* occur is far north Queensland. That, however, is another story and will be discussed in the following chapter.

There is no way of knowing what colour the ancient *Thylacoleo* was, but the vast majority of eyewitnesses said the Emmaville panthers were jet-black. The description given by Sydney businessman Wallace E. Lewis in 1959 was fairly typical: '... slightly larger than a greyhound, jet-black with a feline head and a long tail'.

It seems, then, that the 'average' New England big cat conformed to the following profile:

Shape of body and head: very much like that of a leopard.

Colour: most (but – as will be explained later – not all) of the cats were said to be jet-black.

Feet: the tracks were said to be those of a large cat.

Size: despite mention in 1958 of tiger-sized tracks, most of the New England cats appear to have been no larger than a German shepherd dog: in other words roughly the size of a leopard.

Behaviour: although several sightings were made in daylight most stock losses occurred at night. The creatures were therefore believed to be nocturnal. No more than one animal was seen at a time, and despite the massive number of sheep killed there was no direct evidence of the creatures hunting in packs.

Their method of killing sheep was said to be quite distinctive and unlike the messy practices of feral dogs or dingoes, but no photos appear to be available to confirm this.

Although, as mentioned above, Sir Edward Hallstrom held out some hope that the Emmaville panther was an unclassified marsupial predator, most observers assumed the mystery cats were imported black panthers which had escaped from zoos.

At this point it might be worth mentioning that, contrary to what many people think, the 'black panther' is not a separate and distinct species of big cat. All 'black panthers' seen in zoos and circuses are in fact melanistic (black pigmented) jaguars or, much more often, leopards. More about this later.

No concrete evidence was ever produced to prove that foreign big cats were responsible for the massive stock losses in New England. After the 1969 cat outbreak, however, Arthur Field, the Guyra Chamber of Commerce president, claimed to have received a letter which confirmed the theory. The letter (since lost) was from an 82-year-old ex-trapeze artist who claimed that just before the Second World War a pregnant black leopard and two young males escaped from his travelling circus between Glen Innes and Armidale.

It is, at first, tempting to accept this story as a satisfying explanation for the entire New England cat phenomenon, but on reflection it proves inadequate. First, in Africa and Asia leopards are noted for their fondness for dogs – not as playmates but as food – and have even entered houses in search of their favourite chow. In New England the big cats have rarely, if ever, been accused of killing dogs. Second, the leopard is also well-known for its habit of dragging its kill into a tree. This has never been said of the Emmaville panthers. Third, the New England big cat stories predate the Second World War by many years.

Local lore has it that a panther-like animal was actually shot and killed at a place called Horse Stealer Gully near the Gwydir River in 1902 (some accounts say 1918).

According to the late Dick Farrell the animal was killed by Charlie Leader, a drover who was camped at the gully with his brothers Jack and Harry.

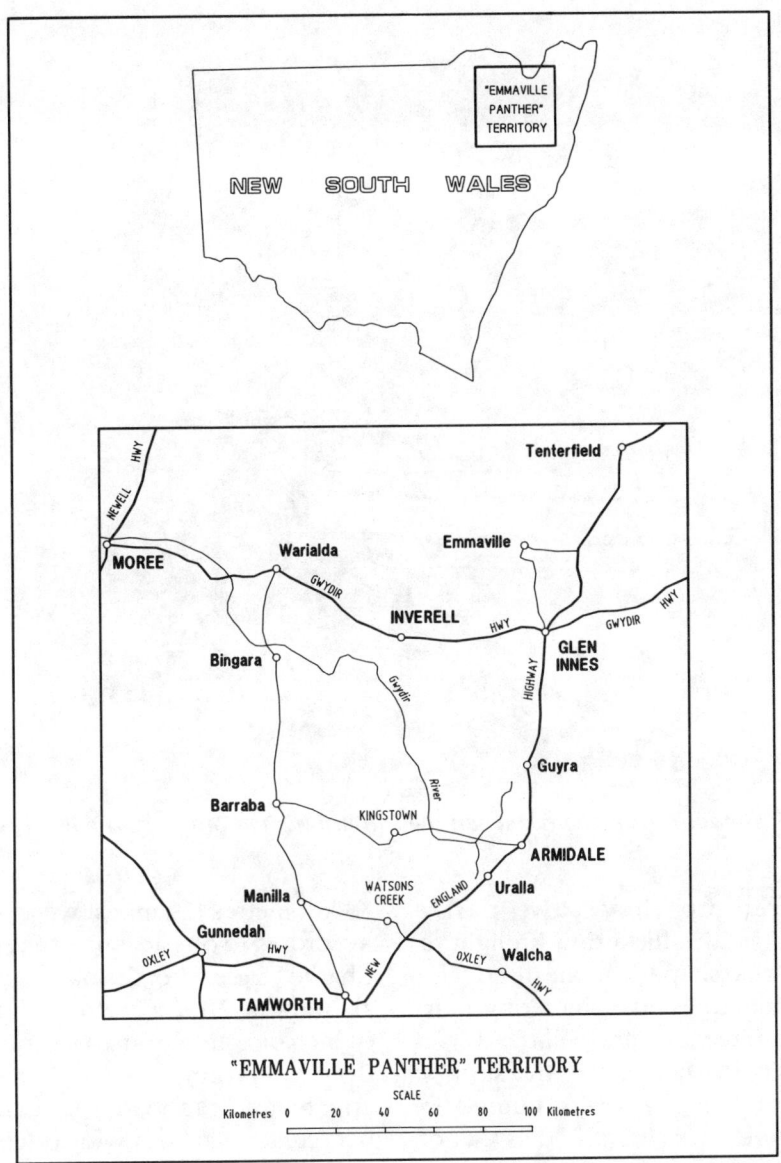

"EMMAVILLE PANTHER" TERRITORY

Since their arrival at the gully the men had been intrigued by strange tracks which frequently appeared around the camp. They were larger than those of a dog and unlike any they had ever seen. Even more unsettling was their discovery of several dead sheep whose skins had been turned absolutely inside out. The carcases had been completely consumed except for the heads.

Finally, one evening while walking back to camp from the river, Charlie was followed by an animal which, though invisible in the gloom, signalled its presence by prolonged low growls and the occasional blood-curdling roar. The camp was only one and a half miles away, but to Charlie the journey must have seemed endless as he scurried along, occasionally turning to throw rocks into the murky shadows.

Bursting into the camp site at last, he grabbed his rifle and yelled at Harry to throw dry bushes onto the fire. As the

'Imagine our surprise when the animal turned out to be a cat ...'

blaze flared up they saw, partly illuminated by the flickering firelight, a looming black shape. Charlie fired, the creature emitted a nerve-shattering roar, staggered a few yards and fell dead.

According to Dick Farrell the skin of the creature was sent to be tanned in Sydney where it was identified as that of a panther. According to others, the skin was brought to Inverell where it was displayed for some time in a shop.

Some versions of the tale end, predictably enough, with the destruction of the shop and the skin by fire. Be that as it may, the skin, if it ever really existed, seems to have disappeared.

In case sceptics and folklorists failed to notice the coincidence, Inverell was also the town where the 'thylacine' skin was supposedly displayed in 1937 (see Chapter Two). Staggy Creek, where the thylacine was supposedly shot, is about 30 kilometres [19 miles] west of Inverell. According to one account, the spot where Charlie Leader shot the black panther was also about 30 kilometres from Inverell (which direction from town is not stated). Both tiger skin and panther skin have apparently disappeared. (Are Inverellians particularly careless with priceless relics or is the 'skin-in-the-shop' a sort of non-urban myth which gets recycled every few years in a slightly different form?)

Although the Charlie Leader story has a ring of folklore – or fakelore – about it, it does suggest that people were at least talking about black panthers in New England prior to the Second World War.

Arthur Field's 'escaped black leopard' theory really falls apart when we consider a final point. Although the majority of the New England cats are said to be black, a significant number of witnesses insisted the animals they saw were sandy-coloured. In 1962, for instance, Mr E. Drew of Sydney spoke of 'a mountain lion or puma ... bounding across the road', and in 1973 C.R. Leigh of Fairlight, New South Wales stated:

At 7 pm (summertime) we were descending to Arrawatta Creek on the Inverell-Emmaville Road when on the left of the road my wife noticed an animal sitting about 30 yards from the road.

We pulled up and backed up to examine same. The animal remained and Mr Budd and myself jumped out of the car with our .22 rifles expecting to see a fox. Imagine our surprise when the animal turned out to be a cat. Two shots failed to hit him as he ran for the bush. It was of a fawn colour with a white-tipped tail; length of body approximately 3 to 4 ft; tail quite long and approximately body length; height 20 inches to 24 inches. In fact about the size of a large dog. The head shape seemed significant and was quite round, similar in appearance to an American mountain lion.

Till the shots were fired the animal seemed quite unafraid but upon being disturbed ran with the gait of a large cat. We returned to the spot next day and found a killed rabbit where the cat had been sitting. Claw marks were apparent on an adjacent tree.

This incident occurred only fourteen kilometres southwest of Emmaville, the epicentre of the New England black panther reports. While leopards may sometimes be black they are never sandy-coloured and spotless. American mountain lions on the other hand, are always sandy-coloured or reddish-brown to grey – never black. No single known species of big cat can account for all the reports.

As early as 1965, in an effort to differentiate the two apparently distinct types of big cat haunting New England, bemused locals had, in addition to the term 'Emmaville panther', begun to refer to the 'Warialda cougar'.

As with the black panther supposedly shot in 1902, there was at least one report of a sandy-coloured big cat in New England many years before the Second World War.

In early 1914 the township of Watsons Creek, near Kingstown, was in the grip of a 'lioness' scare. Large tracks were found and one settler stated positively that he had seen the animal. According to the *Argus* of 12 May, people were too frightened to send their children to school and the mailman had taken to carrying a Winchester repeating rifle.

A sandy-coloured American cougar could, of course, be mistaken for an African lioness.

Despite the 500 pound reward offered in 1958, $1000 offered by Mr Field during the 1969 outbreak and the fact that several experienced big game hunters such as Jim Bergin of Glen Innes, plus every kangaroo shooter and grazier in New England were gunning for them, no big cat was ever brought in for scientific examination.

Over the years the New England panther mystery has been 'solved' in various ways: once when a very black and much bigger than average boar was killed near Emmaville, and again when an old hairless dingo burned black by the sun was shot. But after being repeatedly 'explained', killed and buried, the 'Emmaville panther' refuses to lie down: it continues to pop up in various parts of New England – and sheep continue to die.

The Kangaroo Valley panther

From 1927 to 1930, as sheep were lost and huge cat-like animals glimpsed in the Southern Highlands of NSW, frustrated graziers hunted in vain for a creature or creatures variously known as the 'Tallong tiger' or the 'Marulan tiger'.

The handful of clippings in our files provides little in the way of eyewitness detail but it seems the 'tigers', logically enough, were thought to be striped. As the killings and sightings tapered off the mystery was 'explained' in various ways: by the shooting of a larger than average dingo, by the sighting of a feral Alsatian, etc. But almost 40 years later, in 1968, 'the cats came back'.

The new wave of felids – this time mainly black and therefore dubbed 'panthers' – has as its epicentre the rugged mountains and rainforests surrounding beautiful Kangaroo Valley, just 40 kilometres east of Tallong. Apart from two small villages, Kangaroo Valley is entirely rural and many of its farms back directly into the cliffs which rise, tier upon jungle-clad tier, on all sides. To the west the valley is bounded by the huge wilderness of the Moreton National Park, which is itself just part of a great string of national parks and state forests extending south to the Victorian border and beyond.

Harold McMahon may have been the first person to encounter a Southern Highlands big cat in the modern era. He told of sighting a black panther on two separate occasions at his property on Cambewarra Mountain, overlooking the southeastern end of the valley, in 1968. Mr McMahon, who served with the army in Borneo, said the animal was identical to the black panthers (black leopards) of that island.

Several other reports followed, such as that by Clarrie Hansen, who told of seeing a huge black cat in Meryla Valley and a smaller panther with cubs on another occasion at Yalwal. However, the full extent of the big cat outbreak was not appreciated until a particularly good sighting provided the first tangible evidence.

One damp afternoon in June 1975 a retired naval officer, Raymond Noakes, was relaxing in his house atop

The black leopard

More than 65 per cent of eyewitnesses say the Australian big cats resemble black panthers they have seen in zoos or in wildlife documentaries.

Contrary to what many people believe, the black panther is not a distinct species of big cat. Black panthers are, in fact, melanistic (black pigmented) leopards.

The leopard (*Panthera pardus*) has the widest distribution of all the big cats. Before their range was restricted by the expanding human population, leopards were found throughout Africa, the Middle East, India, China, Manchuria and Southeast Asia. Their range extended right down to Java, only 1200 kilometres from Australia.

The leopard's colouration varies somewhat from area to area and in the wetter, more densely forested portions

of its range, notably India and Southeast Asia, melanism is common.

Like all other leopards, the melanistic individuals are spotted but the spots are overlaid by additional dark pigmented fur so that the animals can appear to be almost uniformly jet-black. In bright sunlight, however, it is usually possible to make out the underlying spots.

Cambewarra Mountain when his fifteen-year-old granddaughter, Rosemary Drinkwater, burst through the door to announce she had just seen a huge black panther emerge from scrub on the edge of their property.

'She was so excited and so adamant,' recalled Mr Noakes, 'this thing had frightened her horse and all the other animals. It had a long streamlined body and a very long tail. It crossed a cleared paddock, heading north.' Because he had himself glimpsed a jet-black, dog-sized, but cat-like animal dashing through some bracken fern only a few months earlier, Mr Noakes questioned the girl closely. This animal, she insisted, was the size of a leopard, about one metre high at the shoulder. Her sighting had occurred around 2 pm.

Three hours later a neighbour who lived a few kilometres to the north arrived in a very agitated state. Just minutes earlier he and his entire family had stood and watched as a 'big black panther' stalked right across their property, leaving hundreds of footprints in a large area of recently bulldozed soil.

Realising the potential importance of the incident, Mr Noakes phoned the National Parks and Wildlife ranger at Barrengarry plus a couple of other neighbours. In all, ten people accompanied him as he inspected the tracks. The trail extended for almost a mile across the bulldozed land to a creek bed, where the creature had paced backwards and forwards before leaping onto a high bank and moving into the bush. Selecting one of the better tracks, Mr Noakes and the ranger made a very clear cement cast which is four-toed and 13 x 14 cm [5 x 5½ inches] in diameter.

Later, when we showed a replica of the cast to the well-known naturalist Harry Butler — that supreme expert on

---

Male leopards can measure 2.4 metres [8 feet] from nose to tip of tail and weigh up to 68 kilos [150 pounds]. Leopards normally hunt alone and by night. They frequently kill herbivores much larger than themselves and occasionally become maneaters. In India, individual leopards have been responsible for scores of deaths. One particularly aggressive animal claimed over 200 human victims.

Whatever their prey, they usually stalk their victim and, after a final leap, kill with a bite to the nape of the neck or to the throat. Surprisingly, some leopards are partial to sweet fruits.

It has often been suggested that Australia's big cat mystery began with an escape into the wild, many years ago, of a breeding pair of melanistic leopards.

There are, however, several weaknesses in the black leopard theory. First, although many witnesses have seen the 'black panthers' in broad daylight and at close range, no one has ever noticed the underlying spots which should have been visible under such conditions. Second, its total extinction in many parts of its former range testifies to the fact that the leopard is not always difficult to hunt or trap. Third, leopards usually only kill what they need to survive — they are not noted for the wholesale slaughter of stock reported at Emmaville and elsewhere in Australia. Fourth, in some Australian eyewitness accounts, the 'black panthers' are said to have run at great speed for considerable distances. Asian and African leopards do not possess that kind of stamina.

Finally, the black leopard theory does nothing to explain the many reports of sandy-coloured, puma-like animals which emanate from precisely the same areas as the black panther reports.

everything which runs, crawls, creeps, cheeps, howls or bites in the antipodean bush – he didn't hesitate for a second: 'Definitely not a dog print,' he declared. 'This was made by a very big cat – something about the size of a leopard.'

Because Mr Noakes, a highly-respected citizen, had the courage to talk to the press about the events on Cambewarra Mountain and because the newspapers treated the story seriously, other eyewitnesses, who had previously been reluctant to talk, now contacted him to share their experiences. He was, he told us, astounded by the number who called: 32 different people within the first few days.

As well as passing on details of panther sightings, some of these people told of mysterious disappearances of farm animals. One family, who lived only about two miles from the Noakes' property, had lost their favourite cattle dog in very grisly circumstances: one morning when they went to feed old 'Tex', who had been tethered to a dairy some distance from the house, they found only his collar and his entrails.

A cow belonging to the same family had been savaged while calving. The mother had survived but the calf's head had been ripped from its shoulders.

Others told of chickens, goats and sheep going missing and local school-teacher Mrs Robyn Neale told of finding the bones of a cow high in a tree, well away from flood-prone areas.

The publicity generated by the Noakes incident also brought forth a second footprint cast. This was made by David Sissens of Barrengarry, whose property lay only sixteen kilometres across country from the Noakes residence. Although he kept quiet about it at the time, a cow completely disappeared from a closed paddock on his property in the same month Rosemary

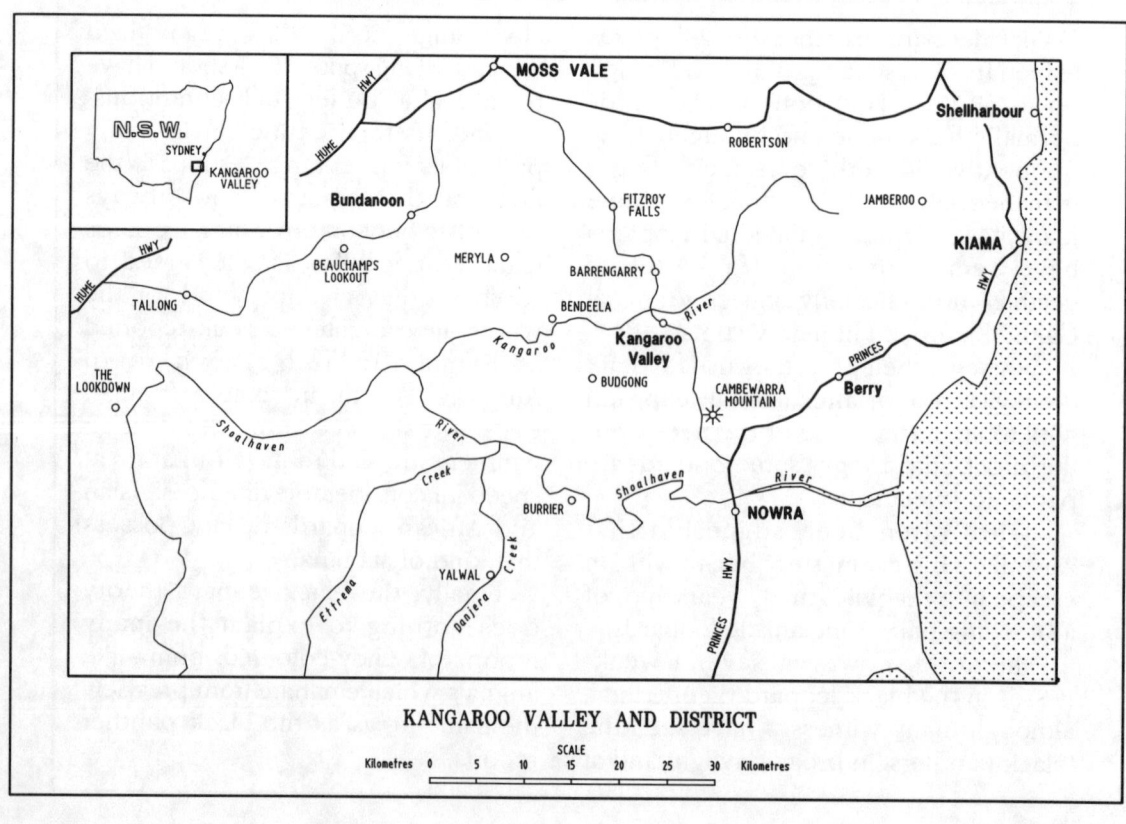

KANGAROO VALLEY AND DISTRICT

Drinkwater saw the panther. Shortly afterwards he found a wallaby in a creek bed with its head torn off. Finally, in February 1976 he found – and made a plaster cast of – a track which, on comparison, proved to be identical to that made by Raymond Noakes.

The decade following the Noakes incident produced a great number of eyewitness reports throughout the valley and surrounding highlands. Motorists reported seeing the creatures on main roads in broad daylight and some people were lucky enough to experience more than one close encounter.

Mrs Maw of 'Kanangra' saw what appeared to be the same black panther on three different occasions. Once while tending goats on her son's property she walked within ten metres of the big cat as it dozed in the sun atop a large boulder. A few weeks later, she stood staring as it calmly inspected her – at a range of only five paces or so and in broad daylight – from the other side of a tall chain-link fence. The creature, she said, appeared identical in every way to black leopards she had seen at the zoo.

Active community member, local historian and delightful character Mrs Doris Blinman, whose property backs onto bushland on Bendeela Road, reported so many sightings in the early 1980s that she became known, for a time, as the 'Panther Lady'. For a couple of months in early 1981, she said, her yard was visited up to three times a week, at night but also in broad daylight, by one or two huge black cats. Although the creatures came as close as her doorstep, she never succeeded in photographing them. They were not picky eaters: one grabbed a flying fox out of a fruit tree and on another occasion a tame koala disappeared. Bizarre as it may sound, Mrs Blinman feels they were drawn to her garden because of her grapevine, which they almost stripped of fruit.

During the period that Mrs Blinman's garden was being raided, Clarrie Hansen, who lives nearby, saw big cats running through a dump a few hundred metres from her property. On searching the area, we discovered tracks which, though much less well-defined, were similar in shape and identical in size to the footprints found by Raymond Noakes and David Sissens.

Other track finds were reported during this period and several valley residents told of being woken at night by terrifying howls and shrieks. Livestock continued to disappear and the carcase of a large dog was dragged from a shallow grave and carried about fifteen metres before being partly devoured.

All these incidents served to raise public awareness of the Kangaroo Valley mystery. However, the panther did not reach its peak of notoriety until, in 1981, it apparently killed a valuable ten-month-old pony belonging to Ron Smith of North Nowra. The pony, worth $2000, had been left with other horses on a property at Emery's Plateau, near Budgong, but went missing on 12 June.

Three days later it was found on a mountain trail several hundred metres from the other horses. Apparently, as it walked along the narrow, overgrown trail, it had been brought down by something which sprang from above and grabbed it by the neck, severing the jugular vein. The right forequarter and offside front leg had been torn off and carried away. Mr Smith found a single paw print 'the size of a man's hand' beside the carcase.

When this story hit the headlines the Kangaroo Valley panther captured the attention of the Sydney TV networks for a few days. Camera teams and well-groomed 'talking heads' dropped out of the sky in helicopters. They interviewed witnesses, filmed the craggy cliffs and wrung as much drama out of the situation as they could. They treated the story reasonably seriously, however, and the publicity did the cats and the valley no great harm. It was said that some gun-toting hunters were drawn to the area because of the TV coverage but on being physically confronted with the ruggedness of the terrain they soon departed.

As with the Emmaville big cats, the Kangaroo Valley panther mystery has been 'solved' from time to time. In 1977 a Wollongong man, Roman Sega, thought he had bagged the panther when he shot a large feral cat. The big cats, however, continued to be seen. Then in 1981, when she captured a jet-black wallaby, Mrs Julie Waller announced she had solved the riddle. 'I can't understand how people were so frightened of such a harmless animal,' she said. In fact, at least one panther witness had also seen the wallaby and recognised it for what it was.

At that time one of the area's greatest sceptics was Mrs Waller's husband Bruce, a National Parks and Wildlife ranger, and he enthusiastically accepted the black wallaby as the notorious panther. As fate would have it, however, Mr Waller, an honest, forthright man, later saw a large cat himself at Danjera Creek. He described the creature, which he observed for ten seconds, as jet-black, the size of a border collie dog and very thick set.

All the eyewitnesses and most interested valley residents reject feral domestic cats, wild dogs, hallucinations and black wallabies as explanations for the mystery. Instead, they favour the theory that the creatures are descended from a pair of black panthers (melanistic leopards) which were supposedly brought to Australia as US regimental mascots during the Second World War. When the

The puma

Also known as the American mountain lion, cougar, catamount, painter and – confusingly – panther, the puma (*Felis concolor*) is one of the world's most adaptable big cats.

In earlier days, its range covered all of South, Central and North America, except for the sub-Arctic and Arctic regions.

The puma is about the size of a leopard. Adult males can grow up to 2.4 metres [eight feet] in length (including a metre-long tail) and can weigh up to 118 kilos [260 pounds]. Its head, however, is smaller than that of a leopard and has a distinctly rounded shape.

The puma's coat is often a tawny-brown, similar to that of the African lion, and if encountered unexpectedly in an alien environment, the creature could easily be mistaken for a lioness. The puma's colour can, however, vary considerably. While most individuals

are sandy-brown to reddish-brown, the coats of some large Patagonian pumas are reddish-grey to silver-grey.

Adult pumas have a black tip to the tail and black spots over the eyes. They have a whitish underbelly.

One melanistic (black pigmented) puma was allegedly shot near the Carandahy River in Brazil in 1843 but the skin was not preserved. Because no other black puma skins have ever appeared in units were sent north to fight, the big cats were released into the bush somewhere in northern Victoria.

On the face of it, this theory is quite appealing. It is simple, plausible and answers most of the questions raised by the sightings. On closer examination, however, it is not so good.

The eating of 'Tex', the unlucky cattle dog, the exhumation of the larger dog, the discovery of cattle bones in a tree and the Noakes footprint all support the leopard theory. There is, however, one factor which argues very strongly against it. As at Emmaville, not all the Kangaroo Valley cats are black: several sandy-coloured creatures have been reported. Although these cougar-like animals are a distinct minority they cannot be ignored. One of the better 'cougar' sightings was made by Mrs Janice Bruem and Mrs Robyn Neale, at about 6 am in May 1978. At the time the women, both respected valley residents, were standing only a few hundred metres from Kangaroo Valley village.

'This very large cat ran across the paddock about 100 yards away,' Mrs Bruem recalled. 'It moved in a kind of stretched-out lope, a nice gentle lope. It was not an Australian animal. We were flabbergasted – we just stood and watched.' The cat was about six feet [1.8 metres] from nose to the tip of its tail, about two and a half feet [76 centimetres] high and 'a sort of fawny-grey' in colour. 'It was a sleek build – not heavy like a lion or tiger. Reflecting on it now, it was more like a puma, like a mountain lion but a bit slimmer. It had a long tail and the tail may have had bands around it.'

---

museums or collections and because no melanistic pumas have been photographed or displayed in zoos, it is safe to say that if black pumas do occasionally occur in nature, they must be so rare as to be virtually non-existent.

Pumas are excellent jumpers, often leaping six to seven metres vertically, but they cannot run quickly for more than 100 metres or so.

The puma, almost always hunts alone, stalks its prey and attempts to kill with a bite to the nape of the neck. It is most active in the morning or in the late evening and is notoriously elusive. They give vent to nerve-rending, caterwauling screams, but unlike leopards they are no threat to humans.

Roughly 30 per cent of Australian eye-witnesses say the creatures they saw closely resembled pumas, and some footprint casts seem to strongly support their opinion. Many people have suggested a breeding pair of pumas must, at one time, have escaped into the bush. There are several factors, however, which make us hesitant to fully accept the feral puma theory.

First, whereas in the Americas pumas are notoriously shy and elusive, in Australia they have frequently been said to approach within a few feet of witnesses and even to walk right around cars full of people.

Second, witnesses have sometimes reported animals with white bands around their tails – markings unknown in the Americas.

Third, unlike some of the creatures described here (notably the two animals which were pursued near Burakin, Western Australia in 1977) pumas are incapable of running at high speeds for more than 100 metres at a time.

Finally, since black pumas, if they exist at all in the Americas, are the rarest of all rare animals, the feral puma theory does nothing to explain the many reports of huge black cats in the Grampians, in southwest Western Australia and in other noted Australian 'puma' areas.

It is very difficult indeed to fit these puma-like animals into the US regimental mascot theory. Are we to believe the Americans released a sustainable breeding colony of mountain lions in addition to a breeding colony of black leopards?

As if to underline the problem, there has been one sighting of a 'panther' and a 'cougar' *running together*. This occurred one summer afternoon in 1979 when sixteen-year-old Peter Bruem (Janice Bruem's eldest son) was rabbit shooting near Bendeela. Knowing a certain gully was frequented by rabbits, Peter approached it in a stealthy manner and cautiously peeked over the edge. This time there were no rabbits to be seen. Instead, to his amazement, there were two large cats, one black and one brown, sitting in the centre of the gully:

Straight away the black one lifted his head and saw me and they were off like a shot. They were that fast ... they headed up the gully into an area of fallen logs and I lost sight of the brown one. It seemed the black one couldn't find a hiding place: he moved here and there and then headed around the side of the hill.

Peter sat in the shade of an over-hanging tree to see if they would show themselves again. After about five or ten minutes both cats reappeared and headed down the hill towards him, cantering almost playfully.

I thought: 'Beauty – I'll shoot one!' When they got to about 100 yards away I lifted the rifle to sight in on them but they must have seen the movement. They veered right around and rushed up the gully and disappeared. They were a fair size. The black one was miles bigger than my cattle dog: it would eat him for breakfast. It had a long tail and was solid but graceful. The other one was fawny-brown and slightly white underneath and up its throat.

While it is just barely possible that US servicemen released pumas as well as

Clockwise from right: Argus – 8 February, 1896; Argus – 4 March, 1936; Wangaratta Dispatch and North-Eastern Advertiser – 29 April, 1885; Argus – 6 October, 1915.

black leopards into the Australian bush, it is more difficult – if not impossible – to imagine cats of those entirely different species hunting together 50 years later.

Leopards are always spotted. Sometimes their spots are overlaid with additional black pigment to create the 'black panther' effect, but they are never uniformly brown or fawn. Cougars, on the other hand, are always brown to grey – never black.

No single species of feline can therefore account for the big black cats and big brown cats seen in such close proximity to each other, not only at Kangaroo Valley but also, as we have seen, around Emmaville, 600 kilometres to the north.

The third major problem with the US regimental mascot theory is this: sightings of big cats in the area predate the Second World War. In addition to the 1927–and–1930 'Tallong tiger' outbreak, we discovered, while researching the Kangaroo Valley mystery, an even earlier reference to Southern Highlands big cats.

In early 1909, according to the *Robertson Advocate* of 23 April, a cat the size of a mastiff dog was said to be prowling the hills just inland from Kiama, only 20 kilometres north of Kangaroo Valley. Although it was said to be jet-black, the creature was known as the 'Jamberoo tiger'.

The Grampians puma

To Australian big cat investigators Victoria presents almost an embarrassment of riches. From late last century to the present day, reports of 'lions', 'tigers', 'panthers' and 'pumas' have come from almost every corner of the state.

The earliest big cat reports, collected by pioneer Australian cryptozoologist R.W. McKay, date from the mid-1880s and refer to encounters at Lilydale (now virtually on the outskirts of Melbourne) at Piper's Creek, Taradale, and at Chiltern. In the early twentieth century, however, most reports appear to have come from a much more zoologically 'logical' area: the fringes of the vast mountainous wilderness in the state's east.

Between 1900 and the 1940s 'lions' were seen at Morwell, at Trafalgar and at Maffra. A 'puma' was reported at Heyfield and a 'tiger' at Traralgon. A nondescript but apparently feline creature called the 'Tanjil Terror' prowled near the village of that name. Between the mid-1930s and the mid-1950s, Rod Estoppey, a dingo trapper and Fisheries and Game officer, doggedly pursued the 'Briagolong tiger' which reputedly could eat an adult ewe in one sitting and which wreaked real havoc in the area, killing 110 sheep on one property alone.

Big cats continue to be reported occasionally from southeastern Victoria but in recent years a much hotter spot has developed in the central west of the state. The area in question is roughly bounded by the towns of Horsham, Hamilton, Ararat, Maryborough and St Arnaud. In the middle of this area – and central to its big cat mystery – are the wild and rugged Grampians mountains.

The Grampians big cat phenomenon is similar in many ways to that of Kangaroo Valley but there are some subtle differences. One is that the Grampians cats appear to be much more inclined than the Kangaroo Valley variety to attack farm animals. Another is that whereas most Kangaroo Valley big cats are said to be black, with only a minority of witnesses reporting brown, puma-like animals, in the Grampians brown animals are reported almost as often as black ones.

Although the black cat reports present something of an identification problem for zoologists, most local residents and most investigators have concluded the mystery predators are American mountain lions. To the press and the population at large, therefore, they are known as the 'Grampians pumas'.

If the creatures really are feral pumas, it would be difficult to imagine a more ideal refuge for them than the Grampians. Roughly 100 kilometres long and 40 wide, the Grampians range has national park status, is well watered, heavily timbered and teeming with wildlife. In addition to native animals such as kangaroos, emus, wombats and koalas, the pumas could feast on the thousands of feral deer, goats and pigs which roam the mountains.

The Grampians rise sharply out of a comparatively level landscape and are bounded on all sides by rich grazing land. If a puma grew tired of dining on wildlife in the mountains it could easily range out into the farmlands by night, perhaps by following one of the many watercourses, to pick off a fat sheep. On many occasions, in fact, the Grampians cats have been accused of doing just that.

Some people tell of seeing the Grampians big cats as early as the 1940s but it was not until the late 1960s and early 1970s, when sightings seemed to increase markedly, that the phenomenon attracted the attention of the press.

So many people have reported sightings from the area in the last two decades that our Grampians file is approaching the size of the Sydney telephone book.

Eyewitness testimony
Les Rentsch, Byaduk, 1969

Mr Rentsch's sighting occurred on his own property, 'Pineview' at Byaduk, 24 kilometres south of Hamilton:

I was mending a fence, when I looked up and saw this beautiful cat-like animal coming across the paddock. He was a tremendous sight – about four feet long and three feet high with a cat-like head and a magnificent silver-grey coat.

It was the coat that first caught my eye. It glistened in the sunlight like nothing I have ever seen before. I must have watched him for five or six minutes and I got a particularly good look at the head. It was just like that of a cat, but had two large fangs jutting from the top jaw.

Rob Wallis, Halls Gap
February 1971

Mr Wallis claims to have sighted pumas in the Grampians area three times in eighteen years: once in 1971 and twice in August 1989.

While his second and third sightings – made from moving cars – are interesting in themselves, the 1971 incident was the most remarkable, and the most frustrating.

On that occasion Mr Wallis and his two sons were photographing birds near Halls Gap, in the heart of the mountains. At 5.30 am, just as he snapped off his last frame of film, his sons called him to 'look at the cats'.

He and the boys then stood motionless as two adult pumas strolled quite casually out of the bush and down the track towards them. Without sparing the flabbergasted spectators so much as a glance, the creatures – one behind the other – walked right past them, across a bridge and into the trees.

Since he was so close to the animals, at one point only seven paces away, Mr Wallis could see they were 'a smoky grey-to-fawn' in colour and virtually identical. Mr Wallis pointed out that he was fairly well qualified to tell a puma from a dog, a fox or any ordinary animal: before coming to Australia from the UK he had worked as a zoo-keeper.

John and Irene Marlow, Lah-Arum, April 1975

The Marlows, an English couple holidaying in the Grampians, were driving on the northwestern fringe of the mountains when they saw a 'black lion'. John Marlow recalled:

After passing Lah-Arum we stopped to look at a map. My son, Tony, said 'Look at that thing. What is it?'. My wife replied: 'Only a black stump'. Then I saw it was an animal. It sat up and started to move.

Tony said: 'It's a great big black cat'. I

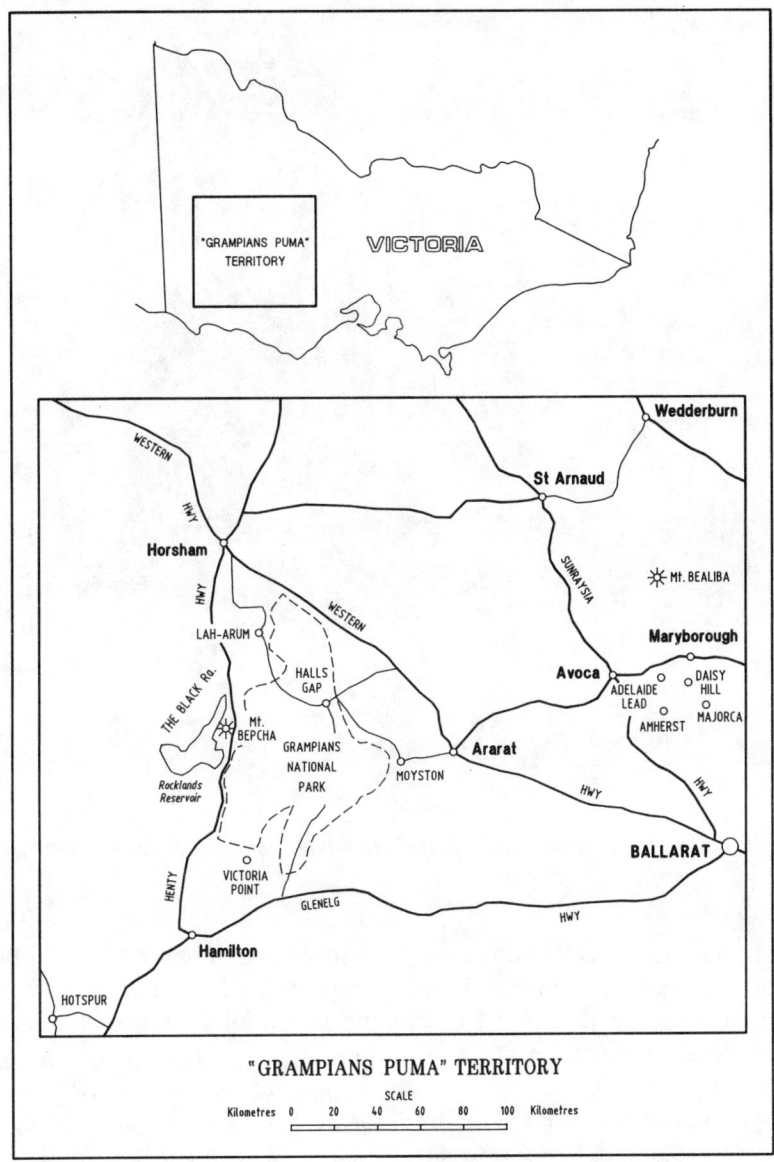

"GRAMPIANS PUMA" TERRITORY

said: 'No, it's too big'. The animal moved carefully, as though it was stalking something. It started to feed. It had a huge tail, heavily-muscled shoulders and was entirely black.

We were 75 to 100 yards away, with a clear view. We watched it for about 20 minutes. Its muscles were so big and well formed they bunched and rippled as the animal moved. I've no doubt it was a lion. It had all the appearance and characteristics of a huge cat.

Irene Marlow vouched for what her husband said: 'It looked just like a black panther, one of those things you see in films.'

Jillian Read, Jim Pitt and Gary Johnston, Syphon Rd, January 1982

One morning, as they drove along Syphon Road in the heart of the Grampians, all three saw a large cat cross the road 90 metres ahead. They stopped the car to investigate and Mr Johnston moved ahead

OUT OF THE SHADOWS

'He walked out of the dunny and stumbled over the three of them...'

of the others into the bush. Before he realised it, he had walked to within about nine metres of what he described as a puma with a head bigger than a man's, sitting in the fork of a tree.

With large, yellow-green eyes, the animal coolly returned his gaze. Mr Johnston, who later confessed to being 'startled', edged his way back to his friends. The animal was easily as big as a German shepherd dog. Its coat was thick and black, not sleek but 'like velvet'.

Ms Read, a local tour guide, said she, her daughter and a car-load of tourists had seen a similar animal at virtually the same spot a week earlier.

Les Farthing, 1985

Just after the 1985 bushfires, when Mr Farthing was living in a caravan next to his burnt-out farmhouse, some large animal began scavenging rubbish around the camp. Then one night, while outside, he heard a harsh, throaty, cat-like purr.

I turned around and here were three bloody whopping great big cats. Jesus, they were big. They looked like female lions to me, so I grabbed the shovel and backed up to the fire.

A little while later, my nephew turned up in his car ... and they bolted. I told him what had happened and he just laughed and said I ought to stay off the grog.

But Mr Farthing had the last laugh. A couple of weeks later the nephew '... walked out [of the dunny] and stumbled over the three of them. He scared the daylights out of the cats and nearly had a heart attack himself. He ducked back inside the dunny and screamed for help.'

Later they saw the cats quite often in daylight and realised the largest – dark brown in colour – was a female and the others were half-grown cubs. The ginger-coloured cubs, a male and a female, were 'about the size of a big Doberman'.

Graham Hunt, Mt Bealiba, 1988

One evening near Mt Bealiba, Mr Hunt and his brother were walking quietly up a forest track towards an open paddock which they knew was full of rabbits. Suddenly they heard 'something running at a great pace'.

It was this bloody great big black cat, bigger than a shepherd or a Labrador, chasing a rabbit ... along the track. The cat got to within about 20 metres and when it saw us it came skidding to a halt and ran full belt the way it came.

We just stood there with our mouths open, we had our guns, but we ... just stood there in shock.

John Middleton and Barry Henderson, Jimmy Creek Rd, 1976

On 29 October 1976, Mr Middleton, a surveyor with the Crown Lands and Survey Department sent a letter (see below) to G.W. Douglas, chairman of the Vermin and Noxious Weeds Destruction Board.

Since, as a surveyor, Mr Middleton was trained to make accurate observations and reports, his testimony would seem to be quite valuable. He is, in fact, not the only trained observer to have reported an encounter with the Grampians cats: at least three policemen have also seen them.

Senior Constable Alan Foskett, Daisy Hill, 1982

One morning Constable Foskett was

```
                        Dept. of Crown Lands & Survey
                                P.O. Box 59
                                Stawell 3380


    Mr. G. W. Douglas
    Chairman
    V.& N. W. D. Board.


    29 October 1976
    Dear Mr. Douglas,
                      Your letter ref. SP 1156 to hand.
                      On friday the 24th. of September this year,
    myself & Mr. Barry Henderson Field Assistant were doing some
    Trig. observations from Mt. William to the Watgania area.
                      At about 2.30 P.M. we were travelling west
    along "Jimmy Creek" road. A quarter of a mile east of "Larram
    Park" road, we came over the crest of a hill, & saw the cat like
    animal sitting up in the centre of the road at a distance of
    70 metres. It turned its head towards us & then sprang off the
    road in one bound, up onto a bank & disappeared into the scrub.
                      In size it was as big as a large Labrador dog,
    with a long straight tail at least 3 feet long. The animal had
    a round cat head, was jet black & sleek, but did not appear to
    be heavily muscled.
                      Both Barry & myself are adamant that the animal
    was of the cat family, but that it was not an over large
    domestic cat.
                                          Yours faithfully,

                                          J.G. Middleton L.S.
```

Mr Middleton's letter to G.W. Douglas, chairman of the Vermin and Noxious Weeds Destruction Board.

'An enormous black cat jumped up and ran in front of my car...'

driving near Daisy Hill, just south of Maryborough:

when an enormous black cat jumped up ... from cleared paddocks on my left, ran just in front of my car and up an embankment on my right.

The panther was nine feet [2.7 metres] long ... and had a powerfully-built body. The head was very small in relation to the body. I can't be sure of its weight, but it was probably more than 200 pounds [90 kilos]. It was huge.

The panther almost ran under my police divisional van.

Shortly afterwards, Constable Foskett picked up Senior Sergeant John Dix.

He was white, shaking a bit and very excited. It was about 9.30 am when we reached the scene. You could see where the alleged incident happened, because of the amount of tyre rubber Foskett had left on the road.

These huge footprints came up from ... the side of the road ... the animal had sunk down deep into the mud, and you could see the muddy prints on the road, and there were deep footprints and slip marks where it had scrambled up the bank on the southern side. On level ground there was no sign of claw marks, but ... up the [southern] bank you could see enormous claw marks digging into the ground.

Senior Constable Les Anderson, Grampians range, 1984

Constable Anderson claimed to have sighted black cats, in pairs, on two separate occasions in the Grampians. His second sighting, on 14 October, 1984, was of a female and cub.

The adult animals, he said, '... were about 60 centimetres high at the shoulder and 1.5 metres long. They were fast ... they could really go'. Constable Anderson became deeply intrigued by the mystery and, until his recent death, made frequent four-wheel drive treks through the mountains in the hope of seeing the creatures again.

Sergeant Dennis Willey and family, near Wedderburn, 1988

The incident occurred at 10.15 on the night of 30 September 1988, on the Calder Highway just ten kilometres from Wedderburn.

'This animal,' said Sgt Willey, 'was off the gravel shoulder ... in short grass in front of a small green shrub which presented a perfect outline ... I had a perfect view because I had my driving lights set to the side to pick up kangaroos. It was definitely not an animal native to Australia. It was fawn in colour and fitted into the category of a puma or mountain lion. It would compare in size to a female Labrador.'

Geoff Woess, Daisy Hill, 1990

Of all the people in the Grampians area Geoff Woess is probably the best qualified to recognise an unusual felid when he sees one. Geoff has worked with big cats for over seventeen years and presently has a small private zoo near Maryborough. In his collection he has a lion and lioness, plus a black leopard and a puma.

I know big cats, and when I was exhibiting at country shows people would look at my black panther and tell me they'd seen one of them in the bush. Despite that ... I was sceptical. But that changed a few months ago when I saw a big black feline crossing the road by Daisy Hill, just outside of Maryborough.

It was bigger than an Alsatian and its tail would have been about a metre long. It looked like a black panther – like my bloke. Unfortunately, because of the angle, I couldn't see its face. I stopped ... and found four good prints in the wet ground ... very big feline prints.

Killing of stock and wildlife

Even if no one had ever seen a big cat in the vicinity of the Grampians, there would still be cause to suspect their existence. Over the past two decades farmers and naturalists have discovered an increasing number of animals – both domestic and native – killed in mysterious ways.

In 1989 a delegation of graziers from the Maryborough district told the Victorian State Minister for Conservation, Forests and Lands that 1000 animals, mostly lambs, were being killed each winter in a way uncharacteristic of normal Australian predators.

The remains of large sheep had been found on top of large boulders and, in one case, in the fork of a tree. One horse had been reported killed and at least one other badly mauled. Several goats had been killed.

The animals were usually killed by a bite or blow to the back of the neck and were eaten in a quite distinctive manner – which will be described later.

Footprint finds

Although few local people are as well qualified as animal keeper Geoff Woess to recognise big cat tracks, several other significant footprint finds have been made in the area.

Rocklands Reservoir, April 1976

A twisting, turning, forty kilometre long body of water, Rocklands Reservoir lies at the foot of Mt Bepcha, just to the west of the main Grampians range.

Just prior to the 1976 hunting season David Hamilton and Wally Smith were camped at the Reservoir, scouting the area for ducks.

The sighting occurred just after dawn on an isolated section of the shoreline and for a short while the animal was unaware it was being observed. Mr Hamilton thinks they caught it off guard because they approached the spot by boat and then walked quietly along the bank.

'Wally saw it first,' he recalled, 'and drew my attention to it as it drank from the shallows ... it was as big, if not bigger than a full-grown Labrador dog. The colour was much the same as a Labrador's but slightly darker.'

When it eventually spotted them it made up for its previous doziness by exploding into action. It burst from the scene in great leaps and bounds. The men managed to keep it in view as it slowed to a loping run and moved across mostly open country towards Mt Bepcha.

They marked two of the better paw prints with sticks and returned later with plaster of Paris. One of the resulting casts, when put side by side with adult puma tracks from Melbourne Zoo, proved almost a perfect match.

Shortly after the sighting a team from Geelong's Deakin University scouted the rocky outcrops on top of Mt Bepcha and discovered several caves. The slope below the largest of these was littered with the gnawed remains of many animals. Some of the bones were from small creatures such as tortoises and rabbits, but most were from larger animals: emus, kangaroos, sheep and cattle.

Cultivation Creek, 1985

On a chilly July morning, Forest Commission officer Bob Hiatt discovered the tracks of not one, but apparently three different big cats. The location was Cultivation Creek in the Grampians: where Constable Anderson had seen a female big cat and cub the preceding October.

This time there were apparently two adults and a youngster. The largest tracks were quite huge: 14 centimetres long and about 10 wide [6 inches by 4]. All three animals had roamed around a picnic area, leaving deep tracks in soft soil and at one point apparently digging under a table.

Bob Lowcock of Cavendish tracked the largest animal on horseback and discovered a place where it had jumped cleanly over a watercourse. The creek was wide enough to halt any Australian animal other than a fleeing kangaroo: 5½ metres [18 feet] bank to bank.

Plaster casts were not made from the Cultivation Creek tracks and it is difficult to tell much from the photos except that they are large and four-toed. Although the toes appear longer than those of the Rocklands Reservoir animal the tracks still look more feline than canine.

Paw prints are not always easy to interpret but we think it unlikely the bushmen concerned would mistake dog tracks for those of a cat.

Near Moyston, 1989

As previously mentioned, Rob Wallis claims to have seen big cats three times in seventeen years. His most recent sighting, at six o'clock one evening in August 1989, was of a huge black animal near Moyston.

The creature crossed the road in front of his vehicle and as he slowed and coasted to within 30 metres of it, he could see it was an extremely powerful-looking beast.

'I was able to have a good look,' he said. It was in sight for probably ten seconds, starkly illuminated by his headlights. 'Incredibly muscular', with 'immense shoulders', it stood two feet [60 centimetres] high, was eight feet [2.4 metres] long – including tail – and looked to weigh about 250 pounds [93 kilos].

Returning to the scene in the morning, Mr Wallis tracked the creature for 2 kilometres into the bush and made a plaster cast of one clear track. Although the print seems very feline, it is unusual for a cat track in that the claw marks are visible. It is also somewhat smaller than what would be expected of a 93 kilo, 2.4 metre long cat. It is more like the tracks of a half-grown puma.

Mr Wallis could, of course, have misjudged the size of the creature he saw. Another possibility is that two or more animals were prowling the area.

Peter's Hill, 1989

This bizarre story was told by a husband and wife gold-prospecting team. A big puma-like cat, they said, approached their diggings and stared down the hole at them. Later, when they retreated to their caravan it leaned on the vehicle, rocked it from side to side, then jumped onto the roof and padded to and fro.

Senior Constable Foskett went to the scene and found paw prints as large as those of an Alsatian on the caravan's window. At a nearby rabbit warren were similar 'enormous' tracks.

Brimpaen-Cherrypool district, 1972

While searching for stolen animals near the Black Range, Bill Hower and some other men found not the sheep tracks they were looking for, but the footprints of a large predator. That, at least, was their interpretation of the tracks which were deeply embedded in the muddy wall of a dam.

The photos they took are not remarkably clear but this incident would seem to be of some significance because of the occupation of the men involved: Bill Hower and his companions were detectives from the Horsham CIB.

The detectives were so impressed by the tracks that they returned to the site and made plaster casts. The casts were apparently a great deal clearer than the photos because they helped convince a federal government vet that there really were strange predators in the Grampians.

In 1971–72 Ian Carmichael, senior veterinary research officer with the Department of Foreign Affairs, had been on loan to the government of Botswana. While in Africa he had been required to track down and kill troublesome lions and leopards. Not surprisingly, then, on returning to his home town of Horsham he quickly became intrigued by the 'Grampians puma' mystery.

During February 1972 he led a party of three into the bush. While scouting the vicinity of alleged sightings they discovered lairs, the remains of kills and a few large paw prints. The tracks appeared very similar to the CIB footprint cast.

When interviewed by the Melbourne press, Mr Carmichael would not be drawn on whether or not he believed in the 'pumas'. Clearly, however, he thought something was afoot. Of a confidential report he prepared for the Melbourne Museum he said: 'I'm sure they'll be very interested ... I think we're on the brink of something exciting.'

The puma hunters

Since the early 1970s several other groups and a few individuals have searched in a methodical way for the Grampians cats.

In 1982 a Queensland naturalist, Gary Opit, camped out for three months at isolated waterholes in the mountains searching for footprints and lairs. Since 1984 the Rare Fauna Research Society has logged and plotted every report from the area. The group also makes regular spotlighting and bush-bashing forays into likely areas.

Every investigator has added a little to what we know about the 'pumas' but the greatest sustained effort to crack the mystery was made by a team from Deakin University at Geelong.

Between September 1976 and September 1977 teams of up to 30 students and graduates led by an environmental science lecturer, Dr John Henry, interviewed witnesses and carried out searches for remains, footprints and faeces. They also researched the habits of pumas in America and sent faeces, footprint casts and bones away for expert analysis.

In caves and on rock ledges in the mountains the group discovered predator droppings which were very similar in size and shape to puma scat from the Melbourne Zoo.

Many predators have the habit of grooming themselves and often their own hair works its way through and is evident in their droppings. Analysis of grooming hairs is one of the best ways of identifying the creature from which the droppings came. Unfortunately, none of the droppings found by the Deakin team yielded puma hairs and all but one of the scats were identified as those of large dogs.

One sample they found at Geranium

Springs, however, was found to contain not only sheep remains but also the fur and foot bones of a fox. The fox bones were up to 6 centimetres [2.4 inches] in length. Hans Brunner, of the Keith Turnbull Research Institute, said the bones were much longer than any he had seen in dog droppings and that the scat was probably from a larger predator.

The university's bush-bashing teams also discovered the remains of many animals apparently killed by large predators. Some of these bones – of cattle, sheep, kangaroos and emus – were found, as previously mentioned, strewn down a slope below a cave at Mt Bepcha.

Several other interesting finds were made in Geranium Springs valley. This valley is heavily wooded and steep-sided but is also quite close to open sheep country.

On the valley's northern face a tree-covered slope rises steeply from a watercourse at the bottom. After approximately 300 metres this slope meets an almost vertical, rocky escarpment which contains several caves. In some of these the team found signs of occupation: depressions, bones, etc.

Along the line where the slope met the escarpment they found the carcases of four sheep. It looked as if the hapless animals had been killed near the creek and dragged or carried all the way to the escarpment.

Calf bones were also found in the valley, but perhaps the most interesting find was the pelvis of a mature emu. In life the emu's pelvic region is surrounded by extremely large and powerful muscles. This animal had been struck with such force that a notch, 29 millimetres deep, 44 wide and 33 long was gouged right out of the bone.

Dr Henry deduced that the bird had been standing at the time of the attack and had been hit from behind with massive force by an instrument – or paw – which had at least three sharp points.

Although they were properly cautious in their assessment of the evidence most team members, including Dr Henry, felt the Grampians were home to large predators, with strong supporting evidence for a population of feral pumas. Interestingly, they did not come to that conclusion solely through fieldwork, but also through historical research. We will return to this aspect of their work later.

The most energetic puma researcher of recent times is undoubtedly John Higgins, editor of the *Maryborough Advertiser*. Since 1984 Mr Higgins has pursued the creatures in the field and has constantly appealed for information from his readers. He has also financed the construction of several cage and automatic camera traps which have been deployed in the area. His files on the big cats are now so massive that to summarise his findings is no easy matter.

He says that not only are sheep regularly taken by pumas but also the occasional calf. On one occasion at least, a horse was mauled to death. The cats, it seems, consider goat meat quite a delicacy: they have sometimes walked right past grazing lambs to take a goat. Sometimes, apparently, kangaroo meat is also preferred to lamb. Informants told Mr Higgins they had seen a huge cat pull down a kangaroo without sparing a glance for nearby lambs. The creatures have also been observed stalking foxes, rabbits, birds and other wildlife.

He says the method of killing is usually by a bite to the neck or by choking. Some animals, including full-grown sheep and goats, had their heads bitten clean off.

Heavy carcases are often moved some distance and occasionally up rock faces before being consumed. One kangaroo was dragged 200 metres (through a paddock full of young lambs) and hidden in a reed bed. A calf was killed right next to a house, then carried over a fence and into the forest.

Mr Higgins says the cats have two quite

distinctive ways of consuming their victims. Both methods are radically different from those of dingoes or wild dogs:

1. Sometimes the predator eats into the carcase through a hole in the groin and consumes all the intestines, flesh and most of the bones. The rib bones are left. Graziers find '... virtually a whole skin, complete with head, legs and feet, but with a hole in it about a foot in diameter, and nothing inside apart from the ribs and possibly the backbone, or part thereof'.
2. The whole skin is 'peeled back to the neck and turned inside out and all flesh is eaten off the skeleton'.

Sometimes the predators have attempted to hide carcases by scratching grass and leaf-litter over them. According to American experts this is classic puma behaviour. Occasionally a carcase and surrounds has 'stunk to high heaven' of cat urine.

Mr Higgins finds that 95 per cent of sightings are of single animals, about 4 per cent involve female and cubs and about 1 per cent involve an adult pair. 'We have,' he says, 'no reports of male, female and cubs – indicating the male does not rear the young'. This, too, conforms to known American puma behaviour.

Like other investigators, Mr Higgins has found the animals seem to appear in two different colour phases. One of these he describes as 'from grey-sand through to ginger and brown' and the other from 'slate blue through to very deep black'.

Interestingly – as at Kangaroo Valley – black and brown creatures have been seen together. For two days in the mid-1970s a black male and a smaller brown female frequented a property near Avoca, where they were supposedly observed by more than twenty people. At Majorca in 1987 a brown female and a black cub were seen and in the same year what appeared to be a black female with a sand-coloured mate were reported at Daisy Hill.

Thanks to his perseverance, Mr Higgins has managed to sight the creatures himself on three occasions. Two sightings were brief but one in 1985 lasted for several seconds, at a range of about 60 metres. Mr Higgins and three companions had placed a bait in a tree beside a dirt track. As they returned to the site a giant cat-like creature sprang from the tree directly into their headlight beams.

It was four feet [1.2 metres] long in the body, plus a tail of almost three feet [90 centimetres]. Its fur was ginger and its eyes '... shone bright moonlight blue'. As it bounded off, its tail flowed out behind it.

Mr Higgins, incidentally, questions the way we have grouped all the big cat reports of central western Victoria under the title 'Grampian pumas'. He feels there are three neighbouring but essentially separate areas involved. The first covers the Grampians and extends down to the plains to the south and west. The second is bounded by state forest and extends from St Arnaud to Bendigo, to the south of Maryborough and through to the Pyrenees. The third covers the central Victorian forests east of the Calder Highway.

Shooting of pumas

Not surprisingly, over the years there have been a few people who claim to have taken pot shots at the Grampians cats.

During the autumn of 1977 Ian Johnson, his son Mark and John Morris encountered big cats on four different occasions. The first sighting was in daylight at the back of the Johnson property near Victoria Point on the southwestern edge of the Grampians, and the second was by spotlight during a shooting expedition at nearby Branch Creek.

As the animal stood dazzled only 50 metres away, the men debated whether to shoot. Eventually Mark Johnson fixed his telescopic sight on its shoulder and fired. He was using hollow point ammunition and all three heard the characteristic thud of the bullet hitting flesh before the creature leapt into the darkness.

The hunters scoured the area later but could find no trace of the animal. Subsequently they saw what appeared to be the same creature again – once by spotlight and once in the daytime. It showed no trace of injury.

When contacted by the Deakin University team the hunters refused to cooperate. They hoped, despite their remarkable lack of success in the past, to see the 'puma' again – and shoot it dead.

In August 1990 a farmer (known to John Higgins, but who requested anonymity) said he shot and wounded a huge felid on his property near Maryborough. The farmer had seen large cats on his property before, but had no intention of shooting them even when a full-grown ram was killed and eaten. When a second ram was killed, however, he lost patience and sat up near the half-eaten carcase for two nights.

On the second night two seven foot [2.1 metre] long cats approached the kill. He fired when one animal actually picked up the remains of the ram. Though it did not fall, the creature seemed to have been hit, because it let out two loud 'yowling noises' before running off.

Genesis of the Grampians cats

Ever since the 'Grampians puma' phenomenon came to the attention of journalists and cryptozoologists in the early 1970s, various local identities, such as the late Dick Saligari, have insisted they knew what the creatures were and where they came from.

The animals, they said, really *were* pumas. They were descended from American mountain lion cubs which were brought to the Mt Gambier area as US regimental mascots during World War II. When the cubs grew too large to handle they were supposedly taken to the Grampians and released.

As we have seen, a similar theory has been put forward to explain the 'Kangaroo Valley panther' mystery and variations of the story have been used elsewhere. It is a theory which contains some very significant weaknesses but in the case of the Grampians mystery it deserves to be seriously considered.

Although the explosion of big cat

The 'pumas' and the powers that be

In the following section we see how the Western Australian government has sought desperately to deny the reality of the 'Cordering cougars'. The official attitude in Victoria has been much more enlightened.

By 1987, John Brumley, the ALP Member for Bendigo, was convinced of the big cat's existence. So was John Radford, the Liberal candidate – and for good reason: his daughter had seen one. In 1989, after receiving a delegation of farmers from Maryborough, Mrs Setches, the Minister for Conservation, Forests and Lands, said she was taking the matter seriously.

These expressions of concern were not just hot air: in 1990 the state government sent Department of Conservation and Environment ecologist Bryan Walters to the US to study with the American Field and Game Department's mountain lion research team. Since returning to Victoria Mr Walters has taken a keen interest in the Grampians puma reports.

sightings began in the early 1970s there are a few on record from the 1960s and Dick Saligari heard rumours of big cat encounters dating from the 1940s. In the 1970s investigators found that while the US mascot theory was widely believed in the area, it was damnably difficult to get to the source of the story. Finally, in May 1989, an elderly Hamilton woman, Irene Addinsall, broke what she said was a self-imposed 46-year silence about the genesis of the big cats.

Miss Addinsall, then 78, said she remembered seeing the regimental mascots several times when she was a Land Army girl on her uncle's property, 'Kangaroo Park', near Hotspur in 1943. An American unit to which they belonged camped on Crown land next to the property.

There was a man among the soldiers with a light-coloured puma. She had four kittens, three light-coloured and a little dark-coloured one. They were always getting twiddled up in sticks or falling over. The army boss down there said he couldn't stand it. She was getting savage because the kittens were being hurt. She was becoming scotty. He told them to get rid of it!

The boss went down to a party at Heywood and got a bit worse for wear. While he was away ... they put the puma on a truck and took her up towards Halls Gap to one of those creeks ... and they let her out there in the middle of the night. She didn't want to stay ... wanted to come back with them. There were some rabbits and she ran after them and the kittens ran after her ... that was the last they saw of her.

A month after Miss Addinsall told her story a Maryborough man told the *Advertiser* he had seen a large cat with a chain around its neck in 1944 or 1945.

He was a child at the time, playing beside the road when he heard the sound of a dragging chain. Looking up, he saw a jet-black felid the size of a large dog 10 metres away. The event supposedly occurred south of Halls Gap in the Grampians.

If we choose to believe that the black 'puma' cub of Miss Addinsall's story was released with a chain still around its neck and that it dragged the chain around as it grew up, then the latter story could, perhaps, be seen as corroboration of her account.

Victorian big cat researcher Bernie Mace had no doubt Miss Addinsall's story was true. He later revealed that in 1987 an elderly man had told him, in confidence, that he had actually taken part in the dumping.

'He even mentioned Miss Addinsall by name ... it all fits'.

It would certainly seem so. As alluded to earlier, some of the most interesting evidence uncovered by the Deakin University team in 1976–77 was found not in the field but in the archives. While attempting to nail down the regimental mascot theory, they eventually discovered the identity of two American units which were stationed around Mt Gambier in 1942. They were the 35th and 46th Pursuit (Fighter) Groups. The units later moved to Queensland and then to the Pacific islands.

Digging deeper, the researchers hit what appeared to be the jackpot: they found that the colour flash emblems of both groups displayed the outline of *large black cats*.

Miss Addinsall's story, the eyewitness account of the dumping, the 'puma with

Colour flash emblems for the 35th (left) and 46th (right) Pursuit (Fighter) Groups.

the chain' story and the 'black puma' shoulder flashes seem, at first glance, to confirm the regimental mascot theory. As Bernie Mace said: 'It all fits'.

But does it?

As pointed out earlier, the only black big cats are melanistic (black pigmented) jaguars, or more often leopards. Only once in the history of North and South America has anyone shot a black puma. Black pumas, if they exist at all in nature, are so rare that they can, for all practical purposes, be considered non-existent. According to orthodox zoological thought, then, Miss Addinsall could not have seen a black cub in 1943.

Whatever the black cats of the Grampians may be, it seems they cannot be pumas. As at Kangaroo Valley and Emmaville, this throws a rather large spanner into the works.

One of the few local observers who has faced this fact was the late Constable Les Anderson. He explained it by saying there must be two types of cat in the district: pumas and black leopards.

If there are two types of big cat in central western Victoria, did the US servicemen liberate viable breeding populations of both kinds? It hardly seems likely. The US regimental mascot theory, appealing as it certainly is as a tidy explanation, really begins to fall apart when we consider this: big cats were sometimes reported in the Grampians area *prior* to the Second World War.

Peter Chapple of Rare Fauna Research has collected reports from the St Arnaud area dating from the early 1900s and from the Grampians range itself from about 1880. During his three months there, Gary Opit heard of a 1907 sighting, and a hunt for a marauding 'lion' was launched around Wedderburn in the late 1930s.

It seems, then, that the 'Grampians puma', like the 'panthers' of Kangaroo Valley and Emmaville, dodges classification as nimbly as it dodges traps and bullets.

The Cordering cougar

Western Australia is the largest, most sparsely-populated and most recently-settled state in the commonwealth. Sporadic guerilla warfare by the hard-pressed Aborigines continued in parts of the state right up to the 1920s, and until quite recently its more remote corners had not been fully explored by Europeans. Western Australia consists in the main of spinifex scrub and searingly hot desert.

In only one part of the vast state – the warm, temperate southwestern corner – is there an agreeable climate, reliable rainfall, fertile soil and significant areas of forest. While other areas rode economic roller coasters of gold, pearl and mineral booms, this corner quietly prospered on forestry, wheat farming and the grazing of huge flocks of sheep. The tranquillity of this green and pleasant area, however, was shattered in the late 1970s by a creature or creatures which threatened to rip the heart out of the sheep industry, terrorised and decimated the native animals and spread dissension, confusion and fear amongst the citizenry.

Graziers in southwest Western Australia have long been resigned to losing a small percentage of stock each year to feral dogs and foxes, and sometimes to dingoes, feral pigs and wedge-tailed eagles. In the mid-1970s, however, farmers in the southwest began to notice much greater than average predation. Not only had the survival rate of lambs on some properties dropped from the usual 95 per cent to 50 per cent but full-grown sheep were also being killed in unusually large numbers.

In the 1977 season alone, Dennis and Ross Earnshaw, graziers in the Cordering area, lost $3000 worth of lambs between them. When sheep are killed by feral dogs or foxes they normally exhibit wounds to the throat and legs and are invariably surrounded by the signs of frenzied attack and protracted struggle: many square

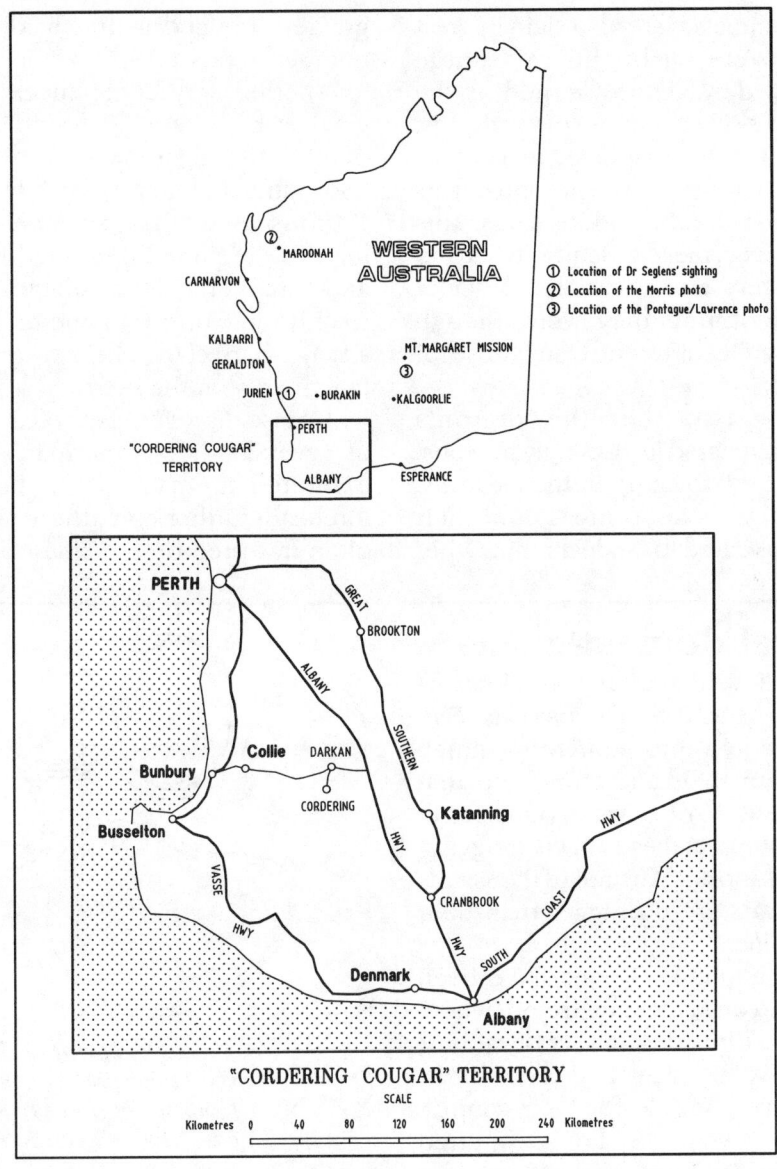

metres of torn and shredded fleece. Dogs, in short, are messy killers.

What concerned the Earnshaws and other Cordering graziers was that the majority of the sheep they lost from around 1977 onwards had been killed in a totally different way: with surgical precision, by a sudden vicious bite which snapped their necks. Several calves, one eleven months old, were apparently killed in the same way.

The new predators appeared to kill for the sheer pleasure of it: most of their victims were not eaten. When they did pause to nibble, however, their eating habits were quite distinctive and radically different from those of dogs, foxes or pigs. The bellies of the victims were neatly slit open and the entrails consumed. When, more rarely, additional flesh was eaten, this was done in an extremely thorough and very unusual manner: the skin was neatly peeled back and the ribs were stripped of every last shred of meat.

Native animals were also slain in great numbers. Veteran bushman George Wheeler, widely acknowledged as the area's most skilled trapper of feral pigs, dogs and dingoes, suspected as early as 1973 that a large, new predator was haunting the scrub. Unlike dogs, this animal was extremely difficult to track and when, on very rare occasions, Wheeler found its footprints they were, though indistinct, quite different from those of dingoes.

He saw also that the region's kangaroos appeared increasingly nervous. They preferred 'to camp in the clearings and avoid some scrub areas' and their numbers appeared to be declining. Other graziers noticed a drastic drop in the number of possums.

Another very experienced bushman, grazier Charlie Sumner, found the carcase of a 20 kilo kangaroo with its neck broken and entrails almost surgically removed. Curious as to the exact nature of its injuries, he partially skinned the animal and discovered its forehead had been cleanly punctured by something, perhaps a long, sharp claw. There were also deep fang marks on the neck.

He also discovered the bleached skulls of several other 'roos, many of which exhibited the same deep hole in the forehead; furthermore, these skulls were often fractured on the side opposite the

Feral domestic cats

Many believe that after several generations in the wild, feral house cats *(Felis catus)* evolve into something much larger than their ancestors, and that most Australian big cat reports result from sightings of these mighty moggies.

In fact, most of Australia's thousands of feral cats are no bigger than their city cousins.

Since about 1811, cats have been living wild on Macquarie Island, where they have thrived on a diet of rabbits, penguins of all sizes and other birds. Rangers responsible for their control, however, have never shot or captured a cat which differed in any significant way from ordinary domestic cats. The same applies on Kangaroo Island, where the animals have been feral for hundreds of cat generations.

Mainland studies have shown that although feral cats living in forested areas or other places where food is plentiful grow fatter than their domestic cousins they are not significantly larger.

The only areas which produce consistent reports of much larger than average ferals are the extremely arid

Above: Footprint of the Kangaroo Valley panther compared to footprint of a large domestic cat. (Both shown at half-size.)

regions, particularly the Gibson and Simpson deserts. These cats are sometimes said to measure up to one metre in length, excluding the tail, to stand twice as tall as domestic cats and to be capable of killing 'well-grown' wallabies.

It has been suggested that the scarcity of prey in desert conditions accelerates the process of natural selection so that larger toms soon dominate the scene, producing larger and larger offspring every year.

puncture mark. Noting that the skulls of many recently killed sheep had been completely shattered, Mr Sumner observed that, while a full-grown man could not fracture a sheep's skull by standing on it, this creature, whatever it was, could easily crush a head between its jaws.

As the killings increased, Dennis Earnshaw and others experienced fleeting glimpses of what appeared to be huge cats, and by 1978 reports of much closer encounters began to emerge.

In July of that year grazier Jim Putland had a confrontation in his own backyard with a cat which stood as tall as a big dog and which he estimated to weigh 200 pounds [91 kg]. The animal appeared out of the dusk and jumped onto a pile of boulders only a few metres from where Mr Putland was feeding his dogs. While his trusty hounds fled in panic, the farmer held his torch on the creature long enough to register its cat-like face, brilliantly reflective eyes, extremely long tail and light brown colouration. Amazingly, the creature, quite unimpressed by its proximity to a human being, dropped nimbly to the ground and moved towards him. That was all it took: Mr Putland burnt up the home paddock in a reckless sprint for the house.

Later, after a special trip to the Perth Zoo, the mystified grazier concluded that

---

Although the theory is full of holes (why, for instance, aren't desert dingoes and other desert predators any larger than their relatives in the forest?) it does appear that some reports of extra-large desert cats are at least partly true.

We doubt, however, that the 'super cats' are quite as large as they are said to be. Bryan Walters, a Victorian government ecologist who has studied the subject for many years, says that the largest feral ever caught weighed only 16 kilos (35 pounds) – about the size of a small fox.

As far as we know, nobody who has shot a 'super cat' has ever preserved the body. We have seen photographs of two or three pelts which appear to be quite large, but because a skin can be stretched by 30 per cent or more in the drying process, and because skins always look much larger off the carcase than on, these photos are not absolutely compelling evidence.

Brief sightings of large feral toms must certainly have prompted a small percentage of Australian big cat reports but there are several good reasons why they could not be responsible for the entire phenomenon.

First, studies have shown that after a few generations in the wild the coats of all feral cats revert to a striped tabby pattern. But, as noted earlier, the vast majority of Australian big cat witnesses describe jet-black or uniformly sandy-coloured creatures.

Second, the 'hot-spots' which produce the largest numbers of panther and puma sightings are hundreds of kilometres from the extremely arid areas where feral domestic cats grow biggest.

Third, as we have seen, in big cat hot-spots many people report encounters with creatures as big as full grown panthers and pumas. Adult pumas can weigh up to 118 kilos [260 pounds], seven times the weight of the heaviest recorded feral.

As can be seen from the accompanying diagram, the entire footprint of a large domestic tom is barely as large as one of the Kangaroo Valley panther's toes.

The largest of Australia's feral domestics would barely constitute a light snack for most of the big cats described in this book.

'... While his hounds fled in panic, the farmer held his torch on the creature long enough to register its cat-like face ...'

he had seen an American mountain lion, a cougar, and a big one at that.

Certainly, the description he gave was very much like that of a cougar – the only difference being that Mr Putland said the creature appeared to have a large tuft at the end of its tail. This could have been a trick of the light: the tails of cougars do have a black tip that could be mistaken for a tuft. The creature's confident demeanour in the face of a human being is, however, entirely uncharacteristic of cougars and will be considered in more detail later.

Shortly after Mr Putland's sighting, Mike Drew of Darkan (20 kilometres from Cordering) was driving home with his wife, three daughters and son-in-law when he saw a pair of eyes 'as big as saucers' in the beam of the headlights. It turned out, said Mr Drew, to be '... a big, thickset, sandy-coloured thing with a small head and a long tail. It moved like a cat with its body close to the ground and showed no fear at all'.

It stayed in the area of the car for around twenty minutes, even when the Drews moved the car to get a better view:

...we moved the car three times. It came up to the car and looked at us. It was definitely like nothing we had ever seen before except a puma. It jumped on a rock 2.4 metres high with no effort at all. Once you've seen it you have to believe it.

During 1977 and 1978 deep scratch marks were discovered on several large gum trees in the area. Because all of these trees had horizontal branches overlooking clearings in the forest, many farmers thought they may have been used as lookouts by big cats.

Because of this evidence, because of the testimony of eyewitnesses and because the stock losses were becoming impossible to ignore, many graziers had become quite convinced by early 1979 that imported cougars were running wild in the area.

The conviction grew when they researched the lifestyle of American

An adult thylacine (Tasmanian tiger).

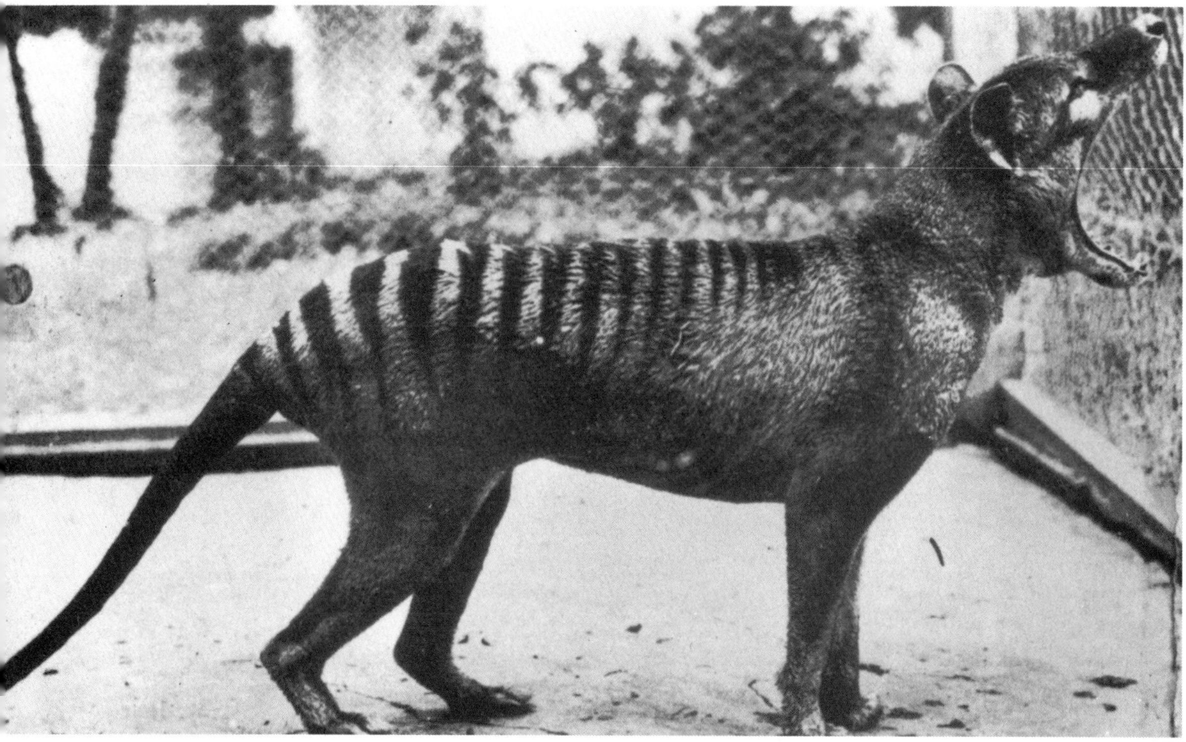

Collection: Queen Victoria Museum and Art Gallery

Above: The thylacine (Thylacinus cynocephalus). Extinct — or merely elusive?

Below: Wilf Batty with the tiger he shot on his Mawbanna property in May 1930.

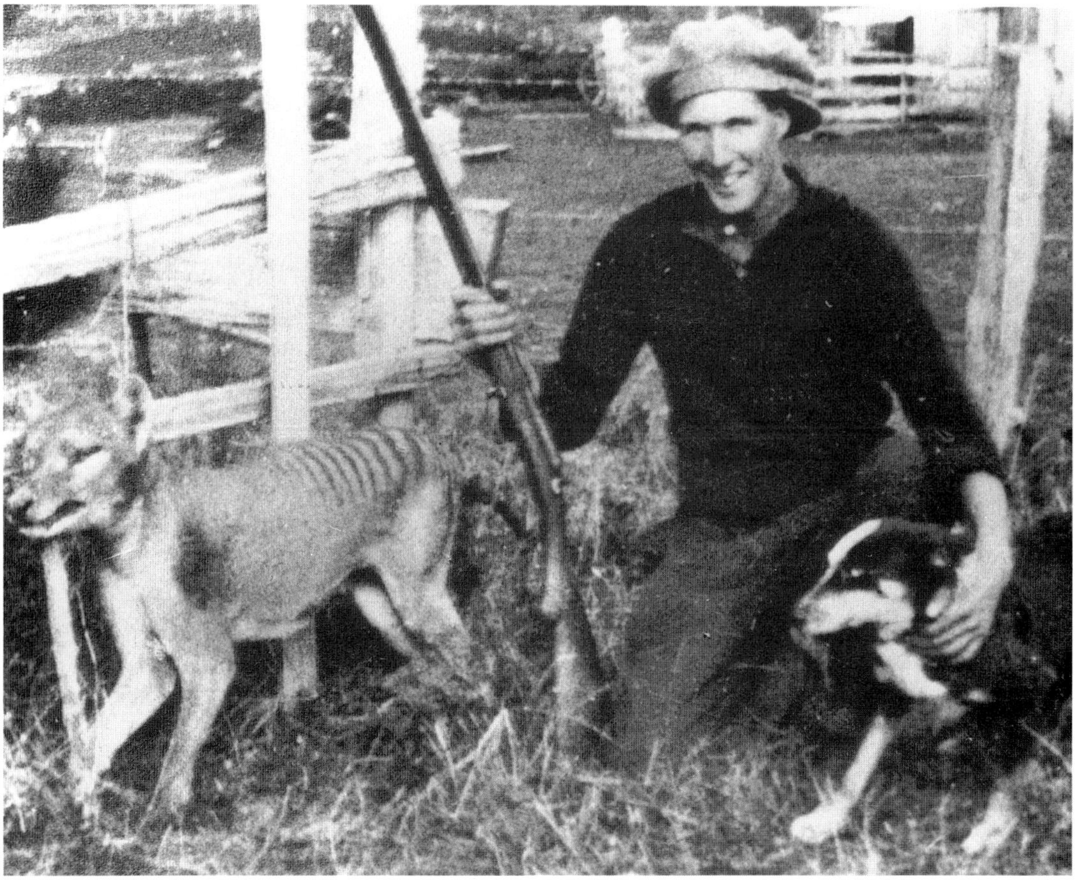

Queen Victoria Museum and Art Gallery

Above: Adye Jordan, veteran tiger hunter. In his book Tiger Man, *Adye claimed to have trapped thylacines in Tasmania as late as 1949.*

Right: Dr Eric Guiler, Australia's leading authority on the thylacine.

Below: The strange, dog-like creature photographed from a helicopter near Birthday Bay on Tasmania's rugged west coast in January 1957.

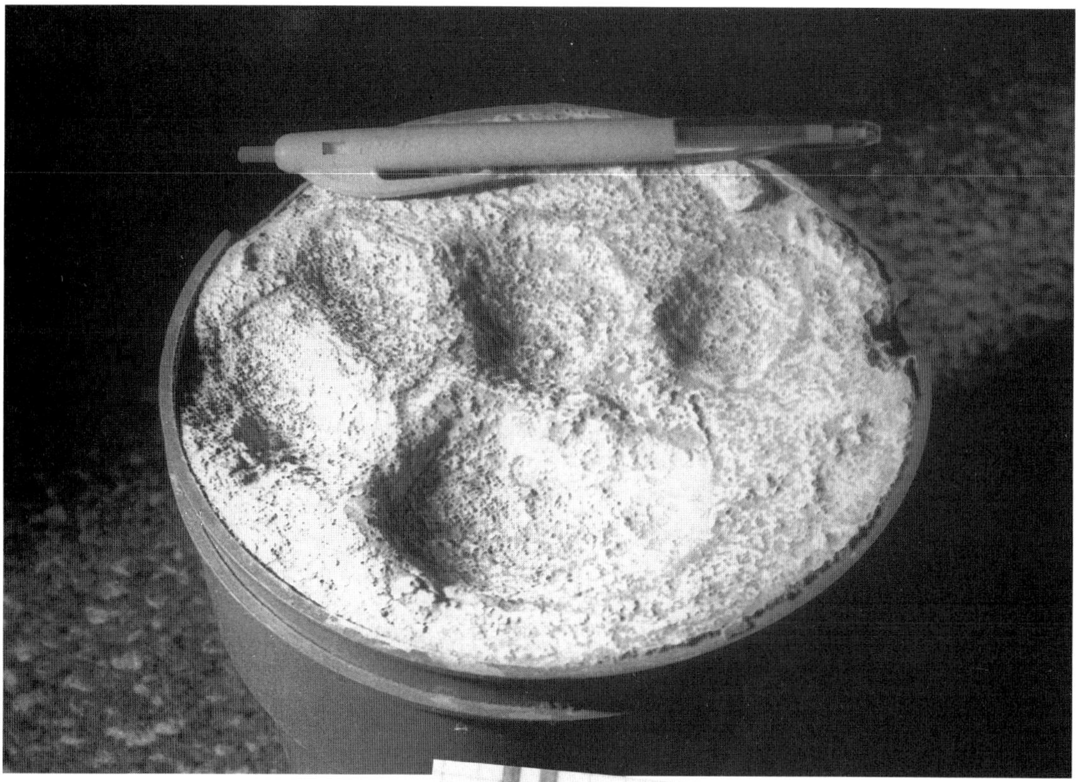

Shoalhaven and Nowra News

Geoff Woess

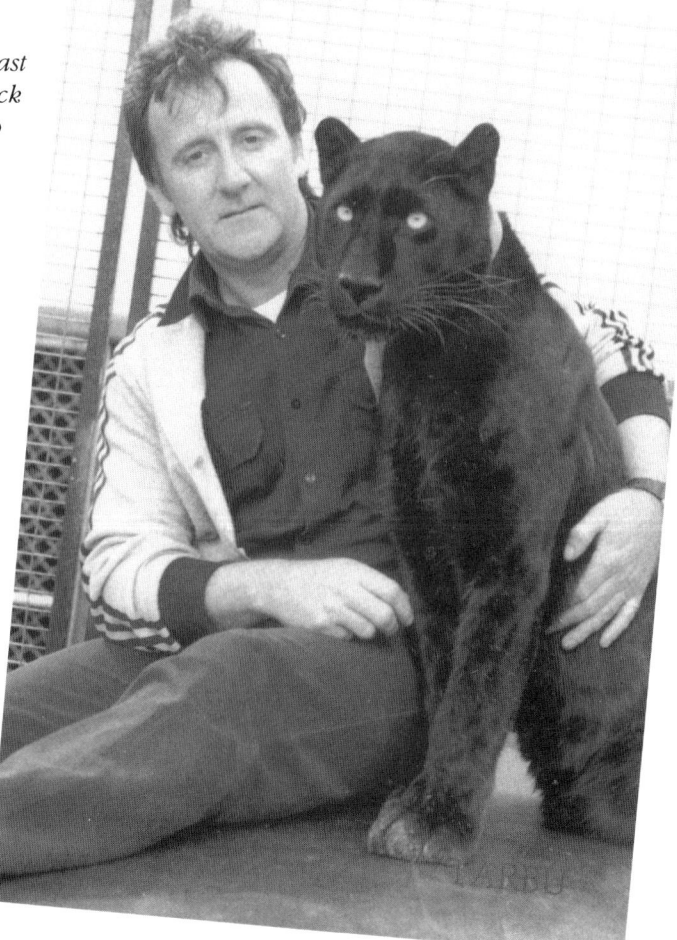

Above: Impression of the track cast taken by Ray Noakes after a black panther sighting near Kangaroo Valley in southeastern NSW.

Right: Big cat handler Geoff Woess and his black panther, Tarbu. Geoff sighted an almost identical animal near Daisy Hill, Victoria in 1990.

John Henry

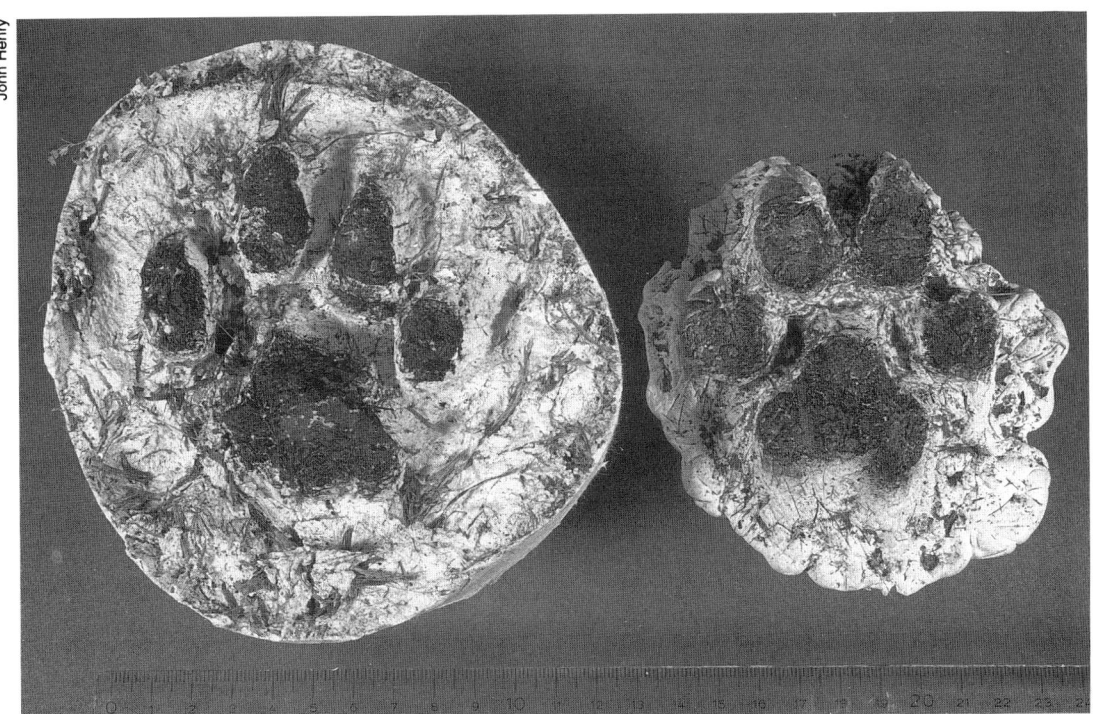

Above: Comparison of a puma cast (left) prepared by Melbourne Zoo and the big cat track found by David Hamilton at Rocklands Reservoir in Western Victoria.

Below: Bob Lowcock and Bob Hiatt measure the jump made by a large cat across Cultivation Creek in the Grampians, July 1985.

Hamilton Spectator

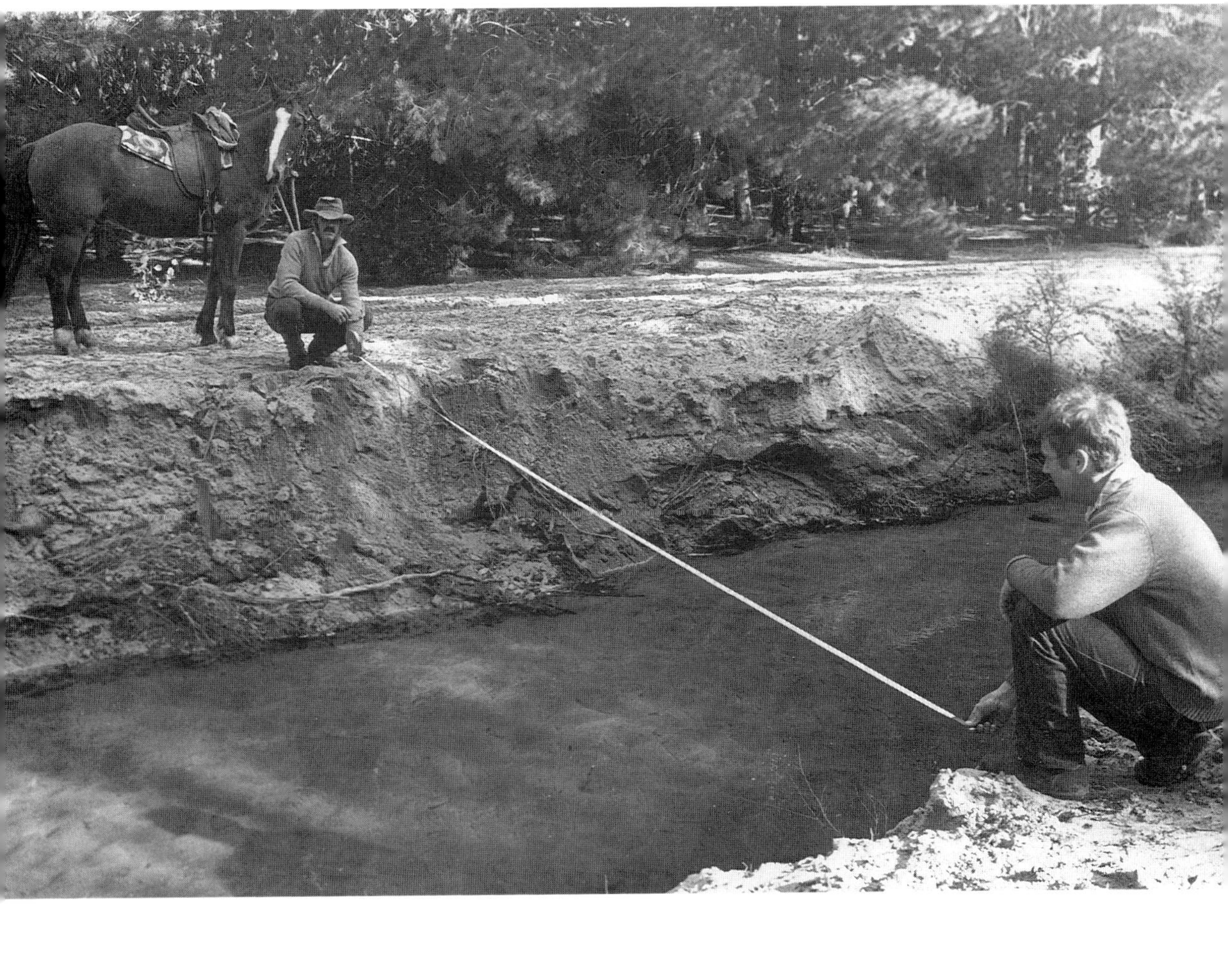

Right: John Higgins, managing editor of the Maryborough Advertiser, *holding the hollowed-out carcase of an angora goat eaten by a mystery predator in April 1987.*

Maryborough Advertiser

Left: Irene Addinsall, who claims to have known of a release of pumas by American servicemen into the Grampians during World War 2.

Hamilton Spectator

Barry Morris

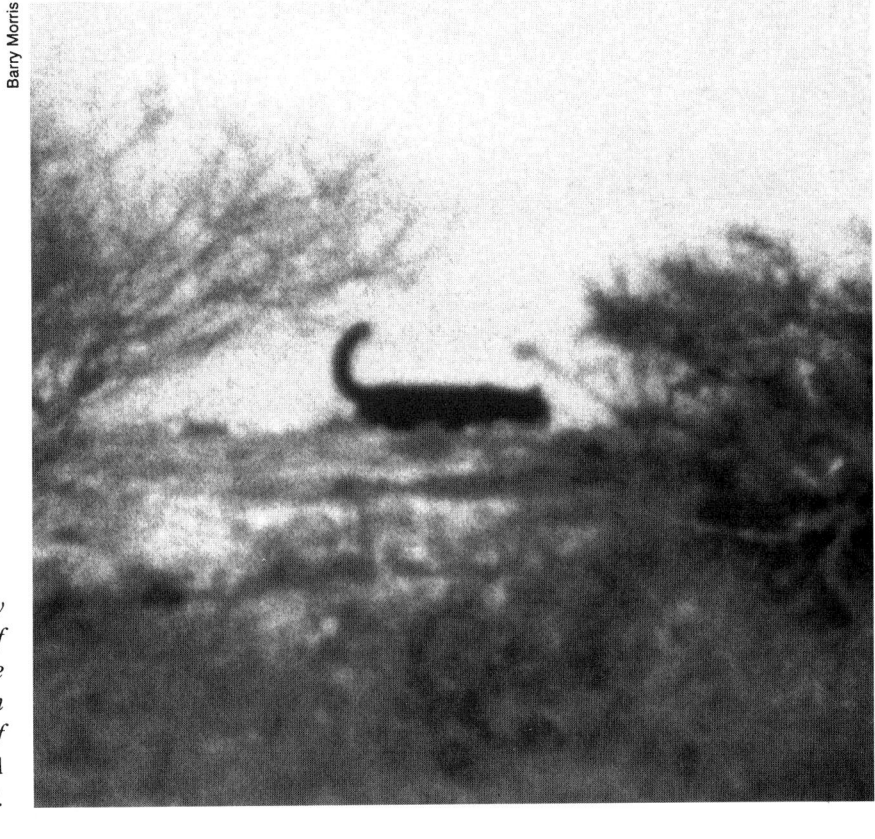

Right: Barry Morris' photo of the giant cat he sighted 200 km northeast of Carnarvon, WA in 1978.

Below: Mysterious black felid photographed by three Perth businessmen near Lake Carey, WA in September 1982. The witnesses all claimed the cat was the size of a German shepherd dog.

Alan Lawrence

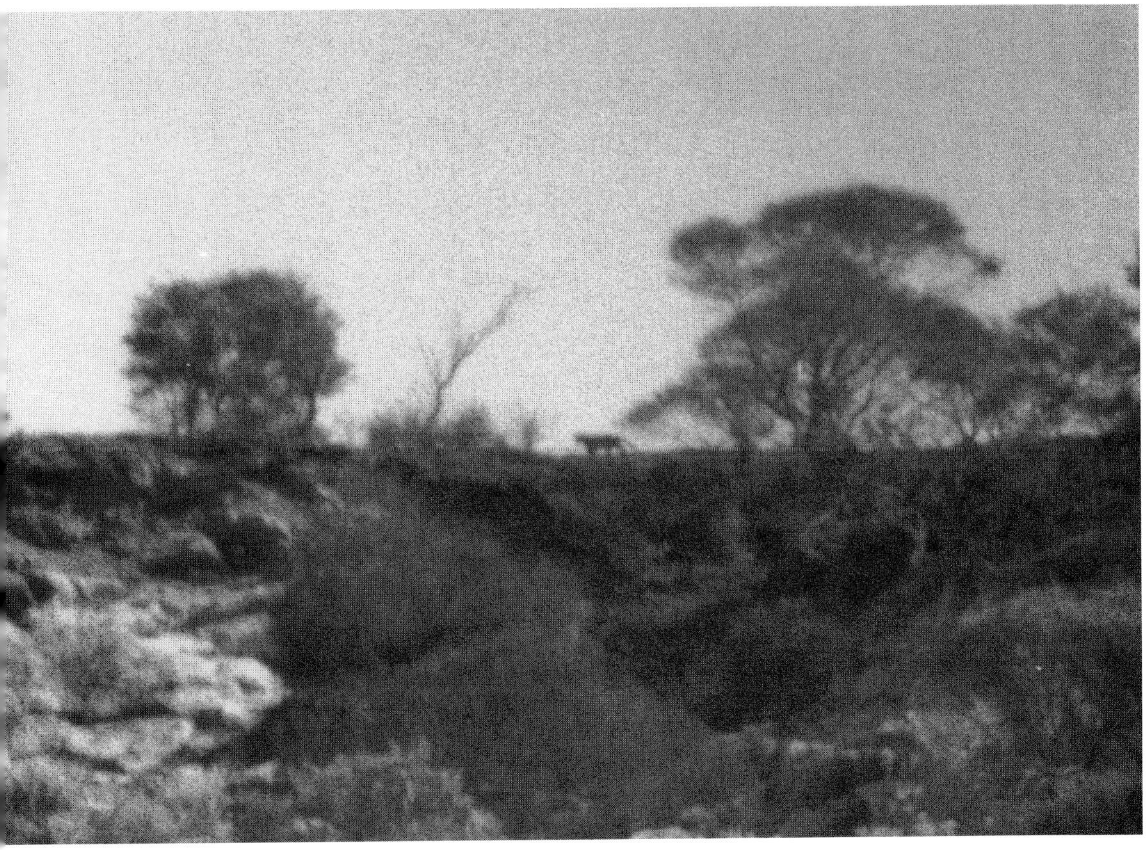

Right: Norwegian naturalist Carl Lumholtz, who was told by Aborigines near the Herbert River, Qld of the existence of a large striped cat which they called the yarri.

Below: Janeice (Kay) Plunkett, one of Australia's pioneer mystery animal researchers. Her extensive fieldwork in Queensland during the early 1970s uncovered many previously unknown reports of the marsupial tiger.

Kay Plunkett

cougars and discovered that the marked trees and the method of sheep killing – by a single massive bite to the back of the neck – were hallmarks of the mountain lion.

For years the farmers had successfully fought wild dogs, dingoes, and feral pigs by spotlight shooting, trapping and baiting, and their first reaction now was to resort to the same time-tested methods. They found to their extreme frustration, however, that such tactics failed miserably with the 'cougars'.

Dennis and Ross Earnshaw and many other farmers spent hundreds of hours patrolling their properties armed with spotlights and high-powered rifles. Although they were assisted for considerable periods by professional kangaroo shooters, and even by a Kenyan big-game hunter, no one succeeded in killing or even wounding the animal.

Remarkably big, bright and wide-set eyes were often caught in the spotlights but almost always at extreme range. Big cats were sometimes glimpsed close up but only when they were partly obscured or running for cover at breakneck speed. On the Earnshaw property it seemed almost as if the cats were teasing the hunters: stock would be killed just before the men arrived at a particular spot or just after they left. Once they staked out a sheep carcase all night only to have it eaten just after they left the scene. After weeks of spotlighting, the noted hunter Bert Pinker mused distractedly that 'It's almost as if it can stay one step ahead of us all the time'.

Pinker, who had rarely, if ever, missed a stationary target, managed to get off one shot at a sitting cougar at a range of only 200 metres but to his absolute consternation the cat bounded off, apparently no worse for wear. Another hawk-eyed professional, Geoff Martin, also missed a sitting shot and, like Pinker, went practically berserk with frustration and disbelief.

Trapping and baiting also proved futile: at times the cats apparently walked off, contentedly smacking their chops, after consuming quantities of strychnine sufficient to kill an elephant. At other times they carefully ate everything except the poison. Traps were found either carefully skirted or sprung to no effect.

In the winter of 1978, David O'Reilly, the young manager of the Western Australian bureau of the *Australian*, became intrigued by the mystery and spent a great deal of time investigating it. He carefully researched the history of big cat reports in Western Australia, photographed the stock and wildlife kills and made friends with Dennis Earnshaw, other graziers and professional shooters. He also went cougar hunting with them and glimpsed one of the creatures himself.

His 1981 book, *Savage Shadow*, describes in an informative and entertaining way all the developments in the mystery up to that year and makes an excellent case for the existence of cougars – or animals closely resembling them – in the Western Australian bush.

To support his case O'Reilly marshalled not only a great deal of eyewitness testimony but also the expert opinions of men and women experienced in hunting cougars in the Americas. Bob Neuman, who had tracked and shot many mountain lions while ranching in Montana, told O'Reilly, after examining many dead sheep and talking to eyewitnesses, that he was certain cougars were to blame. Casey Collins and Estin James, two other American cougar hunters then resident in Australia, and Lyn Hancock – who had written a thesis on Canadian cougars – concurred with Neuman's opinion. Ms Hancock said tree markings she was shown around Cordering resembled the territorial markings of female cougars.

In the Americas cougars are hunted successfully only with the help of specially-bred and trained dogs. There are no such hounds in Australia, but two

German shepherds trained as line trackers were used in the Cordering area.

After being familiarised with cougar scent (gathered at the Perth Zoo) they were set loose at the site of a recent big cat sighting. Although the dogs never actually 'treed' a cougar they did lead their handlers to a marked tree, large cat-like tracks and a recently-killed kangaroo.

O'Reilly's book is well worth reading not only because it deals thoroughly with the history of the phenomenon, with all the physical and eyewitness testimony and with his own involvement in the search, but also because he covers in detail the strange response of the West Australian government. This part of the book is a frustrating yet fascinating tale of bureaucratic ineptitude, stonewalling and buck-passing.

Since Western Australia's Agricultural Protection Board (APB) is responsible for the control of dingoes and any introduced animals which present a threat to stock or pasture it was clearly not in the interests of that organisation to admit feral American cougars were wreaking thousands of dollars worth of damage in the state. As senior APB officer Des Gooding frankly admitted to O'Reilly, if cougars were loose in Western Australia '... it would be our job, I guess, to do something about it and I'm not sure what we could do ...'

Clearly concerned at the prospect of having to pay massive compensation to scores of graziers, the APB (despite the fact that some of its own junior officers agreed with the farmers) attempted from the very beginning to discredit the cougar stories.

Although feral pigs, dingoes and wild dogs had been very scarce in the area for many years, senior APB officers insisted most of the predation was done by those animals. Exploiting the major weakness in the farmers' case – the scarcity of clear cougar footprints – they insisted all of the supposed big cat tracks could have been left by dogs.

On this point the APB was at least partly correct: in their enthusiasm, some farmers had photographed or made casts of tracks which, when examined by Bob Neuman and other experts, were found to be either definitely canine or at least not unambiguously feline.

The APB suggestion that so much alleged cougar activity should have left more tracks does not, at first, seem entirely unreasonable. Research into the lifestyle of cougars in their natural habitat, however, provides an explanation: mountain lions, according to the experts, are easily tracked only in snow. In any other conditions, thanks to their natural caution or to their light footfall, their tracks are virtually invisible.

Compared to much of the cougar's American habitat the Western Australian

Tracing of footprint cast made at Bokal, WA in 1982 (top) compared with a field sketch of an adult puma (below), Olympic Mountains, Washington, USA. (Both shown at half-size.)

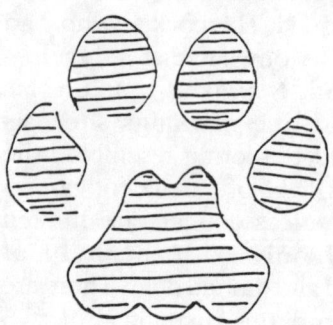

bush – where the ground is relatively dry and stony and snow is unheard of – is not at all conducive to track finds.

Despite this, Dennis Earnshaw and others have over the years occasionally discovered, in mud or sand, well-defined imprints of what are quite clearly big cat tracks. One extremely clear plaster cast given to us by Dennis in 1983 is absolutely identical in shape and size to the forefoot of an adult cougar.

Some of the government's ploys backfired quite badly. The American cougar hunter, Bob Neuman, became involved in the Cordering mystery only because the APB asked him to assess the situation, apparently hoping he would discredit the big cat stories. However, when he announced instead that the animal kills he had examined did indeed look like the work of cougars, the APB chose to ignore him.

Other experts retained by the government were more supportive of the official line. Whereas a highly experienced local veterinarian, Peter Brighton, concluded after scores of autopsies that the single, instantly fatal bite to the necks of large sheep and kangaroos could only have been administered by huge cats, the government vet argued, seemingly in the face of all logic, that feral pigs were responsible.

The APB's attitude caused a great deal of hard feeling and by early 1979 many rural folk were talking bitterly of a government cover-up. Some APB officers responded by wondering aloud if the tree markings and tracks may have been faked, and strongly implied that Dennis Earnshaw – leader of the committee formed to demand government action – may have been one of the perpetrators.

These smears were grossly unfair. Because he had lost more stock than anyone else and because he had been most active in actually hunting the creatures, Dennis, by inclination a quiet and private man, had leadership of the farmers' group virtually thrust upon him.

Our own impression of Dennis is that he is an honest, intelligent, down-to-earth family man. The owner-manager of a large contract harvesting business as well as a highly successful grazier, he would have nothing whatever to gain from perpetrating a hoax. The stubborn, tough-minded farmer was simply determined, from the beginning, to discover what was wreaking such havoc among the local flocks.

Proof of this determination – and a clear indication that he really believed in the big cats' existence – is that very early in the proceedings he purchased from the US a state-of-the-art night-vision device – a starlight scope – at a cost of $7000.

In fairness it must be admitted senior APB officers were not the only people sceptical of the cougar stories. Mr A. Passfield, a retired national park ranger, suggested the Cordering animal may have been merely a big dingo badly infected with mange, and noted wildlife authority Harry Butler, though hopeful that something more interesting might be prowling the bush, told the cautionary tale of the 'Brookton tiger'.

Sightings of a large, unidentified quadruped, coupled with increased sheep predation and the discovery of strange tracks led to the creation of the 'Brookton tiger' legend near Brookton in the 1960s.

Harry Butler tracked it on and off for two years and eventually shot it. The 'tiger' turned out to be a dingo which had apparently been trapped, clubbed, scalped, tailed and left for dead. Against the odds, the much put-upon animal recovered, and its ear-less head, covered with scar tissue and framed by spikey tufts of fur, gave it a weird, alien appearance. Its tail-less body, limping gait and broken, deformed foot which left a large imprint, had added to the effect. So bizarre was its appearance that when Harry, a peerless authority on Australian wildlife, first framed it in his rifle sights he couldn't tell what on earth it was.

Dr Per Seglen's drawing of the animal he saw.

It hardly needs to be pointed out, of course, that while such stories underline the need for caution in accepting every eyewitness report, deformed dingoes could not possibly have been the animals involved in lingering, close-up sightings such as those experienced by Mr Putland and the Drew family.

If you were looking for a person capable of telling a dog from a cat, Dr Per Seglen might be a good man to choose. A research scientist at the Norwegian Radium Hospital near Oslo, he is also a trained zoologist.

After attending a biochemistry conference in Perth in August 1982 he drove to a spot between Nambung and Badingarra, about 300 kilometres north of the city, to collect butterflies. It was there, in broad daylight and at a range of only 100 metres that he saw a creature '... which does not belong on this continent at all':

This big cat ... was loping along and then it disappeared in the bushes. Had I been in Africa I would have said it was a leopard from its gait and size. I could not see whether it had any spots but it had a long, spotted or heavily striped tail.

At 2.30 pm on 24 August, only three days after Dr Seglen's experience, Maurice Lilley, who was patrolling the natural gas pipeline in the same area, happened upon the same or a similar animal. It was a dark, solidly built animal about 80 centimetres high with a very long tail. Mr Lilley could not see any markings but he did say the creature looked exactly like the one sketched by Dr Seglen.

Although we feel sure the strange animals seen around Cordering and other parts of the southwest are not deformed dingoes or wild dogs, we hesitate also to declare them cougars. While the accumulated evidence is more than enough to convince any fair-minded person that animals closely resembling cougars are at large in the area, there are other factors which indicate the creatures, though undeniably cougar-like, are perhaps something rather different.

The first of these considerations is that, as at Emmaville, Kangaroo Valley and in the Grampians, not all the southwest Western Australian cats are classic sandy-coloured 'cougars': some are jet-black. As mentioned earlier, only once in the history of the Americas has a black cougar been killed. This supposedly occurred in Brazil in 1843 but the skin was not preserved. For all practical purposes, black pumas do not exist. So while black cats feature in only a minority of the WA reports they cannot be ignored.

One of the earliest Western Australian 'black panther' sightings occurred near Burakin in 1972 when George Moir saw two creatures rounding up a flock of panic-stricken sheep. At first he thought they were dogs but then saw they were something strange.

According to *Australian Outdoors and Fishing* of April 1977, Mr Moir then hopped into his utility and gave chase:

They did not run like dogs, they loped along with the front feet coming down alternatively about 8 inches [20 centimetres] apart. It was like a canter. They were black all over, at least two feet high, with a long slender body and a tail the same length. My fastest speed was 45 miles per hour [72 kilometres per hour] and I couldn't catch them. When we came to a fence one took it in his stride, and the other, which was lagging, crashed into the wire. It recovered quickly and climbed over like a cat. At the next fence they both went over with no trouble.

Mr Moir gave up the chase when he had to stop at a closed gate. Wongan Hills fauna warden, Don Noble, was called in on the chase and he followed the animals' tracks for another five miles [8 kilometres]. They had not eased up in their flight, he said. Moir had found several of his piglets dead with their throats gashed and their hearts torn out.

Although this 'black panther' report illustrates quite graphically that all West Australian big cats cannot be cougars, the behaviour of the animals as described by Mr Moir is also completely uncharacteristic of leopards. All zoological texts seem to agree that leopards (and cougars too, for that matter) are incapable of sustained bursts of speed.

Possibly the best qualified local 'black panther' eyewitness is Ian Offer, owner of the Wellesley Road Wildlife Park and noted bushman. Mr Offer has now seen large black cats on four different occasions, once in broad daylight at very close range.

Interestingly, he has also found cat-like tracks that he could not cover with his clenched fist. At approximately eleven centimetres in diameter those tracks would have been considerably larger than the adult cougar-sized footprint given us by Dennis Earnshaw and closer to the size of the panther tracks cast in Kangaroo Valley, New South Wales.

Sightings of the West Australian big cats continue to be reported into the mid-1990s and one of the most active investigators at present is Sharon West of the Perth suburb of Gosnells.

Sharon has accumulated an impressive array of eyewitness reports and track casts. Through perseverance, she has also managed to sight one of the creatures herself, at very close range, while spotlighting at a dump near Busselton. The animal was a huge, jet-black cat.

A black panther sighting by Mr J. Cumming is probably the most interesting of all, not so much for the details given, but because of his official position: District Officer with the APB. The document (shown over page) clearly shows that at the very time that the APB was so dismissive of the farmers' complaints about big cats, senior APB officers were well aware of this sighting report by one of their own staff.

Although, as mentioned earlier, Bob Neuman, the American mountain lion hunter, was convinced that cougars were at large around Cordering, he was frankly baffled by the reports of jet-black cats which he knew must be something else. He was also puzzled by another thing which may indicate the Cordering beasts are not true cougars: their habit of apparently killing 'for the hell of it' – behaviour which is fairly unusual in the Americas.

Another thing which makes us hesitant to accept the Western Australian cats as true cougars is their readiness at times to approach humans. The experiences of Mr Putland and the Drew family are good examples of this. In North America we met many people who had spent all their lives in the heart of mountain lion country without so much as glimpsing one, and the animal's extreme shyness and elusiveness is amply documented in zoological literature. The cougar's talent for avoiding humans is reflected in one of the many names given it by the pioneers: the 'North American Ghost'.

Ironically, however, while American cougars are almost never seen by chance, they are easily killed, because when pursued by hounds their reaction is to climb trees and thus present an easy target for riflemen. In the Americas they were also trapped and poisoned to great effect. Hundreds of thousands of cougars were killed in the US and Canada until by the twentieth century they were – apart from a small colony in Florida's Everglades – thought to be extinct east of the Rockies.

The situation in Western Australia could be seen, then, as being the complete opposite to that in the Americas: whereas American cougars are virtually impossible to see by chance but easy to kill, the West Australian variety are easy to see but impossible to kill.

Over the years at least two people claim to have photographed big cats in Western Australia. The first of these photographs was taken by a Perth businessman, Barry Morris, late one afternoon in 1978. The incident occurred well away from Cordering cougar territory, on a track close to the boundary of 'Maroonah' station, about 200 kilometres northeast of Carnarvon.

Mr Morris, his wife and his mother were passengers in a car driven by his father, Alec. The countryside was low, dry and barren, with little underbrush or tree cover.

Barry was the first to notice the animal, which was about 100 metres away, walking along a low, rocky ridge which ran at right angles to the road. The creature was jet-black and all agreed it was 'as large as a Doberman', if not bigger.

When Alec stopped the vehicle, Barry, who had his camera close at hand, took one wasted shot from inside, then rested the camera on the car's roof to take a second shot using a 185 mm lens. The animal did not seem unduly concerned by their presence but continued walking and soon disappeared down the far side of the ridge.

The witnesses were flabbergasted. Alec had been visiting the area for twenty years and had seen nothing like it before.

Barry's second photograph – originally a colour slide – shows a dark, slightly shaggy quadruped in silhouette, but because it was just over the crest of the ridge when photographed, the lower part of its legs are not visible. The animal in the photograph is unquestionably feline and, to us at least, appears to be of considerable bulk. Its long tail curves up and over its back. Although this creates a silhouette resembling that of a domestic cat, leopards have been photographed with their tails held in a similar manner.

Commenting on this detail, Barry remarked that although he would not have expected to see a puma or panther carry its tail as this one did, the creature was definitely of great size: almost 1.2 metres [four feet] in body length, plus the long tail.

Barry and his family were so sure they had seen something extraordinary that they returned to the spot the next day to photograph a measuring stick for comparison and to search for tracks. Unfortunately, they placed the stick in the wrong spot and they were unable to find tracks on the rocky ground. They did, however, manage to locate a possible lair.

The Morris photograph has never been published before but another big cat picture appeared in the Perth *Western Mail* on 13 November 1982.

The photograph was taken while Alan Lawrence of Munster, Fred Pontague of Nollamara and another man were prospecting in 'breakaway' country near Lake Carey, about 200 kilometres north

While the APB appeared dismissive of the farmers' complaints, senior APB officers were well aware of this sighting report by one of their own staff, District Officer J. Cumming.

> AGRICULTURE PROTECTION ADVISER : WHITEHOUSE
>
> Re : PANTHER SIGHTING
>
> Mr. J. Cumming DO at Southern Cross today telephoned to advise that he sighted an animal which he believed to be a panther. Details provided by Mr. Cumming are :
>
> 1. The animal was sighted on the Chesterpass, Cranbrook Road, approximately 12 miles east of Cranbrook.
> 2. The animal was on farming property and moving among sheep – the sheep were not concerned about its presence.
> 3. Colour being black; body long and sleek, had a noticeable bounding gait, appeared to be a very powerful animal and was observed at a distance of from 300 to 400 yards. Tail was carried horizontally for about 15 seconds.
> 4. Mr. Cumming said "the animal looked like a panther."
>
> Details of the above have been passed on to Mr. McKenzie at Narrogin.
>
> I have known Mr. Cumming since his appointment to Southern Cross. I have always found him to be a very thoughtful, reliable and educated I believe that he would not pass on the report without a great deal of consideration.
>
> S.M. Harvey
> SENIOR OFFICER
>
> SMH:MO
> June 18, 1979

of Kalgoorlie. Like the site of the Morris photograph, this is well away from the fertile southwest, but still within a wider zone where big cats have been reported over the years.

At 8 am on 30 September the men were startled by 'an incredible noise – an ungodly howl' from the other side of a nearby rise. The voice was much more powerful than that of a domestic cat and was, says Alan, 'like someone screaming for help, but having their airways restricted'.

The noise continued for several minutes until the animal finally appeared and proceeded to walk around the perimeter of the washaway in which they were working. Interestingly, the first thing they saw of the creature was its tail, carried high like that of the Morris animal.

The animal had 'darkish' fur and Fred said it was about the size of a German shepherd; perhaps 75–90 centimetres [2½–3 feet] long, plus a tail of similar length or longer.

'There was no mistake,' Alan insists. 'It was a cat. It had a cat-like head and walked like a cat.' It was just casually 'poking around' and seemed to be looking into an area of caves and gullies along the edge of the washaway.

The men admit to having been quite apprehensive as the animal approached to within 100 metres. They stayed close to the car and armed themselves with sticks. It was visible for about ten minutes, so Alan, after recovering from his initial shock, was able to take several photographs. The men later found large tracks in a nearby creek bed and met other prospectors who also told of finding big cat tracks.

Because Alan's small camera had only a fixed wide-angle lens, the photographs are not of sufficient quality to prove anything. As with Barry Morris, however, we judged Alan and Fred to be honest, straightforward people. Because of the 'ungodly' howling and large footprints associated with the photographs we are fairly sure they really do show a West Australian big cat.

When the Cordering area depredations began in earnest in 1978 it was rumoured that a pair of cougars had escaped from a wrecked circus truck in the area in the early 1960s. Since what was then considered to be the earliest Western Australia big cat sighting – reported by W. Adams in 1962 – seemed to fit the theory, the circus-accident theory became accepted for a time as the genesis of the southwest Western Australia big cats. David O'Reilly demolished this theory, however, when he discovered reports of two very good, close-range sightings of sandy-coloured cougar-like animals in 1949 and 1950.

Another popular explanation for the Western Australia cats is a local variation of the 'regimental mascot theory'. In the west, the perpetrators are said to have been sailors, not airmen. The cougars, so the story goes, are descendants of ships' mascots released by the US Navy during the Second World War. It seems, however, that in Western Australia, as in NSW, big cat sightings occurred well before the Second World War. Ian Offer has referred to sightings made by old timers, circa 1900–1920, and we have in our files a story of a 'tiger' – of unstated but apparently rather small size – allegedly shot dead near Katanning by a possum hunter named George Sumner in 1905.

If the Western Australia big cats are not cougars and are not black leopards, if they predate the supposed circus truck crash of 1962 and the rumoured naval mascot release of the Second World War, then what are they?

Ian Offer once mused that perhaps the big cats have always been in the bush in very small numbers; that perhaps they were the descendants of the marsupial lion of ancient times – *Thylacoleo*. This is, of course, an attractive idea but if it were true then surely Western Australian Aboriginal lore would be full of stories about the creature. In fact, unless we are badly mistaken, there is no such tradition among the native people of the west.

The true identity of the 'Cordering cougar', then – like that of the 'Emmaville panther', the 'Kangaroo Valley panther' and the 'Grampians puma' – remains a mystery.

References

Age, 14 June 1885; 19 November 1964; 14 October 1969; 23 February 1989
Albany Advertiser, 14 August 1980; 15 October 1981; 21 January 1992
Ararat Advertiser, 15 and 26 August 1989; 26 January 1991
Argus, 8 February 1896; 12 and 25 May 1914; 6 October 1915; 3 November 1933; 14 December 1933; 20 January 1934; 7 March 1934; 23 June 1934; 4 March 1936; 3 December 1937
Armidale Express, 2 February 1962
Australasian Post, 25 June 1981
Australasian, 9 May 1885; 6 June 1885; 16 February 1895; 21 December 1895
Australian Outdoors and Fishing, April 1977
Australian, 5 and 6 June 1978
Bendigo Advertiser, 26 August 1935; 3 April 1987
Butler, H., letter to Dr R. M. Warneke, 5 November 1979
Collie Mail, 4 April 1979; 31 May 1979
Countryman, 3 May 1979
Courier (Ballarat), 17 October 1989
Daily News (Perth), 10 November 1988; 12 July 1990
Earnshaw, D., correspondence with A. Healy and P. Cropper
Glen Innes Examiner, 24 January 1973
Gooding, C., Agriculture Protection Board, internal minute, 12 October 1981
Hamilton Spectator, 13 July 1972; 31 December 1981; 4 July 1985; 2 July 1987; 27 August 1987; 9 May 1989
Henry, J., *Grampians Puma Study Record*, Deakin University, Victoria, 1977
Herald and Weekly Times, 1 August 1990
Kilmore Free Press, 30 November 1988; 1 March 1989
Kyneton Observer, 21 July 1885
Maryborough Advertiser, 22 April 1987; August 1990; 26 May 1992; 23 June 1992; 5 February 1993
McKay, R., letters to R. Estoppey, 5 June 1937; 22 April 1940
National Geographic, June 1943
North Central News (St Arnaud), 15 Sept 1987
O'Reilly, D., *Savage Shadow*, Creative Research, Perth, 1981
Opit, G., Report of an Expedition to Study the Grampians Puma (MS)
Opit, G., Results of a Study of Unknown Cat-like Animals in Australia (MS)
People, 4 January 1961; 20 June 1986
Scone Advocate, 9 January 1977
Sherbrook and District Free Press, 20 June 1990
Shuker, K., *Mystery Cats of the World*, Robert Hale, London, 1989
Shoalhaven and Nowra News, 4, 11 and 18 February 1976; 31 March 1976; 7 April 1976; 9 and 16 November 1977; 7 December 1977
Southern Peninsula Gazette, 6 March 1990
Sun Herald, 15 November 1981
Sun News Pictorial (Melbourne), 25 August 1982
Sun (Melbourne), 21 June 1989
Sunday Observer, 29 November 1987
Sunday Press (supplement), 28 May 1989
Sunday Times (Perth), 4 February 1973; 8 June 1975; 22 April 1979; 6 May 1979; 10 June 1979
Sydney Morning Herald, 9 February 1973
Wangaratta Dispatch and North-eastern Advertiser, 22 April 1885; 13, 17 and 27 June 1885
West Australian, 28 March 1979; 24 October 1981; 24, 25 and 30 August 1982; 11 November 1988
Western Mail (Perth), 13 and 15 November 1982; 25 and 26 February 1984
Willey, D., letter to J. Higgins, 10 October 1988
Wimmera Mail Times, 14 and 21 February 1972; 7 and 30 March 1972; 7 October 1974; 2 April 1975; 7 April 1976; 28 January 1987; 4 February 1987; 12 May 1989

Chapter Four

THE QUEENSLAND MARSUPIAL TIGER

THE QUEENSLAND MARSUPIAL TIGER

'Up here in York Peninsula we have a tiger-cat that stands as high as a hefty, medium-sized dog. His body is lithe and sleek and beautifully striped in black and grey. His pads are armed with lance-like claws of great tearing strength. His ears are sharp and pricked, and his head is shaped like that of a tiger.' – Ion Idriess

During his many years in the tropical north, Idriess, a noted bushmen and prolific author, claimed to have seen the legendary Queensland 'tiger' or 'tiger cat' at close range on two occasions.

Although they are extremely elusive and perhaps now verging on extinction, we will show in this chapter that the creatures have been described in great detail by scores of witnesses from the 1870s to very recent times. They could be, apart from the Tasmanian thylacine, the best documented and most zoologically 'logical' of all the Australian mystery animals.

Since it is – according to all reports – cat-like, we were tempted to include the Queensland 'tiger' in the Alien Big Cats chapter. However, because it may not be a true cat at all, because it differs quite markedly from the mysterious felids of the southern states and because it once came very close to being accepted by the scientific establishment, we feel it deserves a chapter of its own.

While the mystery big cats of the southern states are usually said to be jet-black or sandy coloured, the Queensland 'tigers' are always described as being heavily striped. They also differ from the other cats in that they apparently have a very aggressive nature and a semi-arboreal lifestyle.

The major difference between the Queensland 'tiger' and the southern cats, however, appears to be much more fundamental than colour or lifestyle. Whereas, as we have seen, the 'Emmaville panther', the 'Grampians puma', the 'Cordering cougar' and company might possibly be the descendants of foreign animals released in the Australian bush, it seems that the Queensland 'tiger' is almost certainly a marsupial: a true Australian.

By the mid-nineteenth century Australian naturalists were quite familiar with the phenomenon of convergence: the marvellous way in which nature produced, in isolated Australia, marsupials which resembled many types of placental mammals found on other continents. So when reports of tiger-like animals first began to emerge from North Queensland, they were quite open to the suggestion that there existed in that region a marsupial equivalent of the Southeast Asian big cats.

Another factor which disposed zoologists to take the 'tiger' reports seriously was that most reports came from areas which would have been a suitable habitat for such an animal. Coastal North Queensland is rugged and mountainous with large areas of tropical rainforest, much of it tangled and almost impenetrable jungle. This area was known to harbour strange animals such as the cassowary, the tree kangaroo and the cuscus, and it was for Australia's European colonists, not quite the last, but certainly the most dangerous frontier.

Until the 1870s, European activity in North Queensland was confined to pearling and bêche-de-mer gathering from small coastal enclaves such as Cardwell and Bowen. The steamy tropical north

'My dog flew at it, but it could throw him. I fired my pistol at its head; the blood came.'

seemed in those days a fearsome and alien place. Crocodiles, poisonous snakes and malarial mosquitoes abounded, and of all Australian Aboriginal groups, the North Queensland tribes were the most fierce. From about 1850 to the turn of the century they killed hundreds of European explorers and settlers, in turn suffering thousands of casualties.

Right up to the 1890s whites who ventured into the North Queensland bush unarmed did so at the risk of their lives, and even in the settlements they were not entirely secure. The town of Gilberton had to be hastily evacuated in 1876 and larger towns such as Bowen and Cardwell were sometimes in a state of siege, fearing imminent attack. The North Queensland Aborigines' reputation as cannibals (deserved or not) added to the forbidding aura that surrounded the northern wilderness.

In the late nineteenth century far North Queensland seemed just the place one might expect to discover a large, unknown animal. Even today the nature of the area – still largely wilderness – lends credence to the continuing but now very infrequent claims of 'tiger' sightings.

The tendency of nineteenth century naturalists to take the 'tiger' reports seriously and to conclude the creatures were marsupials was encouraged by the discovery of the subfossilised remains of *Thylacoleo carnifex* – the marsupial 'lion' of prehistoric times – on the Darling Downs in southeastern Queensland.

It seemed reasonable to assume that the North Queensland 'tigers' were the descendants of *Thylacoleo*, or at least a smaller related species.

The earliest sighting of one of these creatures by a European may have occurred in 1864, when a bullock driver employed by W.T. Scott claimed to have come face to face with what he called a 'tiger' just north of Cardwell. This fellow was said to be disreputable – even for a bullock driver – and was therefore not believed, but soon other people provided details of similar experiences.

In 1871, in a letter which was published in the *Proceedings of the Zoological Society of London*, the thirteen-year-old son of police magistrate Brinsley Sheridan described a fight between his dog and one of the animals at Rockingham Bay:

It was lying camped in the long grass and was as big as a Native Dog (dingo); its face was round, like that of a cat, it had a long tail, and its body was striped from the ribs under the belly with yellow and black. My dog flew at it, but it could throw him. I fired my pistol at its head; the blood came. The animal then ran up a leaning tree. It then got savage and rushed down the tree at the dog and then at me. I got frightened and came home.

After this encounter became widely known, several other people, including Reginald Uhr, a police magistrate, told of seeing the same type of creature in the same general area.

That the creatures were powerful carnivores was proven by a native police officer, Robert Johnstone, who found the crushed bones of rock wallabies in a lair after seeing 'this large animal of the tiger tribe' in the jungles of the Rockingham Range.

Its tracks were more than twice the size of the large spotted-tailed quoll (*Dasyurops maculatus*). Johnstone felt the animal was '... a daring fellow, as on two occasions he came into the camp... and took away the salt beef which we had put to soak in the creek'. Once it came in at noon and a trooper who fired at it described it as '... all the same pussy, but big fellow all the same dingo'.

Some years later, in 1909, G. de Tournouer and P.B. Scougall said a 'cat' they encountered one rainy evening between Munna Creek and Tiaro was the size of a mastiff dog. It was eighteen metres away, glaring at them over the body of a dead calf and emitting a growling whine which quite unnerved their horses. They could see the animal was:

... a dirty fawn colour, with a whitish belly and broad blackish tiger stripes. The head was round with rather prominent lynx-like ears, but unlike that feline there was a tail reaching to the ground and large pads. We threw a couple of stones at him, which only made him crouch low, with ears laid flat, and emit a raspy snarl, vividly reminiscent of the African leopard's nocturnal 'wood sawing' cry.

Beating an angry tattoo on the grass with his tail, he looked so ugly and ready for a spring that we felt a bit 'windy'; but on our making a rush and cracking our stockwhips he bounded away to the bend of the creek, when he turned back and growled at us.

Track finds were also common. One night in 1871 near the Mackay River a licensed surveyor, Mr Hull, and his five assistants were startled by loud roars close to their camp. In the morning they found, clearly preserved in soft ground, the tracks of a large predator.

Mr Hull made a 'very faithful' sketch of one track which was duly published in the *Proceedings of the Zoological Society of London*. Comparisons with the tracks of other animals indicated the creature was roughly the size of a Labrador dog.

Mr Hull's sketch (left) compared to the track of dog (right) twenty one inches [50cm] high at the shoulder.

North Queensland Aborigines appear to have been quite familiar with the creatures. When the renowned Norwegian naturalist Carl Lumholtz (discoverer of the tree-kangaroo (*Dendrolagus lumholtzi*) and several other previously unclassified animals) was based near the Herbert River

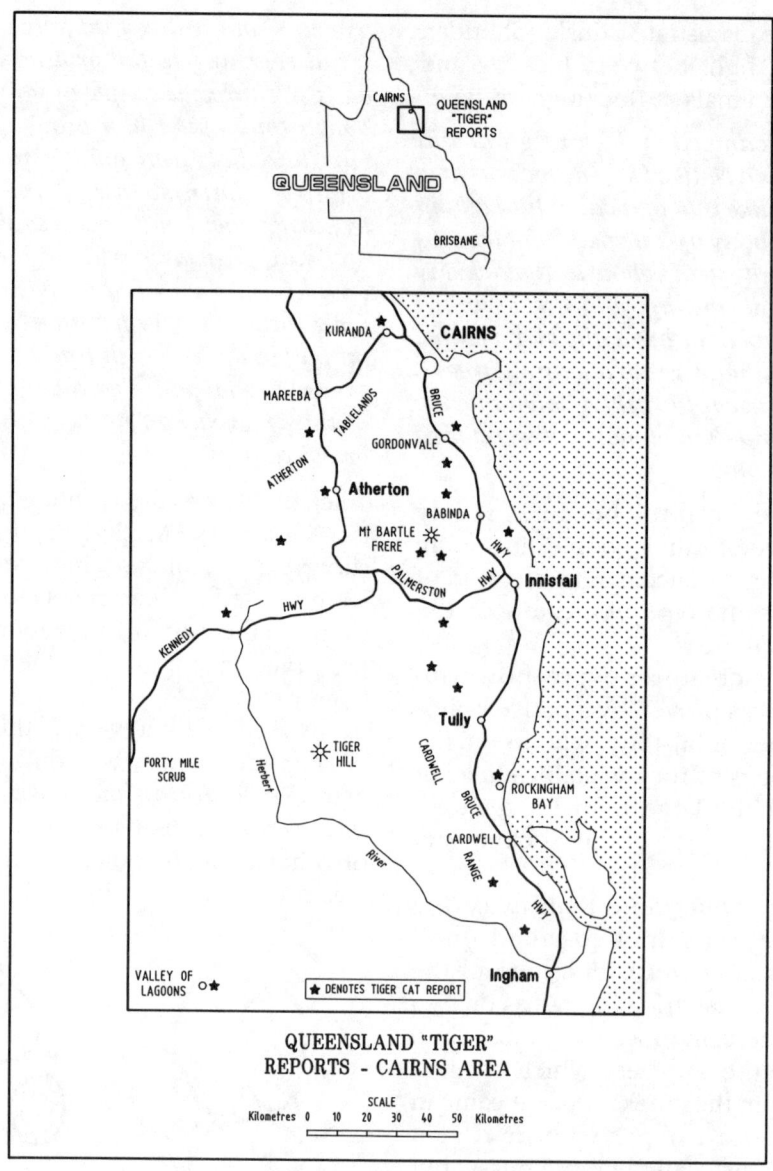

QUEENSLAND "TIGER"
REPORTS - CAIRNS AREA

in 1882–83, local blacks told him of a creature called the *yarri*, which he was convinced must be a large marsupial predator:

It was said to be about the size of a dingo, though its legs were shorter and tail long, and it was described by the blacks as being very savage. If pursued it climbed up the trees, where the natives did not dare follow it, and by gestures they explained to me how at such times it would growl and bite their hands. Rocky retreats were its most favourite habitat, and its principal food was said to be a little brown variety of wallaby common in North Queensland scrubs.

Some North Queensland pioneers thought the 'tigers' not particularly rare and several claimed to have shot them. In the 1960s at Kuranda, one old-timer casually remarked:

Most of the tiger cats which I have killed were four feet long and of fawn colour, with black stripes running across their bodies, which was fairly long, unlike an ordinary cat.

Another reminisced that:

There were a lot of them about early in 1904. My father killed one in our kitchen that year. It was fawny black and yellow stripes. Very large and also savage.

No pelt ever found its way to a museum, but one well-known naturalist, George Sharp, told of examining one at a property on the Atherton Tableland, where a cat which had attacked a farmer's goat had been killed and flayed.

Although the bones and flesh had been consumed by wild pigs, the skin was still intact. It was about five feet [1.5 metres] from nose to tail, but since Sharp had no way of preserving it in the tropical heat it soon rotted away.

By the early twentieth century, because of the consistency of descriptions and the quality of the witnesses, the creatures came very close to being accepted by the scientific establishment. In 1926, the 'North Queensland striped marsupial cat' was listed in Le Souef and Burrell's *Wild Animals of Australasia* and described in considerable detail:

Hair short, rather coarse. General colour fawn or grey, with broad black stripes on flanks, not meeting over the back. Head like that of a cat; nose more pronounced. Ears sharp, pricked. Tail well haired, inclined to be tufted at end. Feet large, claws long, sharp. Total length about five feet, height at shoulder eighteen inches.

In his 1946 publication, *Furred Animals of Australia*, Ellis Troughton, Curator of Mammals at the Australian Museum, also wrote confidently of its existence.

The Queensland marsupial 'tiger' or 'tiger cat' was therefore thought to grow no bigger than, in Ion Idriess's words 'a hefty, medium-sized dog', smaller than a leopard or American mountain lion, but larger, probably, than the lynx – and a lot more aggressive.

The track drawn by Mr Hull lends weight to the marsupial hypothesis. It is different from the tracks of all known cats – but it does bear some resemblance to the hindfoot of the thylacine, or Tasmanian tiger.

Throughout the 1920s and 1930s, people still occasionally claimed – as in the clipping below which describes the supposed shooting of a young 'tiger' – to have killed or captured the beast.

Although animal remains decompose quickly in the steamy jungles of Cape York, it nevertheless began to seem odd to naturalists that after all the shooting and trapping which had occurred in Queensland over the years not a single pelt was ever brought forward for examination. As the years went by, therefore, scientific faith in the marsupial 'tiger' appeared to wane. By the late 1960s even Ellis Troughton was having doubts.

In the early 1970s, however, an eager young naturalist, Janeice Plunkett, became fascinated by the mystery. In the course

SHOT NEAR TULLY

MARSUPIAL TIGER

TULLY, Sunday.—Mr. A. W. Blackman, of Upper Murray, and a party who made a tour of the Kirrima lands, about 30 miles from Tully, claim to have shot what is generally known as a marsupial tiger (called by the aborigines "yaddi"). The animal, which proved ferocious when captured, was half as big again as a domestic cat, and was striped like a tiger. It was captured on the fringe of extensive scrub on the Cardwell Range, and it is thought that with a careful hunt another of the species could be captured.

The party also captured a tree-climbing kangaroo and discovered several new kinds of opossums—brown, brown with white arm bands, and another emerald-tinted (known as tuela). These are thought to be rare specimens.

– *Daily Mail*, Brisbane, 12 December 1932

of fieldwork covering many months and many remote Queensland locations she collected over 100 previously unrecorded eyewitness accounts, some as recent as 1970, and caused a significant revival of interest in the subject.

Typical of the older stories Ms Plunkett collected was one told by a Mrs Woods of Gordonvale.

Between 1928 and 1930 Mrs Woods and her husband worked a property at the head of the Mulgrave River, adjoining rainforest at the base of Walsh's Pyramid.

One night, while investigating a commotion in the hen house, her husband discovered a huge striped cat attacking the fowls. The animal ran out and climbed a tree but Mr Woods went up after it and shook it down. A farm hand waiting below killed it with an axe.

They were amazed to find that the animal, which 'was not like a bush cat (feral domestic cat) nor like a native cat', was the size of a kelpie dog. They intended skinning it the following day but by morning dogs had badly mauled the carcase, ruining the pelt.

Several witnesses told Ms Plunkett the animals were still to be found in remote areas of the north.

A Mr Hair of Stratford claimed to have recently observed seven or eight of the animals living together in boulder country about 65 kilometres northwest of Cairns. He had been within 6 metres of the creatures and described them as cat-like with long tails. They had grey coats marked with dark vertical bands. Their footprints were somewhat like those of a cat but not identical, and three times the size. His aim was to catch one of the animals alive.

Because cows which had died in the vicinity had not been touched, he thought the animals were not interested in carrion. On the other hand, tins of food, such as condensed milk and meat, had been punctured and the contents licked or sucked out.

Another modern sighting allegedly occurred in about 1968 in a rather less likely location: right on the outskirts of Cairns. The witness was a colourful local identity, Nancy O'Brien.

It was perched on my casement window top, growling and snarling and raking the air towards me with its right paw. Its eyes were wide open and a glittering green. So I sat up in bed and shook my walking stick at it and it leapt down. Being bright moonlight, I saw the length of its body and that its tail was as long as its body and the stripes on it, from the small of its back to the butt of its tail. I immediately thought of it as a small, half-grown tiger.

Nancy O'Brien's sketch.

Although Ms O'Brien was rather elderly and her recollections of the incident apparently varied from time to time, her sketch is rather appealing and is perhaps worth including simply because of that.

Ms Plunkett was not lucky enough to sight a 'tiger' herself, but the data she collected added considerably to our knowledge of the creatures. She found, for instance, that although the 'tiger' reports were most numerous in the far north, the range of the creatures extended right down the eastern mountains to about the Queensland border. She collected recent reports in southern Queensland and also some quite old ones.

One veteran bushman, Mr J. R. Cunningham, a fit, lucid 87 year old, told her he had seen striped tiger cats on three occasions between 1900 and 1926. The first incident, which occurred at Gootchie, near Maryborough, ended in the death of the 'tiger'.

I had a good dog and he was a good fighter – dingoes were very bad at that time, and the row he made I thought that a couple of dingoes had him – I was on a horse and I cantered over and this thing was about eight feet up a tree, and the dog was at the bottom, and I had a bullock whip, they have a long handle, and from the horse I hit him on the head and knocked him down and the dog grabbed him and finished him off.

Mr Cunningham was entirely familiar with spotted native cats and feral domestic cats. This, he insisted, was something entirely different.

It was brown to fawn in colour, with black vertical stripes and the hair was sleek, not shaggy. The whiskers, unlike those of a cat, were short, but the teeth in both top and bottom jaws were long. They were arranged like those of a normal cat and bore no resemblance to the weird dentition of *Thylacoleo*. The creature's claws were very long and did not appear to be retractable.

The body was long in proportion to the relatively short legs: 'It would be about from 20 inches to two feet [50–60 centimetres] high at the shoulder and I picked it up to measure it – the tail was pretty well as long as the rest of its body – I held it up like that. I am about 5 foot 10 – so it would be nearly six feet [1.8 metres] long.'

The Gootchie animal apparently lived mainly on scrub turkeys: Mr Cunningham found the remains of many in the area. The second striped tiger cat he saw, at Eungella near Mackay in 1919, was also fond of poultry and this fondness led to its sudden demise.

They got up in the morning and this thing had got into the run, killed almost all of the chickens, ate a lot of them, and he was still in there! Well, this Hardigan grabbed the shotgun, and he blew half his head off. He could have caught him if he wanted to, but he shot him.

At both Gootchie and Eungella Mr Cunningham examined tracks left by the creatures. They were about 6 centimetres [2½ inches] wide and the claw marks were clearly visible. Although it was drawn many years after the event, Mr Cunningham's sketch of the tracks is interesting because it bears at least a general resemblance to the tracks sketched in 1871 by Mr Hull. Like the earlier track, the pad of Mr Cunningham's track is much broader than it is long.

Since Janeice Plunkett gave up the chase in the mid-1970s, Malcolm Smith of Brisbane has become the leading chronicler of Queensland's 'tigers'. Like Ms Plunkett, Malcolm has unearthed several relatively recent reports from the southern part of the state.

He discovered, for instance, that during the 1930s and 1940s a wave of sightings of what appeared to be Queensland 'tigers' occurred in the rugged mountains and dense subtropical forests surrounding the source of the Brisbane and Mary Rivers. This group of sightings gave rise to a local name for the creatures: the 'Yednia tiger'.

In 1939 or 1940, two local timber cutters, Charles and Nigel Tutt, claimed a close encounter with the 'tiger' near Mt Stanley. Charles, who described it as being six feet [1.8 metres] long, grey with very dark vertical stripes and 'shaped like a

The 'Yednia tiger', sketched by Charles Tutt.

light-weight tiger', sketched the animal for Malcolm.

During their sighting, Charles had a .22 rifle in his hands but felt it would have been useless had the creature attacked.

Another recent incident occurred near Bidwell, just east of Gootchie, in 1954 and was related to Janeice Plunkett by a Mrs Gamer.

My husband was riding through the bush when suddenly he rode upon the cat on a high stony bank of a creek. [It] climbed up a wattle sucker and sat there snarling and spitting. My husband was greatly taken by the markings, some of the stripes, he said, were nearly a dark orange and the animal was just like a very large cat in shape and size. It in no way resembled a native cat.

Eventually it leaped out of the tree and faced my husband. He said that he has never seen anything so savage and ... such big fangs on any animal of that size before and since. He thought for a moment that the animal was going to tear him to pieces.

Mr Gamer was by no means the only person who considered the striped 'tiger' dangerous to man.

After relating his own encounter with the beast, a Mr Thurger of Maryborough said, 'I feel sure had it attacked me from behind it could have killed me, it was so powerful'.

Given the extreme ferocity of the creatures, it seems just possible that some of the many people who have disappeared in the Queensland bush over the years have been killed by them.

Be that as it may, Ms Plunkett's files are certainly full of accounts of dogs being ripped to pieces by the 'tigers'.

Several bushmen agreed that the animals were 'inclined to attack a dog rather than run away'. Some stories involve enraged 'tigers' jumping down from trees, right into the middle of packs of dogs, to fight to the death.

A Mr Murphy of Maryborough stated that 'a ['tiger'] could fight and kill any dog. He would go out and meet them. He

Large spotted-tailed quoll

The large spotted-tailed quoll, *Dasyurops maculatus*, which is often referred to colloquially as the 'tiger quoll' or 'tiger cat', is the largest of Australia's native 'cats' but, like its smaller cousins, looks more like a northern hemisphere weasel or marten than a cat.

It is found mainly in the forested coastal areas of the eastern mainland and is plentiful in Tasmania. Built for an arboreal lifestyle, it feeds largely on birds, although it is partial to rabbits and capable of killing small wallabies. It has been known to raid many a hen house.

The head and body length of a large specimen is about 60 centimetres (two feet) and the tail is 48 centimetres (19 inches) long. It is light brown in colour and covered from its ears to the tip of its long tail in distinctive white spots.

Although it is a well-equipped, arboreal carnivore, it is barely capable of killing a domestic tom cat in battle and could scarcely be confused with the daunting, vividly-striped Queensland marsupial 'tiger'.

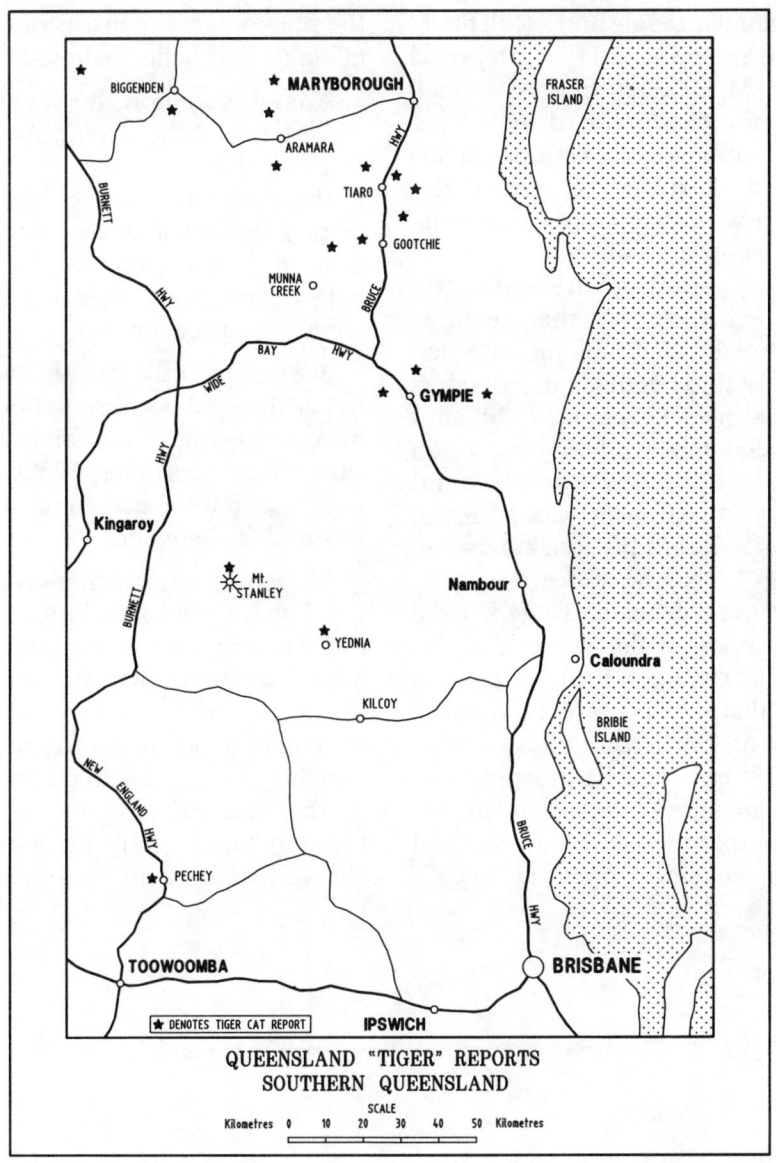

QUEENSLAND "TIGER" REPORTS
SOUTHERN QUEENSLAND

would throw himself on his back, and when the dog attacked he would grip the dog around the neck with his front paws and disembowel the poor dog with his hind feet.'

Mr Murphy lost several good dogs while out possum shooting: 'Several times I heard my dog yelping and often too late – I got to him just in time to see the poor thing disembowelled and had to put it out of its misery.'

One of the most recent 'tiger' reports collected by Ms Plunkett involved a striped nocturnal marauder which mortally wounded a dog on the property of D.G. and D.E. Rodgers near Gympie in 1970.

A full-grown 'tiger' must have been a daunting animal indeed. Ms Plunkett heard a story of one killing a young goat and of another hauling the carcase of a kangaroo straight up an eighteen-metre tree. One bushman told of watching 'a shocking fight to the death between a huge wedge-tailed eagle and a Gulf tiger.'

Regarding the beast's physical description, Ms Plunkett noticed a detail previous investigators had missed: a significant number of witnesses she interviewed remarked on the size of the creature's head, saying it appeared quite large in proportion to the body.

More importantly, she collected additional evidence that the creatures were marsupials. One lifelong bushman and naturalist told her that a pair of tigers he examined near Pechey in 1920, after they had been shot while raiding a hen house, were definitely not placental mammals: '... the female was pouched and the male carried his testes between the rear legs ... like the kangaroo ...'

Because the Queensland 'tigers' were apparently marsupials, it could be as British cryptozoologist Karl Shuker has suggested, that they represent a modern descendant of *Thylacoleo*.

On the other hand, the great number of alleged slayings of Queensland 'tigers' and the complete absence of physical evidence makes one wonder at times if the phenomenon consists of nothing but tall-tales and hallucinations.

We take comfort, however, from the consistency of the descriptions, from the fact that the Aborigines firmly believed in the creatures and from the credibility of many of the witnesses – Magistrate Uhr, George Sharp, etc. – and continue to believe that the Queensland marsupial 'tiger' was a real animal.

We reluctantly use the word 'was' rather than 'is' because although, as we have seen, there are some convincing stories from the 1950s, 1960s and 1970s, such reports are becoming increasingly few and far between.

Hopefully a new sighting, or with great good luck a photo, will prove us wrong, but we fear the Queensland marsupial 'tiger', having survived fire, flood and the ice ages, may have succumbed to strychnine baits meant for dingoes or to that hopping, crawling nemesis of all northern Australia's carnivores: the tasty-looking but lethally poisonous South American cane toad.

References

Burton, M., 'The Supposed "Tiger-Cat" of Queensland', *Oryx*, 1952
Courier Mail, (Brisbane), 17 January 1959
Daily Mail, (Brisbane), 12 December 1932
de Tournouer, G., 'Incident near Tiaro', *Brisbane Courier*, 7 April 1923
Heuvelmans, B., *On the Track of Unknown Animals*, New York, Hill and Wang, 1959
Johnstone, R. A., *Spinifex and Wattle: Reminiscences of Pioneering in North Queensland*
Lumholtz, C., *Among Cannibals, An Account of Four Years' Travels in Australia and of Camp Life with the Aborigines of Queensland*, John Murray, London, 1890
North Queensland Naturalist, 1 September 1938
Scott, W. J., Letter to the Secretary, *Proceedings of the Zoological Society of London*, March 1872, p. 355
Sheridan, B. G., Letter to the Secretary, *Proceedings of the Zoological Society of London*, November 1871, pp. 629–30
Sydney Morning Herald, 30 May 1970
Troughton, E., *Furred Animals of Australia*, Angus and Robertson, Sydney, 1946
Tutt, C., Letter to Malcolm Smith, 5 April 1989
World's News, 11 May 1938
Our greatest single source of information on the Queensland marsupial 'tiger' was Janeice (Kay) Plunkett, who kindly loaned us the maps and files she accumulated during her 1970–73 expedition.

Chapter Five

THE YOWIE

THE YOWIE

When Kos Guines took his sons to Monk Farm, a long-abandoned, overgrown property just 16 kilometres inland from Pambula, NSW in late 1977, he expected to walk a little, do a bit of shooting and enjoy the bright summer evening. Never in a million years could he have foreseen what actually occurred. That afternoon, Mr Guines experienced something he would remember for the rest of his life: a violent encounter with a massive, hairy creature from the Dreamtime.

Just after sunset, with plenty of light remaining, Mr Guines was walking very quietly down a gully when he was startled by a sudden crash in the bracken:

I swung round, startled – anticipating perhaps a kangaroo – and saw the back of a huge black creature like a gorilla making off from only ten metres ... I brought up my shotgun and had a shot at it. No way I'd miss from that range. But it made no noise, just loped off into a cavity in the scrub.

Although upright, the creature was not particularly tall – only about the height of a small man – but much, much broader.

The detail which stayed most vividly in Mr Guines' mind was the way the dome-shaped head seemed to sit directly on its huge shoulders, as if it had no neck at all. Although the animal seemed to have departed, the badly shaken hunter hurried to stand guard over his sons as they cleaned rabbits in a nearby creek. He thought later the creature may have blundered into him while seeking to avoid the boys.

After twenty years in Australia, Mr Guines, originally from Greece, was familiar with all the larger native animals and at the time assumed the creature must have been an escaped gorilla. What Mr Guines saw, however, was no gorilla. It was a semi-legendary creature, possibly ape, possibly man, perhaps something else entirely, which has been reported infrequently, but consistently, by Europeans since the earliest days of settlement and by Aborigines since time immemorial: a yowie.

In some ways the yowie phenomenon is very similar to the better-known bigfoot/sasquatch legend of North America and the yeti (abominable snowman) mystery of the Himalayas. These similarities will be discussed in detail later.

Although the yowie legend stretches back for hundreds of years, documented encounters with the creatures are so rare that until the late 1970s, when the subject began to receive wide publicity, only a tiny minority of non-Aboriginal Australians were familiar with the mystery. When we contacted Kos Guines he was at first very reluctant to discuss his experience. For all he knew at the time, he may have been the only person ever to have seen such a creature.

In fact, over the course of many years, several other people have reported encounters with gorilla-like animals in the same general area. On 23 October 1912, noted Australian poet and bushman Sydney Wheeler Jephcott wrote to the *Sydney Morning Herald* about a series of incidents near Packer's Swamp at Creewah, just 35 kilometres northwest of Monk Farm:

After nearly 50 years in the 'bush' with every sense alert to catch the secrets of the wilds, up until a few days ago not the faintest scintilla of first-hand evidence had reached me that any animal of importance remained unknown in our country.

But about 10 days ago, when riding through the jungle which lies on the eastern slope of Bull Hill (a trig. site, about 12 miles [20 kilometres] southeast of

Summerell rode up close to a strange animal that was drinking from the creek.

Nimitybelle railway station), I noticed on a white gum trunk a series of scratches such as could be made with the point of a dessert spoon. These scratches were in a series of three on one side meeting a single scratch coming from the opposite direction, being exactly such as would be made by three fingers and the thumb of a great hand with abnormally strong and large nails.

Beginning at a height of about three feet six inches [one metre], the series of scratches rose to a height of about seven feet [2.1 metres]. All of these scratches were made by a right hand, suggesting that the creature which made them shared a peculiarity of mankind.

From these indications I judged that some animal unknown to science was at large in this country, but took no further action in the matter. However, on Sunday (October 12), I heard that George Summerell, a neighbour of mine, while riding up the track which forms a short cut from Bombala to Bemboka, had that day, about noon, when approaching a small creek about a mile below 'Packers Swamp', ridden close up to a strange animal, which, on all fours, was drinking from the creek. As it was covered in grey hair, the first thought that rose to Summerell's mind was: 'What an immense kangaroo'. But, hearing the horse's feet on the track, it rose to its full height, of about 7 feet [2.1 metres], and looked quietly at the horseman. Then stooping down again, it finished its drink, and then, picking up a stick that lay by, it walked steadily away up a slope to the right or eastern side of the road, and disappeared among the rocks and timber 150 yards [140 metres] away. Summerell described the face as being like that of an ape or man, minus forehead and chin, *with a great trunk all one size from shoulders to hips, and with arms that nearly reached to its ankles.*

Hearing this report, I rode up to the scene on Monday morning. On arriving about a score of footprints attested to the truth of Summerell's account, the handprints where the animal had stooped at the edge of the water being especially plain. These handprints differed from a large human hand chiefly in having the little fingers set much like the thumbs (a formation explaining the series of scratches on the white gum tree).

A striking peculiarity was revealed, however, in the footprints: these, resembling an enormously long and ugly human foot in the heel, instep, and ball, had only four toes – long (nearly 5 inches), cylindrical, and showing evidence of extreme flexibility. Even in the prints which had sunk deepest into the mud there was no trace of the 'thumb' of the characteristic ape's 'foot'.

Beside, perhaps, a score of new prints, there were old ones discernible, showing that the animal had crossed the creek at least a fortnight previously. After a vexatious delay, I was able, on the Wednesday afternoon, to take three plaster of Paris casts – one of a footprint in very stiff mud, another in very wet mud, and a third of the hand with its palm superimposed on the front part of the corresponding foot. These I have now forwarded to Professor Davis at the university, where, no doubt, they can be seen by those interested.

Anyone acquainted with the nature of mud will not expect to find a cast taken therein three days after imprint as technically perfect as a casting from a regular model, but I believe that any reasonable being will be satisfied by an inspection of these three casts that something quite unknown and unsuspected by science remains to be brought to light.

In 1976, 64 years after Summerell's encounter, Aborigines near Bega were excited about recent sightings of apemen – which they called the *doolagard* – on Brown Mountain, ten kilometres north of Packer's Swamp. Also worth mentioning is the fact that just six kilometres south of where Kos Guines shot the 'gorilla', a steep, stark, rather eerie looking mountain called Egan Peak, or The Jingera, looms high above the surrounding bush. In the early 1970s, Canberra researcher Graham Joyner discovered, in the August 1904 issue of *The Science of Man*, the following note from a section on southeastern NSW Aboriginal dialects: '*Jingara* – a huge mountain, supposed to be haunted by a hairy man or *yahoo*.'

An ape by any other name

In Aboriginal Australia the apemen were known by many names. In parts of northern Queensland, they were known as *quinkin* (or as a type of *quinkin*), in southeastern New South Wales as *doolagarl*, *doolagard*, *gooligah*, *thoolagal*, *moomega* and *yaroma*, in South Australia as *noocoonah* and in Western Australia as *jimbra*, *jingera* or *tjangara*.

When white pioneers began to encounter the creatures they often used the term 'hairy man' and, of the apparently Aboriginal terms, seemed to favour *yahoo*. Place names such as Yahoo Peak in Victoria and Yahoo Valley (a branch of Araluen Valley in southeastern New South Wales) which occur in areas where yowies are said to exist, testify to the widespread and early use of the term.

Although many white pioneers believed that *yahoo* was the most commonly used Aboriginal term for the hairy apemen, it is not entirely clear that this was really the case.

In 1726, in his satirical novel *Gulliver's Travels*, Jonathan Swift called a fictional race of monkeymen yahoos. Graham Joyner, who has researched the matter in depth, also points out that in 1814, when it was exhibited in England, a large ape – possibly an orangutan – was billed as 'the Great Yahoo or Wild Man of the Woods'.

Although Aboriginal use of the word may conceivably have been coincidental, Graham suggests it is more likely that Aborigines picked up the term from the early settlers. Be that as it may, by the mid-nineteenth century many east coast Aborigines were using the term and many whites, believing the word to be of Aboriginal origin, were also using it.

Whether *yowie* is an authentic Aboriginal term for the apemen is also not entirely clear. There is no doubt the word itself was used by some tribes, including the Eora of the Sydney region (one section of Port Hacking is still known as Yowie Bay). However, some old glossaries of Aboriginal terms list its meaning as 'ghost' or 'evil spirit'. In recent years, also, the Aboriginal Black Theatre Arts and Cultural Centre of Redfern has stated quite categorically that the word does not apply to the hairy men of the bush.

On the other hand Mr P. J. Gresser, who took a great interest in the Aborigines of the Blue Mountains and Bathurst area, wrote in 1964 that the Mulgoa and Burragorang people referred to the hairy giants as *yowies*. From at least the 1930s variations of the term, such as *yowroo*, *yowrie* and *yourie*, were certainly used in that context by people in the Batemans Bay to Bega area. Names of geographical features (such as the Yowrie River) and place names (such as the village of Yowrie) still recall this fact.

Rex Gilroy, the New South Wales-based researcher who has been actively searching for the apemen for 30 years or more, favoured the term *yowie* and it is thanks to him that it has become universally accepted, gradually replacing *yahoo* and hairy man in the popular lexicon. Though the term causes a few giggles when people first hear it, it tends to grow on you and probably sounds no more ridiculous than, say, 'bigfoot'!

The yowie and the black man

Although we have studied the yowie legend for many years we do not pretend to know all there is to know about Aboriginal yowie lore.

It seems, however, that Aboriginal belief in the hairy men extends from Cape York right down the east coast to Victoria and occurs in at least some parts of South Australia and Western Australia. It seems the apeman tradition was and is strongest in the mountainous, forested areas of the east coast, from southeast Queensland to northeastern Victoria. While that notion appears to be supported by the pattern of modern sighting reports and while it seems logical in terms of food supply and habitat, it could, of course, merely reflect the fact that most of our own research has been conducted in that region.

Hairy man traditions collected from tribal Aborigines by interested Europeans in the colonial days appeared to be fairly consistent. According to most of those early accounts, the creatures were believed to be the same height as a man or somewhat taller. In rare cases they were described as being *much* taller. In the 1840s a white settler was told by Port Phillip Aborigines that the yowie was as tall as a 'big one gum tree', and in the folk tales of the Yalanji people of Cape York, Turramulli, the giant *quinkin*, towered above the trees.

The yowies were also said to be more powerfully built than men; the legs and arms were long and the hands were equipped with sharp claws. The neck was said to be almost non-existent, so that as with the creature Mr Guines shot, the head seemed to be set right onto the shoulders. They were often said to be mountain-dwelling, nocturnal, man-eating and capable of climbing trees. Frightful screams and growls and an overpowering stench were sometimes mentioned.

Although they were often said to be

THE YOWIE

Several Aboriginal stories refer to attacks by yowies and to violent death on one side or the other.

mortally afraid of yowies there are several accounts of Aborigines besting them in a fight or even killing them. Harry Williams, an old Ngunnawal man, told of seeing a large group of warriors kill one on a hillside below the junction of the Yass and Murrumbidgee rivers, near the present site of Burrinjuck Dam, in about 1840. They dragged it down the hill by the ankles. He described it as '... like a black man but covered all over with grey hair'.

Surprisingly, given their skills as trackers, the Aborigines, as far as we can ascertain, rarely described the shape of the yowies' feet in any detail, saying only, in two accounts, that they resembled those of humans.

One thing the blacks occasionally said about the feet gives a bizarre twist, so to speak, to the whole picture: some Aborigines stated that the creatures' feet were *turned backwards* so that their tracks confused anyone attempting to follow. Readers familiar with the yeti legend will remember that sherpas often say the same thing about the abominable snowman's feet.

Although much of the Aboriginal hairy man tradition recorded in the colonial days and more recently tends to support the modern image of the yowie as a hairy giant, the subject is complicated slightly by the fact that many Aboriginal people also believe in very *small* hair-covered, man-like creatures.

These entities, variously known as *winambuu, waaki, junjadee, nimbunj* or 'brown Jacks' appear to fill more or less the same niche in Aboriginal Australia as leprechauns, fairies and elves did in Europe: they have supernatural powers, guard certain places, punish wrong-doers and protect sick or lost children.

Frank Povah, a researcher, lecturer and writer of mixed Aboriginal/European descent, has collected many stories about the little people. It may be worth noting that the term which he found was most commonly used for the little hairy men, *yuuri* (pronounced 'yawri') does not sound radically different to *yowie*.

While the stories of hairy and rather magical little people blur the picture somewhat, the fact remains that Aboriginal belief in hairy, yeti-like giants was and is quite consistent, particularly, it seems, in the coastal mountains of southeastern Australia.

As Roland Robinson, a noted expert on Aboriginal lore, wrote in 1958:

A doolagarl is a man-like a gorilla. He has long spindly legs. He has a big chest and long swinging arms. His forehead goes back from his eyebrows. His head goes into his shoulders. He has no neck. The blacks from Nowra down to Orbost in Victoria all know of the existence of this 'doolagarl'.

The yowie and the white man

Although it is certain Europeans had been told of the yowie at least as early as the 1830s, it is more difficult to pinpoint the earliest actual sighting report by a non-

Turramulli, the giant quinkin, *as depicted by artist Dick Roughsey.*

The giant *quinkin*

The Yalanji people of Cape York peninsula believe in the existence of strange, usually malevolent creatures called *quinkins*. *Quinkins* come in a variety of shapes and are often said to inhabit cracks and holes in rock faces.

Most *quinkins* are said to be quite small but in earlier days there was said to be one notable exception: the dreaded giant, Turramulli, who towered above the tallest trees.

He resembled a huge hair-covered man but had only three clawed toes on each foot and three fingers, ending in fearsome talons, on each hand. His hideous head was set straight into massive shoulders.

Turramulli slept in a cave for months on end and ventured forth only at the beginning of the wet season, when he strode through the countryside looking for kangaroos or people to devour.

During the 1970s the bushman and writer Percy Trezise and his Aboriginal artist friend, Dick Roughsey, discovered two ancient cave paintings which appear to depict Turramulli. Together they produced a delightful children's book which tells the story of how, long ago, two Yalanji youngsters slew the fearsome giant.

Mr Trezise believes that many thousands of years ago the ancestors of Australia's Aborigines fought long wars of attrition with more primitive hominids – descendants of *Homo erectus* ('Java man'). He suggests that the legend of Turramulli – and, in fact, the entire yowie tradition – could have begun with folk-memories of those ancient conflicts

Aboriginal. For many years Rex Gilroy, Australia's best known yowie hunter, has made passing reference to a sighting near Sydney Cove in 1795, but to date, as far as we know, has not documented the story.

The oldest reference in our files to hair-covered wild men actually predates Rex's story by about five years, but is, unfortunately, an obvious hoax. It is worth looking at, however, not only as a curiosity in itself but also because it might – just possibly – have been inspired by warnings about the yowie by the Eora tribe at Botany Bay. The story is contained in an eighteenth century English handbill entitled: **A defcription of a wonderful large WILD MAN or monftrouf GIANT, BROUGHT FROM BOTANY BAY.**

THERE have been various reports concerning this most surprising wild man, or huge savage GIANT, that was brought from Botany Bay to England, numbers of People arguing and disputing his enormous Size, but to prevent further contending, the following is sufficient to satisfy the Reader as many Thousands have seen him in Plymouth, where he was landed alive and in good health.

... This surprising monstrous giant was taken by a crew of English sailors when they went on shore to furnish themselves with fresh water at Botany Bay. To their surprise they beheld at a distance three of the most surprising tallest and biggest looking naked men that have been seen in the memory of this age, turning towards them, which much affrighted the sailors, caused them to make expedition on board the ship for the safety of their lives, leaving the casks of water and a quantity of good old rum which they had in a cag to refresh themselves and make merry.

When the three savages got to the sea side they stared at the ship for a long time with wonder and admiration, one of them having got the cag of rum, he tasted, spit it out and shook his head, another did the same, but the third drank plentifully, and began to jump about in a frightful wild manner, shouting and making a hideous noise.

The other giants went off and left this one enjoying the cag of rum, who drank to such excess that he dropped on the ground and lay as if dead the sailors went on shore well armed and found this monstrous body motionless!

They bound him fast with ropes and with much fatigue got him on board the ship, where they secured him with iron chains, where he slept upwards of 24 hours before he was awake and was kept

The 'Monstrous Giant' of Botany Bay – a woodcut from the handbill.

chained during the passage. He showed not the least token of illness at sea. He came in the ship Rover, Capt. Lee, to England from Botany Bay, and landed at Plymouth, November 29, 1789.

... He is much tamer, and not so savage in temper as might be expected. He is 9 feet 7 inches [2.9 metres] high, 4 feet 10 inches [1.5 metres] broad, a remarkable large head, broad face, frightful eyes, a broad nose and thick lips like a black, very broad teeth, heavy eye-brows, hair stronger than a horse's mane, a long

beard strong as black wire, body and limbs covered with strong black hair, the nails of his fingers and toes may be properly called talons, crookt like a hawk's bill, and as hard as horn.

In short, he is viewed with admiration and astonishment on account of his huge size.

In several of the reports made by Europeans during the 1870s and 1880s, it is stated or implied that sightings were made by other Europeans twenty or thirty years earlier. One such account appears in the *Lismore Northern Star* of 17 May 1878:

About thirty years ago a shepherd in W. Sutton's employ averred that he had seen a hairy man in a scrub north of Cunningham's Creek, but his story was treated as childish. However, he persisted to the day he died that it walked upright and was covered in hair, and the dogs that hunted everything else ran back from this frightened with their tails between their legs.

The sighting claimed by this unnamed shepherd would therefore date from around 1848, but to find a report in which the witness is named it is necessary to jump forward 23 years. The following report from *The Empire* (Sydney), 17 April 1871, not only identifies the eyewitness but also refers to earlier witnesses by name:

The following particulars have been supplied to us by Mr George Osborne, of the Illawarra Hotel, Dapto, concerning a strange looking animal, which he saw last Monday, and which he believes was a gorilla. It is to be hoped successful means may be adopted to capture the animal, (alive if possible), as it is quite evident it is one of the greatest natural curiosities yet found in the colony. Together with the interest attached to the peculiarity of this strange 'monster in human form', there is something very remarkable and suggestive in the fact, that he should have presented himself to Mr Osborne, while that gentleman was going his rounds, collecting the census. The following are Mr Osborne's remarks concerning the animal:

'*On my way from Mr Matthew Reen's, coming down a range about a half mile behind Mr John Graham's residence, at Avondale, after sunset, my horse was startled at seeing an animal coming down a tree ... and when it got to within about eight feet [2.4 metres] of the ground it lost its grip and fell.*

My feelings at the moment were anything but happy, but although my horse was restless I endeavoured to get a good glimpse of the animal by following it as it retreated until it disappeared into a gully. It somewhat resembled the shape of a man, according to the following description:

Height, about five feet [1.5 metres], slender proportioned, arms long, legs like a human being, only the feet being about eighteen inches [46 centimetres] long, and shaped like an iguana, with long toes, the muscles of the arms and chest being well developed, the back of the head straight, with the neck and body, but the front or face projected forward, with monkey features, every particle of the body except the feet and face was covered with black hair, with a tan-coloured streak from the neck to the abdomen. While looking at me its eyes and mouth were in motion, after the fashion of a monkey. It walked quadruped fashion, but at every few paces it would turn around and look at me following it, supporting the body with the two legs and one arm, while the other was placed across the hip. I also noticed that it had no tail.'

It appears that two children named Summers saw the same animal or one similar in the same locality about two years ago, but they say it was then only the size of a boy about thirteen or fourteen years of age. Perhaps this is the same animal that Mr B. Rixon saw at the Cordeaux River about five or six years ago. The query is, 'Where did it come from?'

The sightings by Mr Rixon and the Summers children would therefore have occurred in about 1865 and 1869 respectively.

As with those given by the Aborigines, reports by Europeans contain many variable features but are, broadly speaking, fairly consistent. Before we attempt to analyse the accumulated reports in any systematic way, however, it might be a good idea to glance through the following stories which, since they span many decades and many hundreds of kilometres, give a reasonably good general picture of how the yowie has appeared to generations of startled bushmen.

A century of sightings

Sutton Forest, New South Wales, 1877

AN EXTRAORDINARY ANIMAL. — Mr. Prosser, manager at Messrs. Amos and Co.'s sawmills at Amos's Siding, near Sutton Forest, has just informed us (*Scrutineer*) that a most peculiar animal has been seen by two men, Patrick Jones and Patrick Doyle, residents of Sutton Forest, in the bush between Cable's Siding and Jordan's Crossing. Mr. Prosser himself has seen the footprints; they are 3 feet apart, and the impression made by the feet is similar to that of an elephant. The animal is described as being 7 feet high, with a face like a man, and long shaggy hair, and makes a tremendous noise. Fourteen of the men from the mill, fully armed, intend starting on Saturday next to endeavour to capture this "wild man of the woods." Mr. Prosser assures us there is no exaggeration about this affair, and every one at the mill believes in the existence of this strange creature.

– Sydney Morning Herald, 12 October 1877

Flea Creek, Brindabella Mountains, New South Wales, c 1885

In *An Alpine Excursion* (Queanbeyan, 1903) veteran journalist and clergyman John Gale referred to the many hairy man or *yahoo* reports which came from the area surrounding the present site of the national capital during the 1800s.

One story in particular convinced him of the creature's reality. It was told to him by his friends William and Joseph Webb, both 'strongminded, experienced, and educated men':

They were out in the ranges preparing to camp for the night. Down the side of a range to the eastward, and with only a narrow gully separating them from the object which attracted their attention, they first heard a deep guttural bellowing and then a crashing of the scrub. Next moment a thing appeared walking erect, though they saw only its head and shoulders.

It was hirsute, so much of the creature as was visible, and its head was set so deep between its shoulders that it was scarcely perceptible. It was approaching towards their camp. Now it was in full view, and was of the stature of a man, moving with long strides and a heavy tramp. It was challenged: 'Who are you? Speak, or we'll fire'. Not an intelligible word came in response; only the guttural bellowing. Aim was taken; the crack of a rifle rang out along the gully; but the thing, if hit, was not disabled; for at the sound of the shot it turned and fled.

The two gentlemen, filled with amazement and curiosity, but not alarm, went to where they had seen and shot at this formidable-looking creature, and sought for its tracks in verification of what had happened. There were its footprints, long, like a man's, but with longer, spreading toes; there were its strides, also much longer than those of a man; and there were the broken twigs and disordered scrub through which it had come and gone. They saw no blood or other evidence of their shot having taken effect.

The descendants of William and Joseph Webb, who still own land in the area, think the incident probably occurred near Flea Creek, at the foot of the Webb Range in the northern part of the Brindabellas.

Other people, including young Alexander Joseph McDonald and his father John (a brother-in-law of the Webbs) were also present during the encounter.

Alexander's account of the incident (as recalled by his son Eric) was collected in 1979 by Canberra historian Lyall Gillespie. It broadly agrees with John Gale's version, but presumably because it was recorded so long after the event, does contain some differences.

Alexander, for instance, stated that the creature was wounded during the encounter: he recalled seeing blood on the rocks among the broken bushes. He also said that nobody actually got a good look at the animal. Despite this, one member of the party sketched the creature 'from memory' complete with spurs, horns and cheerfully grinning visage.

Even though a fair bit of artistic licence was obviously employed, Alexander apparently considered the sketch a valued heirloom and insisted the story was true.

Snowball, New South Wales, 1894

– *Queanbeyan Observer*, 30 November 1894

THE WILD MAN OF SNOWBALL

The Braidwood Despatch *says that on the 3rd of October last young Johnnie McWilliams was riding from his home at Snowball to the Jinden P.O. When about half way the boy was startled by the extraordinary sight of a wild man or gorilla. The boy states that a wild man suddenly appeared from behind a tree, about thirty yards [27 metres] from the road, stood looking at him for a few seconds, and then turned and ran for the wooded hills a mile [1.6 kilometres] or so from the road. The animal ran on for about two hundred yards [185 metres] across open country before disappearing over a low hill so that the boy had ample time to observe the beast.*

The boy states that he appeared to be over six feet [1.8 metres] in height and heavily built. He describes it 'as a big man covered in long hair'. It did not run very fast and tore up the dust with its nails, and in jumping a log it struck its foot against a limb, when it bellowed like a bullock. When running it kept looking back at the boy, till it disappeared. It was three o'clock in the afternoon, and the boy describes everything he saw minutely.

The boy is a truthful and manly young fellow, well acquainted with all the known animals in the New South Wales bush, and persists that he could not have been mistaken. (Queanbeyan Observer 30 November 1894.)

Southeast New South Wales, 1912

In the *Sydney Sun,* 10 November 1912, a surveyor, Charles Harper, described his own encounter with a yowie:

For many years past vague and mysterious rumours have been current of an Australian gorilla, or 'hairyman', or some such animal, seen on and in the wild uninhabited mountains and gorges forming the Currickbilly Range ... from the head of the Clyde River extending southerly to the Victorian border, the eastern slope consists of excessively

THE YOWIE

broken, lateral ridges, deep gorges, and dense jungles, extremely difficult of access for man or beast; therefore its primeval solitude is very rarely disturbed. Scientists assert that this animal, like the bunyip, is a myth, and such animals do not, and never did, exist on this continent, although the old generation of Aboriginal natives assert the contrary in both cases.

In various parts of the southern district of this state on the coastal slopes, and at various times, extending over a long period, I have met men (and reliable men at that) who unhesitatingly assert that they had seen this hairy man-shaped animal at short distances. They were so terrified at the apparition and the hideous noise it made when it saw them that they left their work as timber-getters, and at once cleared out from the locality, leaving their tools and work behind them.

The description of this animal, seen at different times by different people in several localities, but always in the jungle, invariably coincided.

At the risk of being considered by your readers the reincarnation of Ananias or the late Thomas Pepper, I will describe this animal as once seen as briefly as possible. I had to proceed some distance into the heart of these jungles for a special purpose, accompanied by two others, and two large kangaroo dogs with a strain of the British bulldog in each.

On the night of the second day, about 9 pm ... we heard a most unusual sound, similar to the beating of a badly-tuned drum, accompanied by a low, rumbling growl. The dogs were supposed to be able to tackle anything. But in this case they seemed utterly demoralised; they would not bark, but whined, and made to come into the tents.

The 'Bombala anthropoid', drawn by Will Donald from a description given by Charles Harper.

The horrible sounds gradually drew nearer and our thoughts flew to escaped tigers ... We had no firearms, only a scrubhook and an axe ... after much coaxing I induced one of my companions who had a large bundle of leaves and dry kindling to ... place them on the smouldering camp fire ... they flickered up into a big blaze, illuminating the scrub ... when a most blood-curdling sight met our gaze.

A huge man-like animal stood erect not twenty yards [eighteen metres] from the fire, growling, grimacing, and thumping his breast with his huge hand-like paws. I looked round and saw one of my companions had fainted. He remained unconscious for some hours. The creature stood in one position for some time, sufficiently long to enable me to photograph him on my brain.

I should say its height when standing erect would be 5 ft 8 in to 5 ft 10 in [1.7 to

1.8 metres]. Its body, legs, and arms were covered with long, brownish-red hair, which shook with every quivering movement of its body. The hair on its shoulder and back parts appeared in the subdued light of the fire to be jet-black, and long; but what struck me as most extraordinary was the apparently human shape, but still so very different.

I will commence its detailed description with the feet, which only occasionally I could get a glimpse of. I saw that the metatarsal bones were very short, much shorter than in the genus homo, but the phalanges were extremely long, indicating great grasping power by the feet. The fibula bone of the leg was much shorter than in man. The femur bone of the thigh was very long, out of all proportion to the rest of the leg.

The body frame was enormous, indicating immense strength and power of endurance. The arms and forepaws were extremely long and large, and very muscular, being covered with shorter hair. The head and face were very small, but very human. The eyes were large, dark and piercing, deeply set. A most horrible mouth was ornamented with two large and long canine teeth. When the jaws were closed they protruded over the lower lip. The stomach seemed like a sack hanging halfway down the thighs, whether natural or prolapsus I could not tell. All this observation occupied a few minutes while the creature stood erect, as if the firelight had paralysed him.

After a few more growls, and thumping his breast, he made off, the first few yards erect, then at a faster gait on all fours through the low scrub. Nothing would induce my companions to continue the trip, at which I was rather pleased than otherwise, and returned as quickly as possible out of the reach of Australian gorillas, rare as they are.

Although the sketch which accompanied Mr Harper's story looks rather comical, it is evident that the newspaper artist, Will Donald, was genuinely attemping to draw the creature as described by the surveyor. All the various characteristics of the animal are depicted more or less as described, but the end result looks rather odd.

Palen Creek, Queensland, 1928

In November 1980, 76-year-old Bob Mitchell of Redcliffe told the *Brisbane Sunday Mail* of having seen two yowies at close quarters while riding with two mates through rugged bushland along the Queensland–New South Wales border. Their first sighting occurred near Palen Creek:

It was about 10 am – the yowie was standing in a clearing not far from us and in that light there was no mistaking it from something else. It was about seven feet [2.1 metres] tall, with a black human face and a gorilla-like body covered in thick brownish hair. It showed no aggression; it just looked at us for a moment, then turned and disappeared into the bush. It had really big feet and could move fast.

A few weeks later the three men were camped near Widgee Mountain, about 32 kilometres from their first sighting: 'We saw another yowie – it too just looked at us for a moment, then disappeared.'

Lismore, New South Wales, 1935

In July 1977 a 52-year-old man told *Lismore Northern Star* reporter Gary Buchanan of a yowie sighting which occurred many years earlier. He had, he claimed, seen the yowie on his grandfather's farm on Three Chain Road, South Lismore, in 1935 when he was ten years old.

He explained that the area right behind the town had been wild, heavily-timbered country in those days. The incident occurred at about 9 o'clock on a moonlit winter's night.

I was standing on the verandah when I saw a man walking across the paddock

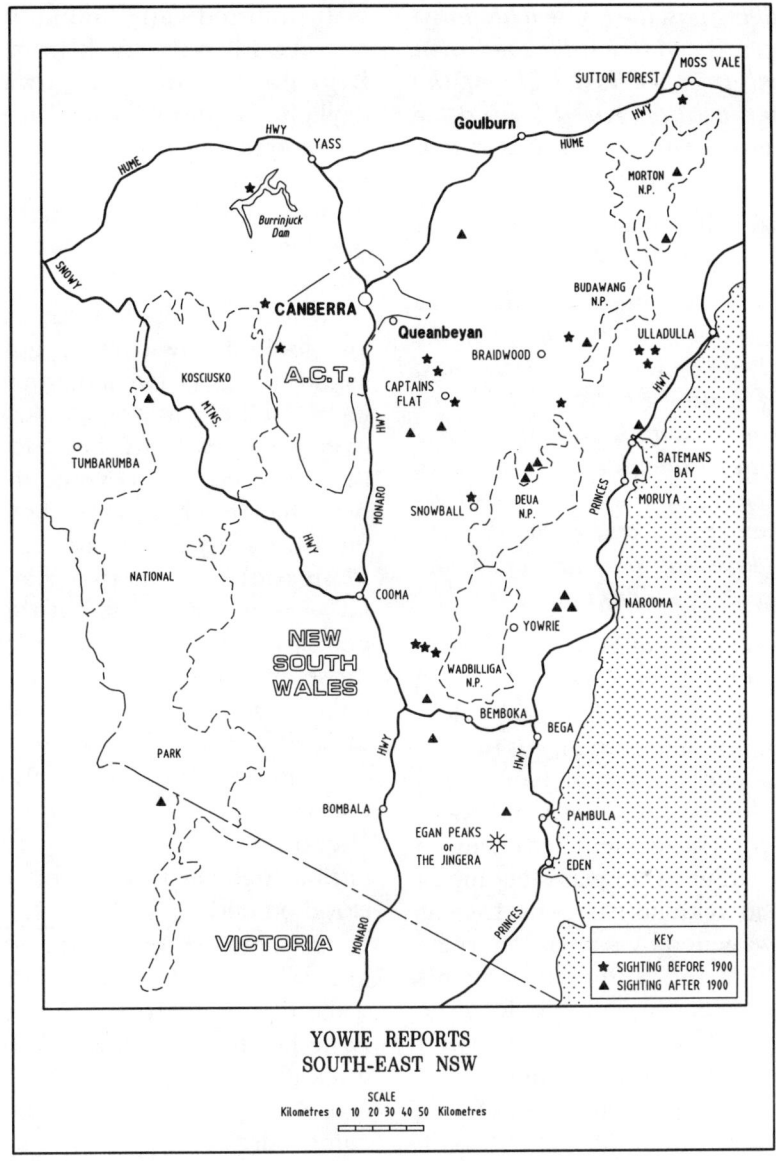

YOWIE REPORTS
SOUTH-EAST NSW

from the direction of the hills ... as it walked towards the house, my grandfather's horse started to kick up a hell of a fuss in its yard. I went inside and told my grandfather that someone was coming. When he saw what it was he pushed me inside, blew out the lamp in the living room and grabbed his rifle.

My grandparents then took me into the kitchen and we all watched through a small window as the creature walked past the house.

The yowie was about 25 yards [23 metres] away and clearly visible in the moonlight. The man noticed the creature seemed to have no neck:

Its head ... was sitting straight on its shoulders. It also looked as if it had a hunched back, but it was standing up straight. It was much thicker around the shoulders and chest than a man.

The animal seemed to drag its feet as it moved.

After walking past the house it hesitated for a few seconds near the sulky shed, then kept on walking. We lost sight of the animal when it disappeared behind the dairy. My grandfather said that it was gone and wouldn't come back.

The man said the yowie was the most frightening thing he had ever seen.

My grandfather told me it was the same creature he had seen up in a gully on the property only a few years earlier. He said he had ridden into a gully to pick some guavas when he saw the creature come down one side of the gully, cross a small creek, then climb up the other side of the hill. I remember him telling me that his horse had played up on him very badly when the creature came into view.

Kookaburra, New South Wales, September 1968

In 1976, George Gray of Kempsey told a reporter from the *Macleay Argus* that he had been attacked by a small hairy creature near the lonely sawmilling settlement of Kookaburra. The incident had occurred eight years earlier as he was sleeping in an isolated hut with his two sons. He was suddenly awakened by something trying to choke him and wrestled with his attacker for several minutes before the creature apparently gave up and left through the back door of the hut.

George described the animal as being small, and very broad 'like a well built little man' and covered with grey, bristly hair. The creature's arms were short, yet they looked powerful. Its neck was short and bullish, and its legs large. He was unable to get a good hold on the animal because its skin was loose and slippery, yet the animal was apparently powerful enough to throw him around with ease.

Cullendulla, New South Wales, early 1970s

Recently, George Birch of Bowral told us of a startling yowie encounter which he experienced about twenty years ago.

It occurred early one morning when he was driving a truck from Nowra to Bega on the Princes Highway. Just on daylight, he stopped near Cullendulla, six kilometres north of Batemans Bay, to check the load. As he was doing so he heard a strange 'screeching' noise from the dense forest on the western side of the road.

When he walked to the embankment and looked down into a gully he was astonished to see two large animals staring back at him from a small clearing about twenty metres from the road. Although the creatures were covered in brown-to-black hair, the hair was rather short, 'not wild-looking or untidy'. The overall impression was of two 'hairy people' rather than two apes, but they had flat noses and arms that were longer than those of a human. Their posture was rather 'stooped' and one animal appeared to have breasts.

Although they were shorter than George (he stands 1.9 metres) he cheerfully confesses they gave him a terrible fright: he is certain his hair actually stood on end.

He quickly moved towards the truck and, glancing back, saw the animals walking away through the bush. In his haste he almost ran into the front of the truck and, once inside the cabin, sat for ten minutes before regaining his composure.

Killawarra, New South Wales, 1974

At around 3.30 one sunny afternoon Mr Alwyn Richards and his sister were riding their horses up a hillside near Alwyn's property at Killawarra, just west of Taree. Ahead of them was a narrow strip of forest, then a cleared firebreak and beyond that a large area of scrub-covered rough country.

The horses normally loved to charge up the slope but on this occasion they shied away from the wooded area, 'snorting and carrying on, with flared nostrils – they wanted to go home'.

Alwyn eventually dismounted and led his reluctant steed through the forest with his sister following. As they emerged on the other side of the trees, they were amazed to see a huge, shaggy creature standing in the firebreak.

It was 9 to 10 feet [about 3 metres] tall, broad-chested, with a very muscular, well-proportioned body and covered in long, untidy-looking hair.

Although its arms were longer than those of a man, it impressed Alwyn as being more human than ape-like. The portion of its face which was not obscured by hair appeared to be black.

The hulking horror stood staring at them for what seemed like several minutes. His sister stayed close to the treeline but Alwyn went within about 30 metres of the animal, which was as close as his terrified horse would allow. A 'terrible burning smell' was evident.

The animal finally turned and walked away. It moved surprisingly quickly considering its immense size and stepped right over a four foot [1.2 metre] tall, four-strand fence without breaking stride.

Alwyn left his horse with his sister and walked straight over to where the animal had been standing. No clear tracks were evident, but plants were squashed and the ground was distinctly warm 'like where a cow has been lying down'.

Oxley Island, New South Wales, early 1977

Killawarra, where Alwyn Richards and his sister encountered the yowie, is near the Manning River, about 12 kilometres upstream from Taree. Three years after the Richards' experience an intense outbreak of yowie activity occurred just on the other side of Taree, on Oxley Island.

Thirty-square kilometre Oxley Island is one of three large, flat, fertile land masses in the estuary of the river, separated from the mainland by narrow, twisting tidal creeks and channels.

It is more densely populated now, but in the early 1970s the island was occupied by only a handful of dairy farming families. Although largely cleared, it was criss-crossed by swampy, tree-lined creeks and scattered belts of scrub. The island's residents enjoyed a quiet, very pleasant lifestyle. They could catch fish from their doorsteps and moor their boats to private jetties.

The first yowie incident occurred at about 11 am one day in February 1977, when Mrs Betty Gee happened to glance out the back door of her house towards her jetty. 'I saw something standing there,' she told us later, 'and I thought to myself "Who's mucking around on the wharf? It looks like a big ape!" I said to myself, "that couldn't be!" Then I got out the binoculars.'

Because of the high river bank, Mrs. Gee could not see the lower part of the creature.

'When I first saw it, its hands were outstretched and it was turning side on. When I looked through the binoculars all I could see was the back of a big, round-shaped head and shoulders with a lot of black fur. It was just like a big ape.'

She could not make out any ears, and the head was set well down on the shoulders: 'It was just a short [neck], you know, just like the back of a real ape-person standing there.'

Mrs Gee did not obtain a clear view of the face; she saw only the animal's profile before fetching the binoculars.

'The wharf is a fair way away. [It was] just roughly a face. Its features were brown, dark brown.'

Although amazed by the sight, Mrs Gee was not particularly frightened. 'I was going down to investigate when the telephone rang and when I returned the animal had disappeared,' she said.

The creature on Mrs Gee's jetty must have been every bit as tall as the three-metre specimen seen by Alwyn Richards.

The 'ape' had been visible from about the centre of its chest upwards, yet when Mrs. Gee's 1.8 metre tall son stood on the jetty not even the top of his head could be seen.

Strange things continued to happen on the property. About a week later the family arrived home to find that on a clear, still day, their massive 6000-litre water tank had been pushed over:

I thought, 'Oh gracious, who doesn't like me?' Then after that we found our fence knocked down. Our field had been freshly ploughed and these big footprints were coming right across it and I called all of the family to have a look. [The tracks] were like a big, big footprint with toes, but I didn't count them because I didn't know what I was looking at. I just thought it was some sort of monster!

I'm not the sort of person who lets their imagination run wild, but I believe in [yowies] definitely; they must be there, because I saw one.

Some of Mrs. Gee's neighbours treated the yowie report as a joke and gently ribbed her about it. One of them, Geoff Nelson, constructed a sign saying 'Caution: yowies next 8 kilometres' and set it up next to the main road bridge onto the island.

At that time Geoff, then 24 years old, was totally sceptical about the yowie. However, he soon had three good reasons to change his mind.

Just two months after Mrs Gee's experience, he and a mate, Alan Merrett, were spotlight shooting next to Scott's Creek when a huge creature suddenly climbed up out of the creek bed about twenty metres in front of the car. It was on all fours and began to stand up just as Alan switched on the powerful spotlights.

The creature was covered in long, shaggy black hair and it remained in a crouched position for a moment, staring straight at the lights before dropping back down the bank. It then appeared to stand up straight and walk away.

The face, unlike that of a human or a gorilla, was almost entirely covered in hair. 'The only skin that was visible,' Geoff recalls, 'was around the eyes, on the nose and maybe a bit of the mouth. Like the hair, the skin was dark, near charcoal colour – but you could see a distinct difference between the hair and the skin because its skin was kind of shiny with the light on it'.

What most impressed Geoff was the intense brightness and colour of the creature's eyes. They were very widely spaced and not large, but were 'vivid, red and glowing, like two flashlights shining back at you. I have never seen anything like them.'

Although, as they later established, the creek bank rose about two metres from the mud flats below, the upper chest, head and shoulders of the creature were visible as it walked away.

Geoff Nelson's sketch of the creature seen by himself and Alan Merrett at Scotts Creek, Oxley Island.

After they had peppered the air with a few expletives and got over their initial shock, Alan suggested that, since they were armed, they try to follow the animal. Geoff, however, declined, with the comment that the massive creature might decide to twist their puny .22 rifles around their necks.

Circumstances prevented Geoff from returning to the spot for three days, but when he did he was surprised to find a 'strong, acrid, electrical smell, like burnt bakelite – like when you blow up an old radio – a sulphury stink' that seemed to permeate everything in the immediate vicinity.

The site of their encounter was about one kilometre from Betty Gee's house.

A little later, while duck shooting at a spot even closer to her property, Geoff entered a thicket of trees alongside a small swampy creek and found an area of crushed grass where some large animal had been lying down. The same 'burnt electrical' smell hung in the air.

Although he had an automatic shotgun with him, Geoff became very uneasy: 'I got cold shivers and felt like something was watching me – I got out of there!'

Although he actively collected yowie reports in subsequent years, Geoff never saw reference to a similar 'burnt electrical' smell until Alwyn Richards' experience was belatedly publicised in 1993.

Geoff's final experience occurred on a Saturday night about a month later, as he drove down Cowans Lane – right beside the Gee family's boundary fence.

On that occasion a huge creature, over two metres tall, suddenly charged across the road about ten metres in front of his car. It was visible for only a few moments but seemed to be a different individual from the one he and Alan saw at Scotts Creek. This one seemed to be covered in rather pale grey or beige-coloured hair.

It appeared to have vaulted the fence on Geoff's right; it crossed the roadway in four or five huge bounds, took the opposite embankment and fence in its stride and appeared to continue at full speed, straight towards the Gees' homestead.

Meanwhile, Geoff had 'hit the brakes, forgot about the clutch', slewed to a halt and stalled the car in the middle of the road.

His main impression of the creature was that – unlike many of the yowie descriptions he has since heard – it did not have a slumped posture: 'Its head was up and its chest was thrust out, just like an athlete heading for the tape.'

The whole incident was over in a flash, but Geoff was left with one other, rather more vague impression: he felt that the creature's arms moved oddly – they did not seem to swing quite like those of a human being.

All the Oxley Island incidents, therefore, occurred within a few hundred metres and within a few weeks of each other. Curiously, the locations involved also form a more-or-less straight line.

Geoff Nelson subsequently talked to a local man who told of seeing a yowie walk across Old Bar Road on the mainland, a few kilometres to the south.

The creature had '... its chest thrust out, just like an athlete heading for the tape ...'

Woodenbong, New South Wales, November 1976 and August 1977

The next two incidents occurred within the residential section of Woodenbong, a small town right at the foot of the McPherson Range in far northern New South Wales.

On a bright moonlit night in November 1976, 49-year-old Thelma Crewe watched in amazement as two hair-covered apemen walked onto her lawn and approached her house.

Mrs Crewe had gone to her kitchen at about 1 am because she couldn't sleep:

I didn't turn on the kitchen light straight away because it was such a moonlit night, and stood at the open kitchen window looking at the view. Suddenly this creature walked onto our lawn from the next door vacant lot. He stood there outside for two to three minutes just looking towards me.

He was sort of flexing his arms in a circular movement in front of his face – first one, then the other. The creature then moved down the side of the house about ten feet [3 metres] towards the bedroom where my husband was sleeping. There was another creature of exactly the same height and appearance standing under our bedroom window.

Both animals stood under the window for a few seconds, then moved off across the yard into nearby Richmond Street. Mrs Crewe rushed in to wake up her husband, but by the time she returned the creatures had disappeared. She said the animals stood about five feet [1.5 metres] tall and were covered in tan-coloured hair.

The interesting part was that the hair on the arms was about six inches [fifteen centimetres] longer than the shorter hair over the rest of the body. Their heads seemed to be sunk low into their shoulders, but I couldn't describe them properly. You couldn't see the facial features properly because the head was only a dark rounded outline. My first impression was that they looked like an Afghan hound because of the long hair on the arms, but they weren't dogs because they were too big and walked on two legs. I also noticed that they had a shuffling kind of walk.

I was much too close to mistake it for anything I have ever seen before. It just isn't possible to compare them with any other animal.

Mrs Crewe said she was mesmerised by the creatures as they stared back at her through the window. 'Although I wasn't afraid at the time, I can't say I did not feel scared afterwards.' She checked the lawn early next morning but did not find any footprints. 'The thing that struck me as strange at the time was the unusual quiet', she said. 'We have a street full of dogs that usually bark at anything that moves, but there was no sound at all.'

In August 1977 another yowie sighting occurred in Lindsay Street, only about 270 metres from Thelma Crewe's house.

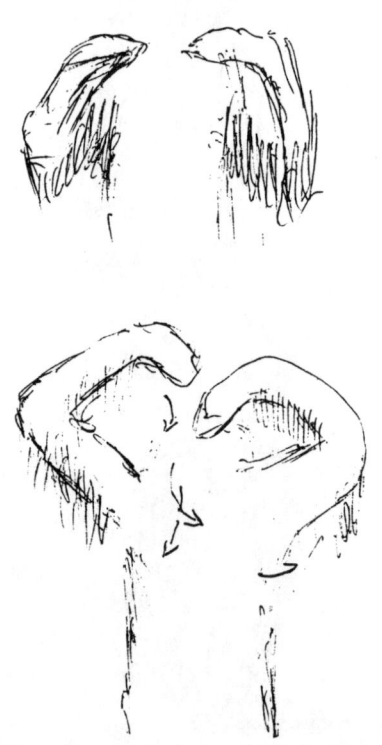

Thelma Crewe's sketches of the creatures she sighted in November 1976.

Because her husband wanted to avoid publicity, the lady who saw the creature kept quiet about her experience for a couple of days. Finally, however, she contacted the *Lismore Northern Star* because she felt the matter 'was too darned interesting to keep to myself'. She said she had been awoken around 2.30 am by the sound of her Australian terrier yelping in her backyard. As well as the dog's yelping, she could hear a high-pitched screaming sound. Jumping out of bed, she ran to the back porch and switched on the 200-watt yard light.

I went down the stairs and ran into the backyard when I suddenly saw the creature directly in front of me. I was within six feet [1.8 metres] of the jolly thing and I think I stopped breathing for a moment because of the fright. It was sitting on its haunches and had my dog completely crushed up against its chest. The dog was almost completely covered by the creature's arms which were wrapped around the dog, one above the other. It looked as though the creature was trying to crush the life out of her.

The creature looked straight up at me for a few moments then dropped the dog, which I thought was dead at this stage because she fell to the ground and did not move. It then backed away from me towards the grape trellis, but it never took its eyes off me. It backed away to the left side and wrapped its right arm around the trellis post. The creature stayed there for a few moments making these strange, deep grunting noises. The noises were very loud. It then ran off to the right, down the side of the house between the garage and disappeared towards the front street.

The woman claimed the creature stood about six feet [1.8 metres] tall. Long ginger-coloured hair hung from its arms and the rest of its body was covered in shorter brownish hair. It had a small head and no neck. Its face was ape-like, with its head appearing very small in comparison to the rest of the body. The animal had a wide chest, powerful-looking legs and long, slender arms. She also noticed a strong, offensive odour. 'The only thing I could compare it with would be a ferret,' she said.

The woman later examined the terrier and found it was bleeding from scratch wounds to the chest and the back of the neck. 'I thought the dog was going to die,' she said. 'She could hardly walk, and if you moved her too much she would yelp. I also noticed that she was badly bruised on the chest.' The dog's hair felt very greasy and stank so badly that she had to be washed in Dettol.

The woman's daughter later found three distinct footprints alongside the house but two of these were destroyed by rain. The remaining print was examined by *Northern Star* reporter Gary Buchanan. He described it as being 22 centimetres long by eleven centimetres wide, with five toes of roughly equal size. Buchanan also spoke to a next-door neighbour who confirmed that he and his wife had heard both the dog's screams and loud grunting noises coming from the woman's yard.

Springbrook, Queensland, October 1977 – March 1978

Within a period of five months from October 1977 at least five separate yowie incidents were alleged to have occurred either in, or on the edges of, Lamington National Park near Springbrook, in southeastern Queensland.

The first incident is of particular interest because the principal witness, Bill O'Chee, is now a National Party senator for Queensland.

October 1977: According to the *Gold Coast Bulletin* of 17 November 1977, twenty students of the Southport School, after returning from a two-day camp near Springbrook, claimed repeated sightings of a three-metre tall hair-covered creature.

They said the animal approached their

camp on several occasions, at one stage coming within ten metres of the cabins. One of the many students who saw the creature was young Bill O'Chee. He told the *Gold Coast Bulletin*:

About 20 of us saw it. It was about three metres tall, covered in hair, had a flat face and walked to one side in a crab-like style. It smashed small saplings and trees like matchsticks as it careered through the bush. We spotted it several times and once watched it through binoculars, so it definitely was there. We first saw the yowie at 12.30 pm on October 22 and last saw it just before we returned back to Southport on the afternoon of October 23.

When we dug this clipping out of our files and telephoned Senator O'Chee for confirmation, we didn't know what his reaction would be. Most politicians, we suspected, would twist and turn, bluster and lie themselves blue in the face rather than be connected to the yowie. On the other hand, we knew that Bill O'Chee, Australia's youngest senator, international-standard athlete and general super-achiever, had a reputation for guts and integrity.

He didn't let us down. Although he obviously rued the day he spoke to the *Gold Coast Bulletin*, he met the issue head on, confirming the story and providing us with further details. He also put us in touch with a former classmate, Craig Jackson, now a resident tutor at their old school.

The following is a composite of their separate recollections of the incident.

The camp site, known as 'Koonjewarre' and then newly established, was in open grazing land right on the edge of dense forest. Thirty boys aged twelve to thirteen and two teachers were lodged in cabins and it was from the window of one of those that the first sighting occurred. Bill and Craig were among the first to see it.

The creature was uphill from the camp and at first lying on the ground. Eventually it stood up and moved slowly around. It was right out in an open, almost treeless area and no grass or underbrush obscured the view. Although it was about 400 metres away, the animal was so gigantic that the boys could see it clearly with the naked eye. It remained in the same spot for several minutes as the boys passed a pair of binoculars backwards and forwards. Each had time for a couple of good, long looks.

It was 12.30 pm, the day was bright and sunny and through the binoculars the creature stood out in sharp detail.

'There was no doubt about it,' Bill recalled, 'it was like nothing we'd ever seen – and it was *huge*.'

Its whole body, including its flat face, was covered with black or very dark-brown hair which appeared to be about six centimetres long. Bill noted that it appeared to have no neck, as its head sat squarely on its shoulders.

'It was not really like a gorilla,' said Craig. 'In fact,' he added with a laugh, 'it was more like Chewbacca out of *Star Wars* – except that its hair was not so long and its body was much broader; it was very heavy around the shoulders.

'It looked rather slumped or hunched over. Its arms hung down past its knees and it took a couple of steps here and there with a sort of swaying, sideways movement. It seemed to be just looking around.'

The creature was standing right beside an excellent reference point, an isolated bush densely covered with white flowers. The boys carefully noted that the bush came up to about the animal's waist. Finally, a couple of boys stepped outside the cabin. The apeman spotted them immediately and ran for the nearby treeline. By this time at least 20 of the 30 boys had observed it.

The boys told the teachers what they had seen and one of them, Kevin Brooks, an adventurous ex-soldier, decided to lead a party up the hill.

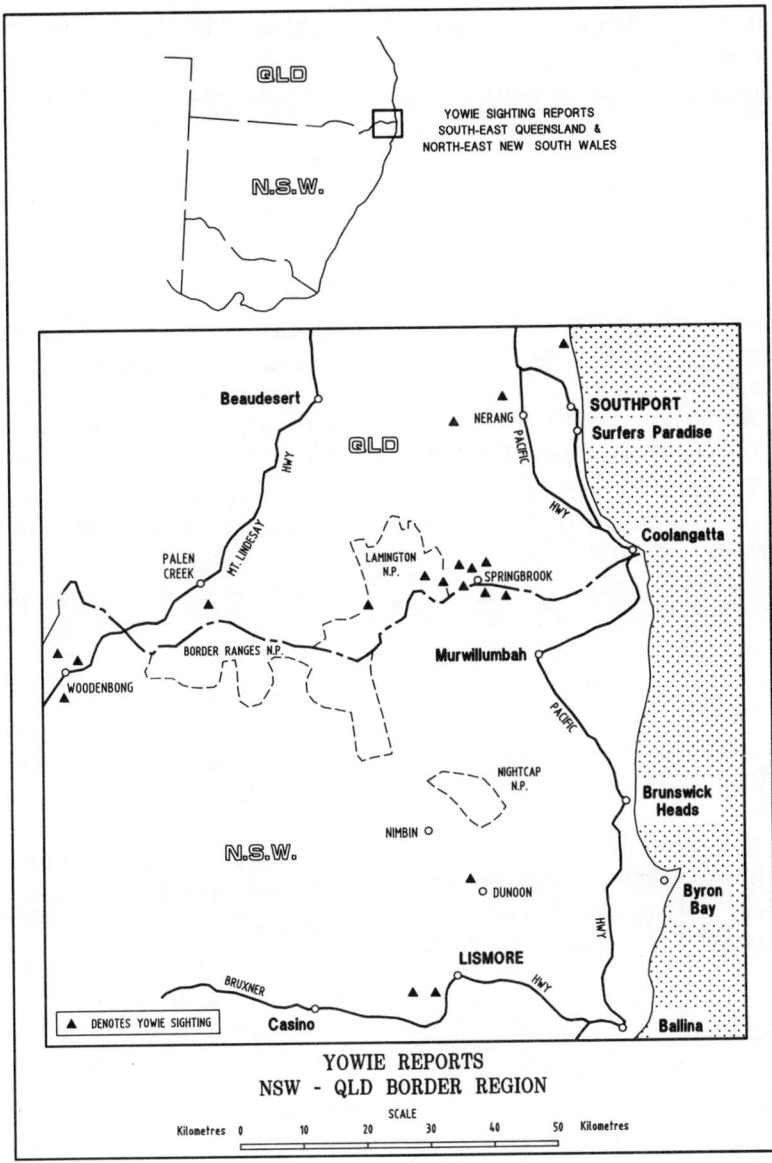

YOWIE REPORTS
NSW - QLD BORDER REGION

Craig said the reaction of the camp site's caretaker was interesting. 'When he heard what we'd seen his jaw dropped, he looked really frightened, and he urged us not to go up the hill.' At the time Craig suspected the caretaker had seen the creature himself on an earlier occasion – and his suspicions have now been confirmed.

The present caretaker recently told us that before his retirement his predecessor had spoken of encountering a yowie in the vicinity of the camp shortly after it was built.

Ignoring the caretaker's warning, Mr Brooks and four boys, including Bill and Craig, advanced up the hill. To their amazement they found that the white bush which had been waist high on the yowie was four or five feet [about 1.5 metres] high.

'The thing would have to have been eight feet [2.4 metres] tall at least,' said Bill. Craig thought it was even taller.

The creature had left a trail of widely-spaced imprints as it bounded, slipping and sliding here and there, across the hillside.

Craig admitted to being more than a little apprehensive as, armed with sticks, they entered the treeline, following a trail of pulverised underbrush. 'A whole lot of saplings had been freshly twisted, shredded and broken off above head height. I started to think it might have become enraged.'

Eventually they came to a large impression in the ground where they assumed the creature slept. 'Something very heavy had compressed the grass and twigs. They were packed down very tightly.'

Meanwhile, the other boys back at the camp saw the creature emerge from the scrub near where the party had entered. It moved away along the treeline. All through the afternoon grunting noises were heard and the creature was glimpsed intermittently.

'That night', Bill recalled, 'it came back. There were the most incredible noises and crashing sounds all around the camp.'

'It was no joke,' Craig insists, 'we were shit-scared.'

In the morning they again found footprints and also metre-high native shrubs which had been ripped right out of the ground.

Both men insist no human, however strong, could have budged the bushes, which were strongly rooted in hard ground. 'There were huge clods of dirt still attached to the roots and they'd been hurled all over the place.' Because the ground was so hard, the creature's tracks, though quite visible, showed no detail.

Although the headmaster, Peter Rogers, later searched the area himself and did not dismiss the reports as imagination, the boys were ordered, on their return to Southport, to say nothing about the incident. An article about it in the school paper was also censored.

Annoyed by this and feeling the story was too important to conceal, Bill, even then a strong-minded fellow, risked expulsion by contacting the *Gold Coast Bulletin*.

Since he has entered politics, Bill has often regretted that rash move. Sooner or later a researcher or journalist was bound to stumble over the old story.

Bill is, of course, extremely lucky in one respect: far from being alone at the time, he was just one of 20 to 30 people involved in one of the best multiple-witness incidents on record. He is probably lucky, also, that the story of his yowie encounter was not rediscovered by some big city tabloid. Instead, it can be read here, in context, as just one of many well-documented cases going back 120 years and more.

While researching this case we have been mindful of possible damage to Senator O'Chee's political career. Some of the human yahoos in parliament will, no doubt, give him hell for a while. We are confident, though, that his natural good humour and candour will carry him through.

Craig and Bill's other old classmates will back him all the way.

'Just write the truth', Craig advised us. 'It'll take more than this to stop Bill.'

January 1978: A Springbrook man known only as 'Scott' claimed a yowie entered the open door of a house one evening in January 1978. He told Howard Smith, then owner of the Natureland Zoo in Kirra, that he had been alone at a friend's home one evening, when the strange creature wandered up to the front door, and stood peering down the corridor. After overcoming his initial shock, 'Scott' threw a chair at the animal, which then hopped or limped away.

Mr Smith said the man had described the animal as being black in colour and around two metres tall. Its head was egg-shaped with deeply-set eyes and a small

THE YOWIE

After overcoming his initial shock, Scott thew a chair at the animal ...

'screwed-up' nose. The animal smelt like a 'badly kept public lavatory'. Mr Smith also noted that several other people claimed to have sighted a similar creature during the preceding week.

March 1978: A Queensland National Parks and Wildlife ranger encountered a yowie while stalking what he thought was a pig, not far from the Antarctic Beech tree grove at the 'Best of All' lookout.

The man, who insisted on anonymity, spoke about the incident to Frank Hampson of the *Gold Coast Bulletin* and later to us.

People in this area know me and would probably lose a lot of respect for me if they read about me making what they think is a crack-brained claim like this. But it's perfectly true. I met a yowie about a fortnight ago – and I've never been so scared in my life.

I thought a pig had gotten loose and was scrubbing amongst the trees. I went into the forest to see if I could find it. I heard the grunting again, but I couldn't find any tracks. Then something made me look up and there, about twelve feet [four metres] in front of me, was this big black hairy man-thing. It looked more like a gorilla than anything. It had huge hands and one of them was wrapped around a sapling.

He was close enough to see hair on the back of its fingers. The skin underneath was shiny and dark, and the fingers were basically 'human like'.

The ranger, who stands over 1.8 metres, estimated the creature was about 2.5 metres tall. 'It had a flat, black shiny face, with two big yellow eyes and a hole for a mouth. It just stared at me and I stared back. I was so numb I couldn't even raise the axe.'

As he stood there, paralysed with

'Then something made me look up and there, about twelve feet in front of me, was this big, black hairy man-thing.'

shock, he could feel sweat streaming down his back. 'We seemed to stand there staring at each other for about ten minutes before it suddenly gave off a foul smell that made me vomit – then it just made off sideways and disappeared.'

The creature had a short, thick neck and was very muscular and solid. Its hands, feet and body were covered with short, black hair. As with the creature described by Bill O'Chee and his party, the face was partly covered with hair. The animal appeared to be a male.

The man reported the sighting to his boss, but was told to keep it quiet for fear of hunters entering the national park. He later heard, from a Springbrook resident, of another sighting of an apparently female yowie.

'The point I want to make is that there is no fiction about my experience,' he said. 'I saw this beast in daylight, about 2 o'clock in the afternoon. Before I might have agreed they were comic-book stuff – but no more. They exist alright. The reason they aren't seen more often is that most people who go for bushwalks make a noise. I didn't make a noise because I was trying to stalk what I thought was a pig.'

With regard to the 'big yellow eyes', it may be worth pointing out that many gorillas have light brown, honey-coloured eyes and that some Madagascan lemurs – nocturnal animals – have large glaring eyes with striking yellow irises.

Generally speaking, yowie incidents occur

at random locations up and down the mountainous areas of eastern Australia and many years often elapse between reports. However on rare occasions, and for reasons we can only guess at, dramatic outbreaks of activity occur which seem to be concentrated on small, fairly well-defined areas.

The Springbrook incidents of 1977–78 provide a classic example of this phenomenon and we have therefore covered them in some detail.

The sightings were very tightly grouped geographically as well as chronologically. ('Best of All' lookout, the site of the face-to-face encounter reported by the ranger, is less than three kilometres from 'Koonjewarre' campgrounds, where Bill O'Chee and his friends saw their yowie.)

Besides involving highly credible witnesses, the Springbrook incidents also provided details of unusually good close-range encounters and, in the case of the 'Koonjewarre' incident, one of the best multiple-witness incidents on record.

It can also be seen from the previous map that the Springbrook area is quite close to Woodenbong, Palen Creek, Dunoon, Lismore and Nerang, the sites of other notable yowie incidents.

Nerang, Queensland, August 1978

A thirteen-year-old schoolboy told of sighting an enormous hairy creature in bushland near his home at Nerang in early August 1978. Shaun Cooper told *Gold Coast Bulletin* reporter Des Houghton that he had been riding his bicycle at about 2.30 one Sunday afternoon when he came across the animal stripping bark off a tree.

'Bark was falling down around its body,' he said, 'then suddenly it turned and looked at me, putting its arms by its side. It looked at me from about 50 yards [46 metres] away for no more than three seconds. I turned and went for my life. My dad wasn't home and my mum didn't want to go back and look for it.'

Shaun described the creature as about eight feet [2.4 metres] tall and covered in thick fur. Returning later with some friends, he found several footprints that went up a nearby hill and through a fence to a waterhole.

Gold Coast Bulletin staff later found and photographed a tree with bark torn from the trunk, as well as several large three-toed footprints.

Wentworth Falls, New South Wales, April 1979

In April 1979, while bushwalking near their home in the Blue Mountains west of Sydney, Leo George and his wife Patricia found a dead kangaroo with all the flesh ripped from its hindquarters. A few minutes later they stumbled across a 'massive' footprint in the sand.

'It was very eerie,' said Mr George. 'The print was four-toed, about 30 centimetres long and we started to get a strange feeling we were being watched. We walked further along a creek bed, then suddenly

Shaun Cooper's sketch.

saw a shaggy grey mass disappearing through the trees.'

'The beast was at least three metres tall,' Mrs George added, 'and was too long-haired for a kangaroo – its fur was about six centimetres long.'

'It shambled away silently – I'm certain that what we saw was a yowie.'

A few days later, while spotlighting in the same area, Mr George and his seventeen-year-old son picked up a pair of red eyes 'the size of tennis balls'.

'We were a bit afraid,' he confessed, 'but we left the spotlight on the car and walked toward the apparition.'

The eyes disappeared as they approached. 'But once again we had the feeling we were being watched.'

'Suddenly tremendous crashing noises came from a thicket behind us ... and we broke records getting away from the spot.'

Kilcoy, Queensland, December 1979

Warren Christensen and Tony Solano, both sixteen, said that in late December 1979 while pig shooting at Sandy Creek four kilometres from Kilcoy, they encountered a three-metre tall yowie.

They were having lunch when the huge creature, covered in dirty, chocolate-coloured hair suddenly appeared twenty metres away.

If the yowie thought the boys might share their sandwiches it was badly mistaken. Warren grabbed his .22 rifle and fired from the hip. 'I think I might have hit it,' he said, 'but it just took off. It definitely wasn't a cow or any other animal like that.'

The creature left a faint sulphureous smell behind it.

The boys then followed the 'thump-thump' of the yowie's giant strides along the creek until suddenly there was silence.

'Then we heard the thumping noise behind us – it had doubled around. We jumped down into the creek bed so we could have a clear line of fire in case it attacked us.'

They later spoke to their biology teacher at Kedron State High School, Mrs Jenny Bolman, who returned to the spot with her husband John.

Several 50 cm x 15 cm 'distinctly three-toed' tracks were discovered and plaster casts made.

Dunoon, New South Wales May 1981

One of the most widely publicised modern yowie incidents occurred on 20 May 1981 when three young bushwalkers told reporter Gary Buchanan of the *Lismore Northern Star* that they had encountered two strange animals in rugged bush six kilometres west of Dunoon.

The encounter took place when the boys, aged fourteen, thirteen and eleven, were exploring thick scrub on the top of a range of hills. Around 12.45 pm two of them saw a hairy man-like creature cross the bush track from right to left. Shortly afterwards a second creature appeared from the same direction.

'The second animal seemed to stumble, stopped behind a tree standing on the left side of the path, and peeped around the tree towards us,' said the oldest boy. 'It kind of squatted behind the trees on its legs and looked at us for about five seconds before running across the path behind the other animal, which had its back towards us and appeared to be waiting for its mate to catch up.' Both animals then disappeared, but could be clearly heard moving through the undergrowth.

The boys claimed the animals resembled nothing they had ever seen before. Their dog had 'gone berserk' when they sighted the first creature, making a crying sound and then chasing both animals down the bush path.

The boys laughed off suggestions that they had misinterpreted a sighting of ordinary bush animals. They pointed out that the creatures were about two metres

THE YOWIE

tall and walked on their hind legs. 'I've never seen a wild pig walk down a hill on its hind legs,' commented the eldest lad.

'They weren't wallabies either, because they hop, not run, and these definitely ran. They moved quickly, but looked slightly awkward, and bent forward a little as they moved.'

On being asked whether the animals resembled gorillas, the eldest of the boys said, 'Yes, but these weren't gorillas. Gorillas are black and bow-legged. These had straight legs and were brown, more human-like.'

Cooma, New South Wales, June 1981

In early 1981, at their property on the banks of Cooma Creek just two kilometres north of town, the Marion family found several of their horses slashed on the sides and back as if by a large animal. One mare almost died from her injuries.

Mr Peter Marion later heard, coming from a scrubby hillside overlooking the horse paddock, a curious, deep throbbing noise 'like someone shaking a big sheet of galvanised iron'.

Finally, on the same hillside, at about 1 pm on a sunny June day that same year, Adam Marion and his friend Shane Goodwin, both twelve years old, ran into a hair-covered giant.

'It was just standing there beside a tree,' said Adam. 'We could see it real clearly. It was huge, very broad, solid.' Its arms were longer than a man's and 'the head was stuck straight into the shoulders'.

It was covered, but not densely, with dark-brown to reddish hair. 'You could make out the chest muscles.'

From where the boys stood, 25–30 metres downhill, the creature's eyes were obscured by a tree branch (later found to be almost two metres above ground level) but they could clearly see its mouth.

'We just stood there looking at it,' said

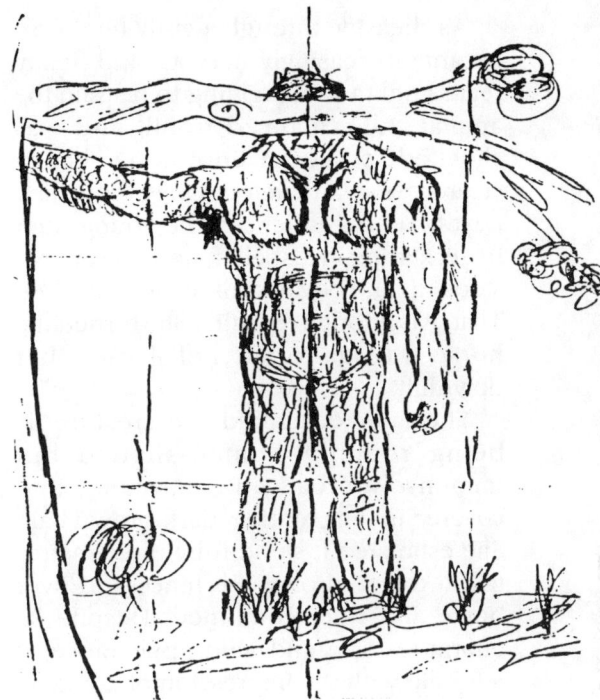

The Cooma yowie as sketched by Adam Marion and Shane Goodwin.

Shane. 'Then it bent to look at us ... and it stepped ... and so we turned around and ran straight down the hill without worrying about falling over.'

Adam seemed to be in a state of mild shock. His mother told us that after blurting out the story he went straight to bed and slept soundly for two hours – something he was never known to do in daylight.

Krambach, New South Wales, 1990

On a wet winter's afternoon in 1990, thirteen-year-old Julie Clark had a brief but unforgettable encounter with a giant yowie near the tiny town of Krambach, about 25 kilometres southwest of Taree (and about seventeen kilometres south of Alwyn Richards' 1974 sighting).

It happened at around 2 pm as she was riding across a mountainside on a property owned by a family friend, Pat Mullins. The slope had been largely cleared of trees but scattered areas of bush remained.

As she rode through a gully her horse became increasingly nervous and finally reared right up. Struggling to restrain the animal, Julie glanced uphill and was shocked to see an enormous shaggy creature only ten metres away, crouching next to a broken fence. The young rider froze, staring in disbelief, until the animal stood up and began walking towards her. That was enough for Julie. She turned the horse and galloped hell-for-leather downhill.

She later described the creature as being roughly human-shaped but immensely broad and muscular, and covered in long, untidy, dark-brown hair. She estimated it stood fully three-metres tall: it towered over the fence and over horse and rider combined. Despite its enormous size and wild appearance, it left Julie with the impression of a hugely overgrown person rather than an ape.

Julie later returned to the hillside with her mum but was still so shaken by her experience that she would not allow her mother to get too close to the actual site of the encounter.

Analysing the Reports

As can be seen by these cases, no single yowie report tells the whole story: one may describe an encounter with a man-like, six foot tall ape while another may make no mention of size or some other important feature. In an attempt to create a composite picture of the average yowie-in-the-street, we analysed 85 reports. Only 43 reports specifically mention estimates of height.

Height in feet	No. reports
3-4	1
4-5	3
5-6	12
6-7	10
7-8	7
8-9	5
9-10	1
10-11	4
Total	43

These figures yield an average height estimate of about seven feet one inch [2.15 metres]. However, since many other reports strongly imply the creatures were much larger than a man, we could probably hazard that the 'average' yowie looms close to seven and a half feet [2.3 metres].

Many reports imply that the creature's hair was darkish, but only 33 specifically mention colour:

Colour	No. reports
Black	8
Mixed (black and brown)	5
Brown	10
'Dark'	1
Reddish brown	2
Red	1
Grey	5
White	1
Total	33

It would seem, then, that most yowies, if they indeed exist, are brownish or black in colour.

The 'slender' yowie encountered in 1871 by Mr Osborne must have been a mere slip of a lad: almost all other witnesses (20 in all) who have specifically described the creature's build have used terms like 'very heavy', 'huge', 'enormous', 'very powerful', 'thickset' or 'heavily muscled'. One witness estimated the creature (over eight feet [2.4 metres] tall in that case) would have weighed between 600 and 800 pounds [about 300 kilos].

So based on the information available to us, the following Identikit description of the yowie emerges:

They are very thickset, powerfully-built ape-like men (or man-like apes), averaging 2.3 metres in height, covered all over in longish brown or black hair. They are normally bipedal but may sometimes drop to all fours. Juveniles may climb trees.

They have rarely if ever been observed in the act of eating, but assuming Mr and

Mrs George were correct, then the creatures seem to enjoy kangaroo meat. We have another report of a creature raiding a potato patch and several accounts of them stripping bark from trees, possibly in search of grubs.

Not surprisingly, then, for large animals trying to eke out a living on a harsh continent, the yowies appear to be omnivorous.

Given the long periods which often elapse between sightings, it is tempting to assume the creatures are largely nocturnal. The fact that their eyes are sometimes said to reflect light from headlight beams and spotlights tends to support that notion.

Occasionally they exude a devastatingly foul odour. The head is small in proportion to the body and appears to be set right onto the shoulders almost without benefit of a neck. The ears are not visible and the nose is flat. The face is that of an ape or man minus forehead and chin, and when the skin is seen it is normally said to be brown or black. Two large canine teeth may be visible.

As with gorillas, the sex organs of the males are not prominent and the breasts of females apparently almost unnoticeable. Probably because of this, nearly all yowie witnesses have assumed the creatures they saw were males. We assume the smaller individuals are juveniles.

We know of no reports of family groups. Such sightings may have occurred but we suspect they are very rare. Our records indicate quite strongly that the yowies, even juveniles, are solitary by nature. Of our more than one hundred reports, only five refer to pairs of yowies, and only one refers to a group of three. We have no reports which refer unambiguously to four or more seen together.

The creatures grunt and growl and may occasionally beat their chests, King-Kong style. The arms are very long – hanging down to knee level – and muscular. The hands are roughly like those of a human except that the little fingers may be opposable, rather like a second thumb, and the fingers are sometimes equipped with long, fearsome nails. The legs, unlike those of a gorilla, are straight – more like those of a human being. The feet are ... ah yes – the feet ...

The composite picture of the yowie is fine down to ankle level but then becomes a little blurry. Like the Aborigines, white percipients seem to have rarely taken notice of the creature's undercarriage. In the 85 reports examined there are only four in which eyewitnesses whose names are known to us have made any reference to the feet.

In two of these, detail is meagre to say the least. In 1894, trusty young Johnnie McWilliams said only that, while running, the wild man of Snowball 'tore up the dust with its nails' and in 1878, in a report which is curious in many ways, Pat Wring told of a hairy, man-shaped monster with 'three claws on each foot'. Both of these stories were reported at second-hand.

The two other accounts – told at first-hand – provide considerably more detail. In 1871, Mr Osborne said the feet were '... about eighteen inches [45 centimetres] long, and shaped like an iguana, with long toes'. Although he could glimpse the feet only occasionally, Charles Harper gave a more detailed description: '... the metatarsal bones were very short, much shorter than in the genus homo, but the phalanges were extremely long ...' In other words, the main part of the foot was short but the toes were very long.

In contrast to the situation in bigfoot and yeti stomping grounds, yowie footprint finds are much fewer than claims of actual sightings, and none of the descriptions of these tracks seems to fully corroborate Harper's description of the feet. Take what seems to be the best track find of all, that made by Jephcott in 1912.

Jephcott was, as we have seen, drawn to the tracks after a neighbour, Mr Summerell, claimed to have actually seen a yowie at the spot the day before. Because he was a veteran bushman and because he had a score of footprints to examine, we consider his statements to have high credibility, but although his description of the toes seems to tally with Harper's, he states that the main part of the foot was 'enormously long' rather than 'very short':

...resembling an enormously long and ugly human foot in the heel, instep, and ball, had only four toes – long (nearly 5 inches), cylindrical, and showing evidence of extreme flexibility ...

To make matters worse, in the 22 other statements about feet or footprints there are only three other references to four-toed tracks.

Traditional Aboriginal belief has it that the yowie's feet 'resembled those of a human'. This implies five toes, and some non-Aboriginal testimony supports this view. Three reports of track finds specifically mention five toes and three others strongly imply five toes. For a moment it is tempting to hope that the tracks found by Jephcott may have been left by a deformed individual ... until we dig deeper into the footprint file and find four accounts that refer to only *three* toes. In one of these cases the witness, a biology teacher, remarked that the 50 x 15 centimetre tracks were 'distinctly' three toed.

Annoying as the references to three-toed tracks may be, worse is to come. Consider these other excerpts from the footprint file:

... like those of an emu's feet, but there was one claw which penetrated several inches into the ground.
... similar to those of an elephant.
... like those of a young camel, but with a broad flat toe more than eight inches long.
... almost eight inches by six inches ... they had three front pads – two with three toes and one with two toes. There was also a rear pad, or it might have been a heel ...

The great muddled mixture of different shapes and sizes of tracks raises many questions, especially when several of the weirder examples, were allegedly discovered immediately after sightings of yowies.

The weirdest foot shapes of all are contained in a story from *The Australian Town and Country Journal*, 4 November 1876. Although told at third or fourth-hand it is interesting to read as the possible discovery of a dead yowie, and even if it is a hoax, as a reflection of how everything about the yowie's appearance has become more or less known, and amounts to a more or less coherent picture – but only down to ankle level – where contradictions, uncertainty and confusion set in:

The Milbury Creek correspondent of the Bathurst Free Press says:- A resident of this place returned from the Fish River some forty miles from here, a few days ago, and told me he had been informed by a respectable settler in that quarter that a party of sawyers, working in the Walla Walla scrub, came upon the dead body of an unearthly looking animal, human or inhuman they could not tell. It stood about 9 feet [2.7 metres] in height, with head, face and hands, similar to a man's; one of its feet resembled the hoof of a horse and the other was club shaped; the body was covered with hair or bristles like a pig.

For many years past it had been believed by the settlers of that wild part of the country, that the Walla Walla scrub was inhabited by a monster called 'the hairy man of the wood', or what all the blacks stand so much in dread of – the yahoo. Horses and cattle are said never to have been known to enter or remain in the scrub.

Much as we value the testimonial evidence and much as we would like to prove the creatures exist, we must admit that at this stage it does seem, at times, that the yowie has feet of clay. Hopefully, as the years go by, if the creatures really do exist, more and better tracks will eventually be found, photographed and cast, and the vexed matter of foot shape will be solved.

Before leaving the question of yowie tracks we must mention again the veteran yowie investigator Rex Gilroy. Whereas the authors admit to being rather uncertain of the yowie's foot shape, Rex has no such doubts. He claims to have made plaster casts of their footprints on at least three different occasions. Rex's casts tend to be extremely broad as well as long. Apart from the fact that they have five toes, they are nothing like human tracks. If we could be certain they were really left by yowies they would, of course, be of great interest.

Rex Gilroy

No discussion of the yowie mystery would be complete without devoting some space to the work of Rex Gilroy.

A self-taught naturalist now 49 years old, Rex has been hunting the yowies since about 1958 – far longer than any other investigator. Although fascinated by the subject since childhood, he says his interest increased markedly after an experience he had on 7 August 1970.

While resting below the Ruined Castle rock formation near Katoomba that day, he was startled to see a five foot [1.5 metre] tall, bipedal, hair-covered ape-like creature burst from the undergrowth and run across a clearing about 40 metres from where he was sitting. The creature, he believes, was a juvenile yowie.

We have no doubt Rex truly believes in the creatures' existence and we know he has spent a great deal of time actually out in the bush looking for them. When checking out reports of new sightings we have often found he has beaten us to the punch. He has persevered with his quest in the face of considerable ridicule and has – through his many press releases and appeals for information – almost single-handedly brought the yowie phenomenon to the attention of the modern, urban Australian population. As mentioned earlier, he is also responsible for the widespread acceptance of the term yowie.

No gun-toting thug, Rex should be applauded for his peaceful approach to the search. He hunts the creatures armed only with a camera and urges others to do the same.

Since the mid-1970s he has been issuing appeals for information about yowies through popular magazines and country newspapers and as early as 1977 was claiming to have accumulated an enormous number of sighting reports – over 3000. For many years he was based in the Blue Mountains west of Sydney, right in the heart of yowie country.

With such a wealth of data in his files, Rex should be in a better position than anyone in Australia to legitimise the subject in the eyes of the scientific establishment. So far, however, most scientists seem quite unimpressed.

It is not only the outlandish suggestion that giant apemen roam the Australian bush which upsets them. They are equally perplexed by some of Rex's other pronouncements – which seem to veer even more sharply away from orthodox scientific thought.

To give just one example: for some time Rex had on display at his Mt York museum what he claimed was a fossilised *Gigantopithecus* footprint, which he found near Kempsey, New South Wales. The remains of *Gigantopithecus* – a huge man-like ape which has been extinct for about 500,000 years – have been found only in southern China, Vietnam and northern India. Since those remains consist only of jawbones and teeth it is very difficult to see how Rex could identify his artefact as the footprint of one of the creatures.

Rex has also stated repeatedly that *Gigantopithecus* was 20 feet [six metres] tall. In fact, no one can say how tall they were. John Napier, one of the world's leading anatomists and primatologists, stated that even if they were bipedal – which he doubted – they would have stood well under nine feet [2.7 metres].

Even more perplexing is the remarkably high number of personal sightings of unknown animals which have been attributed to Rex. Perhaps he has been extensively misquoted, but at various times he has been credited with having seen:

- one, two, possibly three – or even four yowies
- a Tasmanian tiger (in New South Wales)
- The Lake Taupo (New Zealand) monster
- The Kangaroo Valley panther

(*Canberra Times*, 5 April 1976; *Sun*, 31 July 1979; *Queanbeyan Age*, 26 October 1979; *Australian Penthouse*, September 1983; *Daily Telegraph*, 5 December 1984)

As indicated above, it is, in fact, difficult to work out exactly how many yowies Rex has actually seen. At times (for example in the September 1983 *Australian Penthouse*) he insists he has claimed only one sighting (the 1970 encounter already discussed).

At other times he is quoted describing at some length and quite unambiguously two other sightings: one of '... what I am certain was an 8 ft [2.4 metre] tall, hairy, two-legged ape-like animal' near Mt York in July 1979 and another of a tall, bipedal creature which approached his camp in trackless 'unexplored' country near Katoomba in October of the same year.

Perhaps most puzzling of all is Rex's reported sighting not of a live yowie but of a *dead* one. In 1979 *The South East Magazine* quoted him as saying that during the preceding year, at 'a southern New South Wales location' whose owner 'wishes to remain anonymous', skeletal remains including a huge non-human arm, hand and finger bones were found on a snow-covered hillside. Rex was quoted as saying that the bones, which were still attached to long brownish hair, '... now confirm that the length of a full-grown yowie's arms does indeed reach down toward the knees and that the animals do reach a height of 12 ft [3.7 metres].' Curiously, we have never seen another reference to the yowie skeleton.

Before Rex approached the press with his claims, theories and appeals for information in the mid-1970s only a small proportion of the Australian population had so much as heard of the *dulagarl/yahoo/hairy man*. We feel that anyone who had the moral courage to stand up and declare the existence of the creatures in the mid-1970s and who has had the physical courage to venture repeatedly, often alone and unarmed, into as many of the isolated, spooky and dangerous areas as Rex has, really deserves to succeed.

Unfortunately his pronouncements about *Gigantopithecus*, about the yowie carcase and about even stranger matters (such as the Egyptian pyramid he supposedly discovered near Gympie, Queensland) have now proliferated to such an extent that, much as we would like to, we are hesitant to endorse any of his theories.

Other yowie investigators

Although Rex Gilroy has put by far the most effort into the quest and is the best known yowie researcher, several other people have, over the years, taken a considerable interest in the subject.

The founder of the *Queanbeyan Age*, John Gale, collected several first-hand accounts in the area of what was later to become the Australian Capital Territory and mentioned the matter in print as early as 1903. As we have seen, after examining the tracks near Packer's Swamp in 1912,

Sydney Wheeler Jephcott collected many reports (now mostly lost) from southeast New South Wales and Gippsland. Sydney researcher R. W. McKay and Rod Estoppey of Briagolong, Victoria, exchanged correspondence on the matter in the 1940s and historian Errol Lea-Scarlett also took an interest.

From the 1930s to the 1970s, Roland Robinson, a bushman and authority on folklore, noted the widespread Aboriginal belief in mountain-dwelling apemen. Canberra historian Lyall Gillespie has also been researching the subject for some time.

One of the most notable modern investigators is Graham Joyner, a Canberra resident whose main interest, before he became intrigued by the yowie mystery in the early 1970s, was the history of science. Once employed as an archivist, Graham has a great talent for unearthing references to the yowies – or yahoos, as he prefers to call them – in old documents and nineteenth century newspapers.

In 1977 Graham produced a booklet, *The Hairy Man of South Eastern Australia* which contained 29 early references to the yahoo, twelve of which included eyewitness descriptions. Because every item in the collection was thoroughly documented, because Graham's own brief comments were modest and to the point, and because he would always cheerfully share the fruits of his research with others, he succeeded in making the yahoo an acceptable subject for discussion in some sections of the scientific establishment.

Another very active investigator is Geoff Nelson of Taree who, after experiencing two sightings himself in 1977 has collected many yowie reports, mostly from the New South Wales central coast.

Although he is planning a book on the subject himself, Geoff generously put us in touch with two of his star witnesses, Alwyn Richards and Julie Clark, and provided us with some excellent sketches.

Although we had been interested in the sasquatch and yeti legends for some years previously, our own involvement in yowie research did not begin until 1975. Since then we have walked many mountain tracks and library corridors in search of the hairy giants.

We take the yowie mystery seriously and believe the great majority of eyewitnesses are decent, rational, truthful people. Sometimes – particularly after interviewing an exceptionally good witness – we come very close to accepting that, preposterous as it sounds, giant apemen really do roam the forests of Australia. However, unless we have the freakish good luck of actually seeing a yowie ourselves, we will probably never believe unreservedly in their existence.

Most of the time we simply try to remain open-minded while retaining a degree of what we hope is healthy scepticism. Most of the time, too, we can't help but see a humorous side to the yowie mystery. For some reason the very suggestion that shambling, three-metre tall rock apes may be lurking out there somewhere, peering around trees as yuppies drive by in their Pajeros, strikes us as very funny.

Basically, our position is this: the yowie itself may or may not exist, but the long, consistent sequence of yowie reports by apparently honest, credible witnesses definitely exists and the ancient Aboriginal tradition definitely exists. We collect the evidence, and without necessarily categorising it as either fact or folklore, go where it leads us. So far it has led us to many remote and interesting corners of the country, to many little known areas of Australian history and to many interesting people.

Who or what is the yowie?

Many bigfoot buffs like to think that in ancient times *Gigantopithecus* might have crossed from Asia into the Americas via the Bering Straits land bridge, and that modern sasquatches are descended from those ancient apes. Some yeti investigators like to think the same about the abominable snowmen who, after all, are reported today in areas quite close to the former range of *Gigantopithecus* in southern China and northern India.

There is nothing to suggest the giant apes ever ventured as far as Australia. Even had they moved south, they would have found not a land bridge to the Lucky Country but a considerable water barrier. During the Ice Ages Australia was joined to New Guinea but never to Asia: it was one of the great triumphs of the Aborigines that their settlement of Australia was the first colonisation of a continent which involved seafaring.

The nearest large apes to Australia are the gentle, and tragically vulnerable, orangutans of Sumatra, some 3000 kilometres away. It has rarely, if ever, been suggested that the reports of the fearsome yowie are the result of orangutans which have somehow found their way to Australia. As against the many reports in which the yowie has been compared to a gorilla, orangutans are mentioned only once. In 1985 a Braidwood grazier phoned Sydney's Taronga Park Zoo to tell how he and his son saw two creatures resembling orangutans – a 'large one' and 'a small one' – in a remote, scrubby corner of their property.

Although Australian palaeontologists have provided us with no fossilised great apes, they *have* uncovered remains of a type of supposedly primitive man who just might have had something to do with the yowie legend.

In 1967 during the digging of irrigation canals, about 40 very unusual skeletons were unearthed at Kow Swamp, between Swan Hill and Echuca. The skeletons, between 9000 and 14,000 years old, were robust, large-toothed and appeared radically different from those of modern Aborigines.

The jaws were among the largest human jaws ever found – one almost equalled that of Heidelberg Man – at that time the world's largest. They appeared, in some respects, quite similar to those of Java Man (a southeastern form of *Homo erectus*).

It is important to note, however, that although they appeared so primitive, the Kow Swamp skeletons were by no means the oldest discovered in Australia. Remains of a more slender 'modern' type – clearly one of the ancestors of the modern Aborigines – have been dated at 30,000 years and it is generally accepted that such people lived in Australia for at least 20,000 years before that.

Although Dr Alan Thorne of the Australian National University has suggested that the ancestors of the 'Kow Swamp people' may have entered Australia as long ago as 120,000 years, there is no way of proving, as yet, which group arrived first. What is certain, however, is that the 'Kow Swamp people' shared the continent with the ancestors of the Aborigines for at least 5000 years, until as recently as 7000 BC.

It is impossible to tell from the skeletons how hairy the Kow Swamp people were. It is possible they were no hairier than modern men but it is also possible they were very hairy indeed. They may have possessed only the most primitive technology. If so, the memory of them, preserved in Aboriginal folklore and handed down from generation to generation would have formed a good foundation for the legend of the wild, hair-covered yowie.

The suggestion that the folk-memory of the Aborigines could stretch back 9000 years is not entirely unreasonable; in the colonial era Aborigines in southeastern South Australia were found to have legends pertaining to great fire and destruction coming out of Mt Gambier, an extinct volcano which last erupted 3000 years earlier.

Anthropologists have long noted that

one of the most widespread themes in Aboriginal folklore is the contest between eaglehawk and crow. It has been suggested that these battles, in which the eaglehawk is almost always triumphant, recall a centuries-long contest between the ancestors of the Aborigines and an earlier wave of more primitive people. It is just possible that the 'crows' were the Kow Swamp people/*Homo erectus*.

Several Aboriginal tales about the yowie recorded in the nineteenth century refer to yowies attacking Aborigines, culminating in violent death on one side or the other. One very interesting story spells out a tale of intermittent warfare in which the Aborigines ultimately emerged triumphant:

Then they [the Aborigines] have a tradition about the yahoo they say he is a hairy man like a monkey plenty at one time not many now but the best opinion of the kind I heard from old Bungaree a Gunnedah Aboriginal he said at one time there were tribes of them and they were the original inhabitants of the Country before the present Race of Aboriginals took possession of the Country he said they were the old Race of blacks he was of Darwin's theory that the original race had a tail on them like a monkey he said the Aboriginals would camp in one place and those people in a place of their own telling about how them and the blacks used to fight and the blacks always beat them but the yahoo always made away from the blacks being a faster runner mostly Escaped the blacks were frightened of them a lot of those were together the blacks would not go near them as the yahoo would make a great noise and frighten them with sticks. He said very strong fellow very stupid the blacks were more Cunning getting behind trees spearing any chance one that Came near them this was his story about those people.

(From R. Millis (ed.), *The Wallabadah Manuscript. Recollections of the Early Days by William Telfer Jr: The Early History of the Northern Districts of New South Wales*, Sydney, 1980.)

If *Homo erectus* really did inhabit Australia in considerable numbers and if they were defeated by the Aborigines in skirmishes spanning hundreds of years, it is reasonable to expect the tattered remnants of the race would withdraw to the most remote and inhospitable areas of the country – just the kind of places where yowies are allegedly encountered today.

There are, of course, certain major problems with the *Homo erectus* = yowie theory. The most important perhaps is the fact that in the last few years some prehistorians have challenged Dr Thorne's assertion that the Kow Swamp skeletons have skulls similar to those of Java Man. The shape of the skulls, they suggest, may have been the result of artificial skull manipulation (similar to the binding of infants' heads which produced the distinctive skull shape of the Flathead Indians of Montana) practised by a group of otherwise normal *Homo sapiens*. At least one anthropologist, Gail Kennedy, argues that, in the femur at least, the Kow Swamp skeletons are perfectly modern with no trace of *Homo erectus* characteristics.

Another consideration is that the Kow Swamp skeletons do not appear to display the very long arms or the extremely short neck we have heard so much about in yowie reports. It is also important to note that their remains have been found in actual graves, that one skull was adorned with a kangaroo-tooth headband and that shells, quartz chips and stone artefacts were found at the site. Given these finds, and the assumption that the ancestors of the Kow Swamp people must have used boats or rafts to island-hop from Asia, it seems they must have been reasonably intelligent people.

The composite picture we have built up from eyewitness accounts of the yowie, however, hardly suggests they would be capable of navigating vast stretches of water. Yowie technology appears to be a little basic, to say the least. Our files contain only three references to them using sticks as weapons or walking aids and three references to them hurling stones at humans. The yowies may be physically large but they are no mental giants. To borrow Lyndon Johnson's phrase, it seems as though they would have trouble walking and chewing gum at the same time.

Is the yowie a hoax?

Over the years we have interviewed two or three people who we feel may have fabricated their yowie stories for one reason or another. In one case the story began to fall apart when the teenage 'witnesses' inadvertently contradicted each other, and in another our suspicions were aroused when the 'witness' pretended to have had no prior knowledge of the yowie phenomenon when we knew from another source he did.

Although we have over the years learned various techniques for spotting hoaxers there is no guarantee that we have not been successfully conned on occasion. At the risk of sounding outrageously gullible, however, we maintain that certain people are quite transparently honest. When someone looks you in the eye and tells you, in their own home, in the presence of their spouse or children that they have seen a strange creature in the bush it is very difficult to disbelieve them. Similarly, if people are obviously very reluctant to be interviewed and request or demand that their names not be published, one is also strongly inclined to take them at their word.

While they do not destroy our faith in the genuineness of the yowie phenomenon it is nevertheless true that hoaxes have played a small part in the saga from the very beginning.

As mentioned earlier, the first written reference to hairy giants in Australia, the handbill depicting the 'Monstrous giant from Botany' was clearly a hoax (although it may have been prompted by rumours of yowies near Botany Bay). Since it was never really meant to be taken seriously, 'hoax' is almost too strong a word for the only photo of what is claimed to be a yowie. That picture of, possibly, a small stack of straw, was published as a prank by the *Coffs Harbour Advocate* on 7 August 1979.

Similarly, the following story from the *Goulburn Evening Penny Post*, 28 October 1893, seems to be a rather laboured practical joke although, once again, it may have been prompted by an outbreak of genuine yowie sightings in the area:

Says the Braidwood Dispatch: *Mr Arthur Marrin, cordial manufacturer, met with a rather awkward reception as he was going in to Captain's Flat on Friday last with a load of cordials.*

Shortly after getting upon the turn off road from the Cooma Road, within two or three miles [about 4 kilometres] of the Flat township, he noticed his dog running up out of the bush at full tear and clear off down the road in a terrible scare. He got down to see what had frightened him, when a formidable animal with which he was entirely unacquainted jumped up the lower bank on to the road. It frightened him quite as much as the dog, as it was standing up on its two hind legs with its two fore feet stretched out like the two arms of a man.

The road being a cutting on a hill side, was narrow, and the animal was making for him, either to follow the dog or spring upon himself. Being unarmed, having only the whip in his hand, which would have made very little impression upon such an antagonist, he dropped the whip and picked up a stone which lay close to him, which he threw at the beast, striking it on the temple, bringing it to the ground. He then ran up to it and finished it with the butt end of the whip. After he killed it he left it on the road, and on his return to

Braidwood put its body in the cart and brought it home with him.

We paid a visit to Mr Marrin's factory on Saturday and inspected it. It was four feet [1.2 metres] long, 11 inches [28 centimetres] across the forehead, with a face very much like a polar bear. It weighed over 7 stone [45 kilos]. Its forearms were very strong, with great paws that would be capable of giving a terrible grip. It was a tan colour like a possum with strong hair on its skin. When Mr Marrin encountered it it stood between 6 or 7 feet [about 2 metres] high.

Some people think it is identical with a beast which has frightened several teamsters travelling through Parker's Gap on the Cooma Road at various times, so much that they have left their horses and run away ...

Anyone who has seen a bear in the wild or a gorilla at close quarters in a zoo must find the idea of Mr Marrin slaying a comparable creature with a stone to be nearly incredible.

One or two odd references to 'giant wombats' in a follow-up article and some apparent attempts at humour also make us suspect this particular story was a load of clap-trap. In our more sceptical moments we sometimes wonder, uneasily, if other venerable old reports are also hoaxes. It seems, however, that a key part of the enjoyment for people who play practical jokes is gained from, in the end, revealing the joke to the unfortunate dupe. None of the other old stories, which are, in any case, more restrained in tone and much less dramatic in content, have that kind of follow-up.

Ironically, Alexander Harris, possibly the first European to write about the yowie, assumed he was being hoaxed by the Aborigines who warned him of the creatures in the 1830s:

The river, on the banks of which we now were, rises and for a long distance winds to and fro among the mountains of the country of Durham; at length it falls into the Hunter, not a great way from the mouth of that stream. It is now well settled, but at that time we were there spoiling it of its cedar, only here and there amidst the lonely wilderness was there to be found a settler's farm or stockman's hut. The blacks were occasionally, but not often, troublesome. The stories they used to tell us about the brush thereabouts being haunted by a great tall animal like a man with his feet turned backwards, of much greater, however, than the human stature, and covered in hair, and perpetually making a frightful noise as he wandered alone, made me sometimes doubt whether they were themselves really terrified, or were merely endeavouring to scare us away; but I very strongly incline to the latter opinion.

In suspecting that the Aborigines did not really believe in the creatures however, Harris is the odd man out. It is quite evident from all other accounts that they believed absolutely in the creatures. Our own conversations with Aborigines convinces us the belief is still strong and very widespread.

In Canada there was a case of a man in a gorilla suit successfully hoaxing most – but not all – of a bus load of witnesses, but the hoaxer could, of course, not resist talking about it later. There has been no suggestion of gorilla suits being used in any Australian incident and in any case, judging from the reactions of Kos Guines and the gun-toting teenagers of Kilcoy, wearing a monkey suit in the Australian bush could be a very hazardous pastime!

If the yowie phenomenon is a hoax it must be a very, very elaborate one. It would, in fact, have to be a long *series* of hoaxes, involving Aborigines and Europeans stretching back for centuries, if not for millennia. No, hoaxes have played a part in the yowie saga, but only a small part. What veteran Canadian sasquatch hunter, Rene Dahinden, once said about the bigfoot mystery applies just as well to the yowie: 'Anyone who thinks the sasquatch is a joke is ignorant of the facts – it's as simple as that.'

Are the yowies feral humans?

In *Cryptozoology*, vol. 8, 1989 the energetic Brisbane-based researcher, Malcolm Smith, argued that reports of 'hairy men' in the Australian bush refer to just that: 'hairy men, isolated Aboriginal males whose physical features were sufficiently striking to confuse the credulous anglo settler.'

He points out that during the nineteenth century, when the Aborigines waged desperate guerilla wars against the whites and were decimated by epidemics of imported disease, tribal society in many areas broke down completely. At that time, he argues, 'degraded and antisocial individuals are likely to have been fairly common'.

Since Aborigines are just as hairy as Caucasians, Malcolm argues that the yowie reports could have been the result of unexpected encounters with solitary Aboriginal individuals – males with unusually profuse body hair as well as untended beards and long hair.

While Malcolm raises several interesting points his 'feral man' argument contains several rather serious flaws:

- In the nineteenth and early twentieth centuries most Europeans in frontier areas were quite familiar with the sight of naked or near-naked Aborigines.
- In those days the majority of Aboriginal males sported full beards and long hair.
- Only one report – detailed later – refers to the yowie having a beard.
- Only three reports state or imply that the creature's head hair was longer than that on its body.
- If the yowies were merely Aborigines disorientated by the frontier wars and epidemics, why are the creatures still seen today?

Malcolm's arguments, aimed mainly at explaining why nineteenth century Anglos reported seeing yowies, do little to explain why *Aborigines* have believed in the creatures for hundreds of years. (As a point of interest, however, it might be worth mentioning that one European suggested as early as 1842 that Aboriginal encounters with dishevelled white castaways or runaway convicts might have started the *yahoo* legend.)

Whatever the yowie may be, Malcolm, like the rest of us hapless investigators, is only human and like the rest of us he is, at times, rather selective in which material he presents and which he rejects. Because George Osborne's 1871 account described in detail a creature which was absolutely non-human, Malcolm rejects it as a hoax. This is not to say he is being dishonest; in fact, he wryly acknowledges that 'to dispose of inconvenient data in this manner may seem like special pleading...'

In our view Osborne's story, unlike the accounts of the yahoo allegedly killed by Mr Marrin, contains nothing to suggest a hoax.

Malcolm is also very selective about the modern yowie material. Out of the dozens of reports more recent than 1920 he chooses only two. It must be admitted, however, that one of these cases does support his argument very strongly. This concerns a family which claimed a yowie encounter in, of all places, the Northern Territory. The *Centralian Advocate* of 18 February 1987 told the story:

Phyllis Kenny and friend Frank Burns were hunting with Phyllis' nephews when the sighting occurred about 5 pm Saturday. They were driving through Yambah Station about 50 kilometres north of Alice Springs when they stopped at a favourite spot called Top Bore. The kids went to the toilet while Phyllis shared around some kangaroo meat.

'Suddenly this thing jumped out of one of the empty tanks,' Phyllis said. 'At first I

didn't know anything about it until one of the kids screamed. This thing started walking towards the ute and I shouted at the kids to get on. The kids in the back of the ute had a better look at it and say it was half man/half animal. Frank just put his foot flat to the floor.'

Nephew Daniel Kenny said the thing looked like a gorilla. 'It was huge and was covered with hair,' he said. 'The hair on its head grew to its elbows and its beard reached its chest. It had a large forehead, big eyes and it was red around the mouth. The red bit couldn't have been blood 'cos you would have seen it dripping'. Daniel described the creature to be about two to three metres in height and 'very fat.'

'It ran after the car the way monkeys run. It caught up and grabbed the tail of the ute and tried shaking the car. It was very strong. I noticed there were no cattle around so it must've spooked them too.' Daniel said the creature chased the group for about 60 m before it gave up. 'It didn't make any noise or speak. I had a nightmare about it on Sunday night. I don't think I'll go out bush any more, not to that place anyway.' Phyllis said no one had been drinking alcohol. 'We usually take a few beers with us but not when the kids are with us,' she said.

When the group arrived in town Phyllis contacted the police but received a negative response. 'They said they were too busy in town to go chasing monkeys through the bush,' she said. Phyllis told her relations and several went to look at the site where the beast was seen. Karen and Henry Bloomfield drove to the site and said it was not a hoax. 'There were human-shaped footprints in the sand but they were huge, about a foot or so long,' Karen said. 'There was a lot of long grass and a big area had been flattened where something had slept. I think it must be eating things raw because there was no fire either. When we arrived we could sense something was watching us but we didn't see anything.' Karen said anyone could be in danger going to Yambah Station.

Karen said the property owner, Arron Gorey, told people he had been chased by a similar thing while riding his motorbike. Mr Gorey was not available for comment.

Apart from the details of the extremely long head hair, the long beard, the aggressive behaviour and the fact that it supposedly occurred in the Northern Territory (we have no other cases from anywhere near the NT) there are some things about the story – the description of the 'thing' as 'half-man/half-animal', 'covered with hair', 'two or three metres in height', its monkey-like gait, the 'spooked' cattle, the child's subsequent nightmares, the 'huge' footprints and even the claim that 'we could sense something watching us' – which sound very compatible with 'normal' yowie reports.

One all-important detail, however, was included in a later report by a Brisbane paper: unlike Phyllis and the children, Frank Burns thought the entity was a man: '… it looked like a man to me'. Sure enough, the following night in the same area police took into custody a behaviourally-disturbed, two metre tall man who they estimated weighed about 145 kilos. They found him sitting by the roadside completely naked.

Malcolm's second modern account does far less to bolster his argument. It concerns a yowie report from the Heathcote National Park which was supposedly debunked when investigating police were told that a Yugoslav hermit, Franjo Jurcevic, had been living in the park for years.

While admitting to doubts about this case – Heathcote National Park is uncomfortably close to the Sydney metropolitan area – we fail to see how the fact of a human living close to nature in a particular locality proves that yowies could not also, occasionally, visit the same general area. Certain elements of the story still have a ring of authenticity about them.

Malcolm's 'feral human' theory suffers from the fact that apart from the two atypical modern cases detailed above, his source material is limited to the twelve eyewitness accounts (the most recent being 1912) contained in Graham Joyner's 1977 booklet *The Hairy Man of South Eastern Australia*. Since 1977, Graham, ourselves and others have uncovered many more nineteenth and twentieth century reports, and although a small number of those could at a stretch be interpreted as encounters with wandering, isolated Aborigines, most could not.

In considering the feral human argument we invite the reader to turn back to our 'century of sightings' and to look again at the 1976–77 Woodenbong incidents and at the March 1978 report from Springbrook. These sightings were made at point-blank range in well-lit conditions by competent witnesses with absolutely no desire for publicity and no prior interest in the yowie phenomenon.

We have personally interviewed them and have total confidence in their veracity. They are quite definite about what they saw: not pathetic, wandering 'feral' human beings, but large, powerful gorilla-like animals.

An undiscovered marsupial?

Graham Joyner, the most careful of researchers, is not particularly interested in modern yowie reports. He feels the press releases of Rex Gilroy from 1975 onwards, representing the yowie as an enormous primate related to the sasquatch and yeti, have provided potential hoaxers with so much information (accurate or otherwise) about the creatures that all modern reports must be considered suspect.

While we feel he is rather rash in ignoring all the modern reports we respect his right to investigate the mystery in his own very productive way.

Dismissing the yowie as '... a recent fiction', Graham rejects even the term 'yowie' – preferring 'yahoo' which he considers to be more correct. He feels the creature may now be extinct and favours the theory that it was 'an undiscovered marsupial of roughly bear-like conformation.'

We agree that, if the yahoos were – or are – real flesh and blood animals, then it is quite possible they were – or are – marsupials. The thylacine was a marsupial that resembled a dog; why should Australia not have had a marsupial that resembled a large bear?

Graham favours the idea of the yahoo being roughly bear-like because, unlike ourselves, he feels Mr Marrin's account of having slain the creature near Captain's Flat to be genuine. Apart from the Marrin story there are three other reports where the creatures were said to be bear-like.

On the other hand, a far greater number of reports (21 in all, and eleven of these prior to 1975) specifically compare the creatures to apes, gorillas, orangutans or apemen. Because of this we feel that the yowie/yahoo, if it is a marsupial, is a marsupial which is much more ape-like than bear-like.

Apeman legends worldwide

Legends and modern reports of hairy apemen are not a purely Australian phenomenon. Over the years, with cameras clasped tightly in shaky hands, we have crept through many supposedly sasquatch and yeti-infested locales in North America and Nepal. We have also made expeditions to less well-known apeman hot-spots: to peninsula Malaysia (seeking the dreaded *orang mawas*) and to Andros Island, Bahamas (the equally dreaded *yay-ho*).

Hairy apeman reports have come from many other areas as well. Guatemala, Panama, Colombia, Brazil and Argentina have all produced reports of creatures locally known as *sisemite, shiru, ucumar*

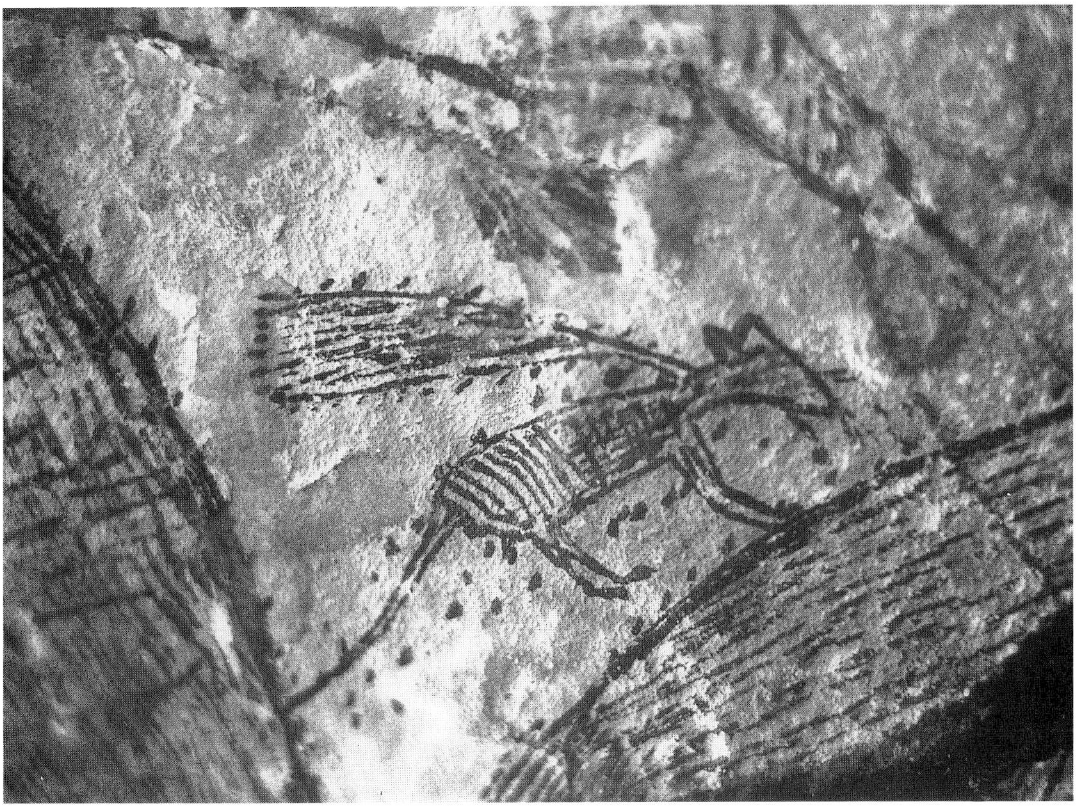

George Chaloupka

Above: Aboriginal rock painting of a thylacine from Arnhem Land, Northern Territory.

Below: Rilla Martin's 1964 photograph of the Ozenkadnook tiger, taken near Goroke in western Victoria.

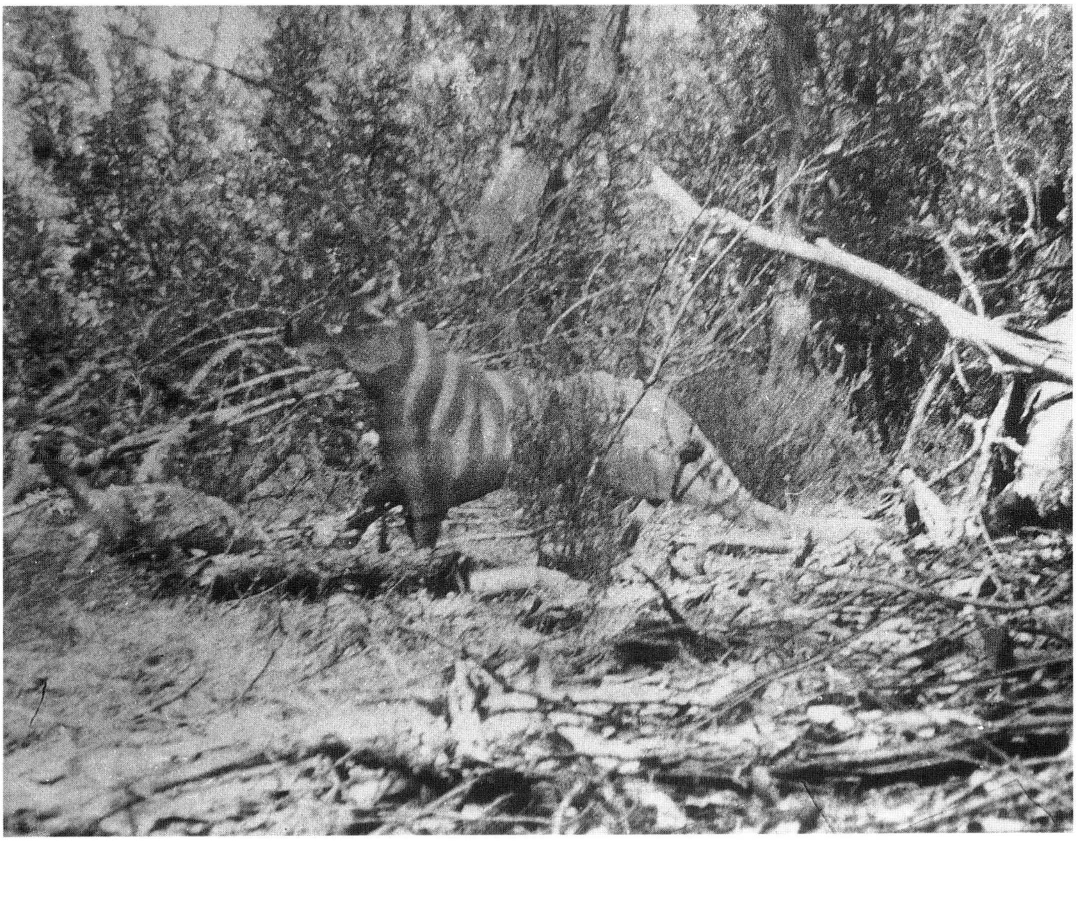

Left: WA farmer Sid Slee, who claims that thylacines have regularly visited his property, 'Hillside', since the early 1940s.

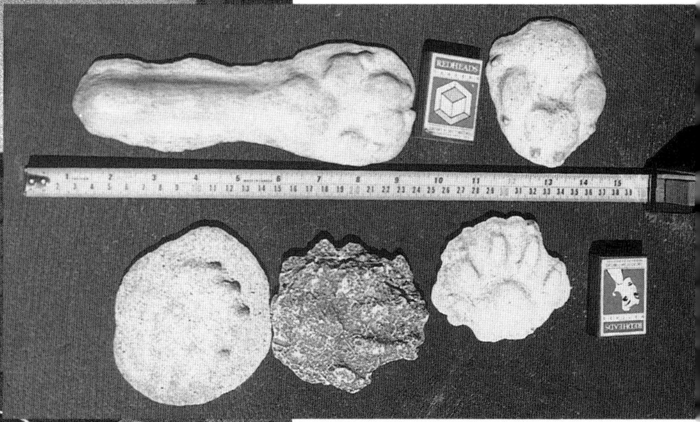

Inset: A selection of track casts taken from Sid Slee's property.

All pics Sid Slee

Below: Kangaroo killed by a mystery predator on the Slee property. Note the long pad mark near the lens cover.

Above: The Tantanoola tiger.

Right: Conservation and Environment officer Ian McRae with the Tasmanian devil found dead near Harcourt, Victoria in April 1991.

Above: The mummified carcase of a thylacine discovered in a cave on Mundrabilla Station near Eucla, WA in 1966.

Above: Joseph (left) and William (right) Webb, two brothers who shot at a yowie in the Brindabella Ranges in 1885.

Left: The Webb brothers' yowie as sketched by 'an eyewitness'.

Below: Alwyn Richards, who sighted a huge yowie near his property at Killawarra, NSW in 1974. The three-metre tall creature stepped over this wire fence without breaking stride.

An Aboriginal rock painting of Turamulli, the giant quinkin. The Yalanji people of Cape York, Qld said that Turamulli was a giant, hair-covered man who towered above the tallest trees.

Peter West/AUSPIC

Clockwise from above: National Party senator Bill O'Chee, one of many witnesses to a remarkable yowie incident near Springbrook, Queensland in October 1977; Adam Marion and Shane Goodwin indicate the height of the yowie they saw near Cooma, NSW. The creature's head was partially obscured by the branch; Kos Guines, the Melbourne greengrocer who shot a yowie while hunting with his sons near Pambula, NSW in 1977; Yowie witnesses Julie Clark and Geoff Nelson.

Tony Healy

Sunday Press

Tony Healy

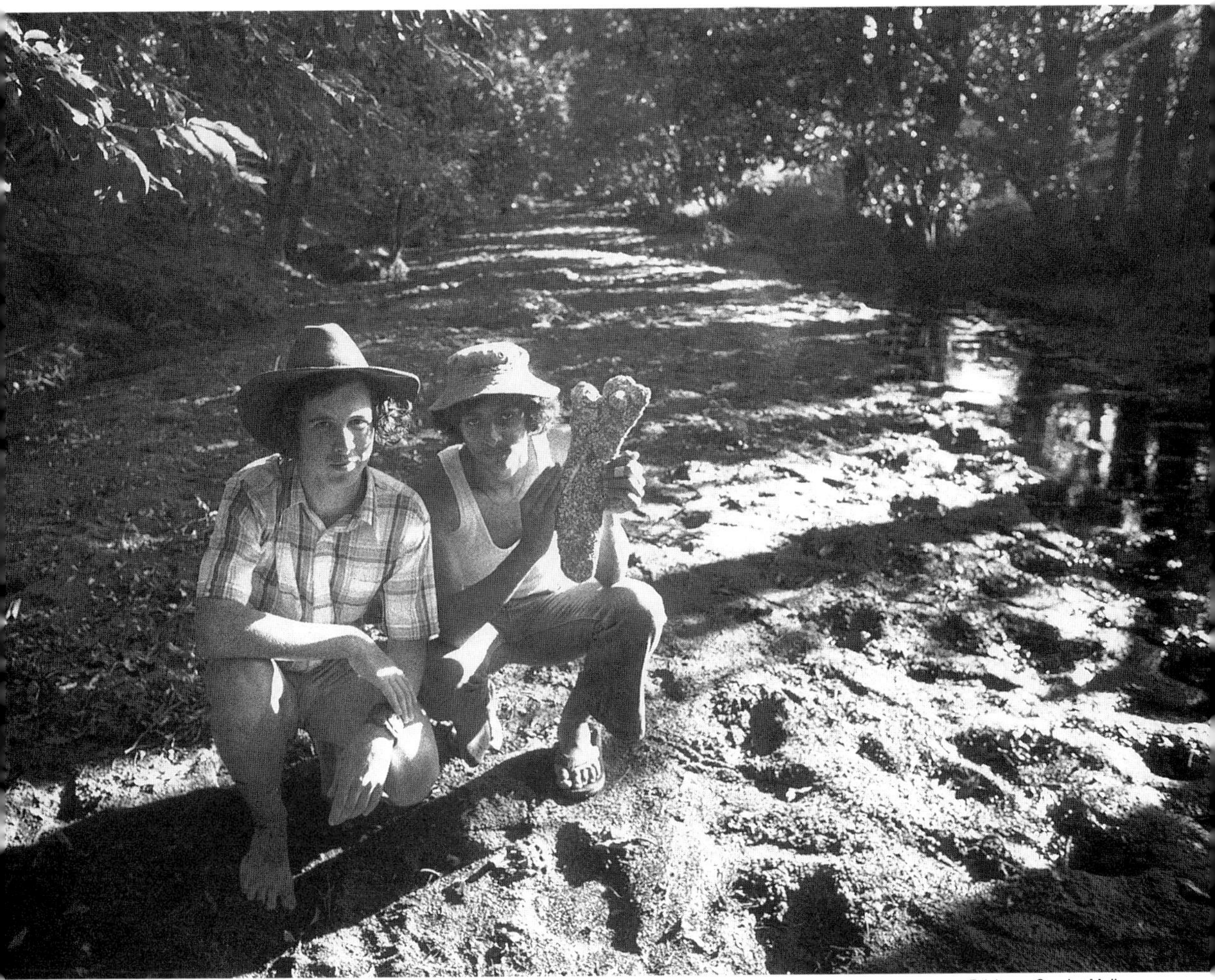

Brisbane Courier Mail

Above: Warren Christenson and Tony Solano with a cast of a three-toed track found after their yowie sighting near Kilcoy, Queensland in December 1979.

John Green

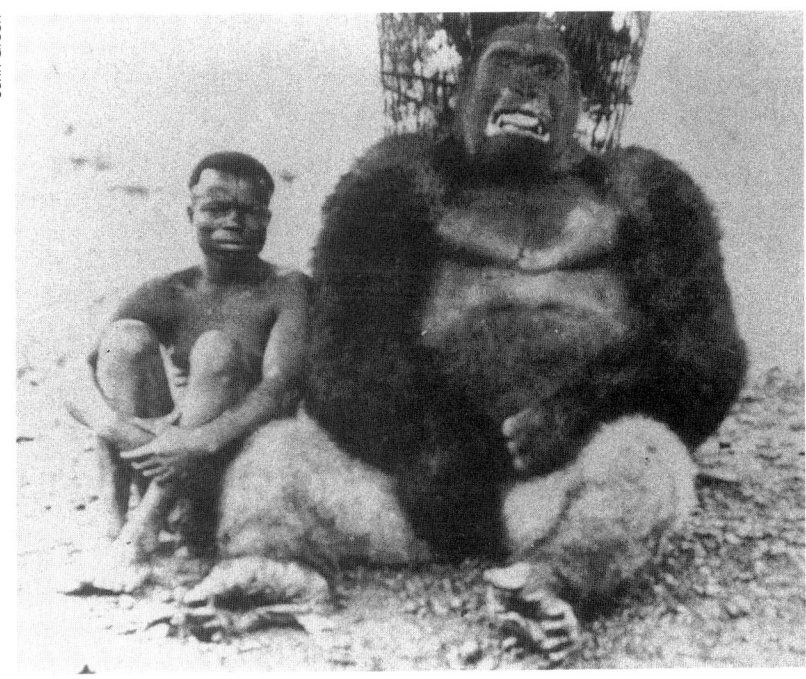

Right: The idea of giant, eight foot tall yowies striding through the Australian bush may seem fantastic, but a large male gorilla like this would be a similar height if his legs were of similar proportions to those of a man.

Above: An Aboriginal carving which may depict a bunyip from Bantry Bay, NSW.

Left: Captain Sam Southwell, who saw a bunyip basking on the edge of the Murrumbidgee River in the late 1800s.

Lyall Gillespie

Right: Student Brian Vercoe and his impression of the mooluwonk, an ape-like creature said by the local Aboriginal community to live near Murray Bridge, SA.

Adelaide Advertiser

and *mono grande*. In Sumatra the hairy, man-like *orang pendek* continues to elude its pursuers and since the 1950s, Russian scientists have been searching intermittently for the sasquatch-like *almasti* of the Pamir and Caucasus mountains.

Like American sasquatch hunters, the Russians have come up with huge amounts of testimonial evidence, a little hair plus some casts and photographs of footprints.

Throughout 1976 and 1977 a hundred-strong team of science workers and army scouts, organised by the Chinese Academy of Sciences, scoured the mountains of northeastern Hubei Province, hot on the trail of hairy 'wildmen' which were mentioned in Chinese writings as early as 300 BC and which continue to be reported by startled forestry workers into the 1990s.

The Chinese, who thought they would have the *yeren* in the bag after only a few weeks, have been able to produce nothing more tangible than casts of footprints, hanks of hair, heaps of dung and the type of photograph so familiar to Australian yowie hunters: pictures of bemused witnesses pointing into now-vacant landscapes, saying: 'It was seven feet tall and it was right over there – so help me!'

Our filing cabinets now overflow with apeman reports from New Zealand, New Guinea, Kenya, India and even Japan. (Surely you've heard of the 'A-Beast' of Mt Hiba, near Hiroshima?)

Even after weeding out the dreaded 'A-Beast' (let's hope *that* one was a joke) and other fringe reports, we are still faced with the inescapable fact that reports of giant, hairy, always uncatchable apemen are a worldwide phenomenon – which seriously begs the question of whether or not the yowie, or any of the others, are at all real.

Whether any of them are real or not, however, it is probably worthwhile, if only as a study of folklore in the making, to briefly review here the various ways in which the yowie legend agrees with or differs from other apeman traditions. To keep things relatively simple, we will compare the yowie mainly with its best-documented (by far) cousin – the North American bigfoot/sasquatch.

We don't believe, by the way, that modern media coverage of the bigfoot/sasquatch legend has greatly influenced the descriptions given by Australians who see or think they see yowies. Our view is that since Australian media coverage of the sasquatch phenomenon was almost non-existent before 1975, the American legend can have had only a marginal effect on perceptions of the yowie. Descriptions of the yowie have, after all, been pretty consistent for well over a hundred years.

The yowie's big brother

Since the mid-1950s the Canadian investigator, John Green, has collected and rigorously analysed over 2000 Sasquatch reports. In his definitive work *Sasquatch – The Apes Among Us*, he has provided us with a composite description of the sasquatch distilled from hundreds of reports spread over 150 years.

Strong similarities between the 'average' sasquatch and the 'average' yowie are readily apparent – but first the differences:

DIFFERENCES

Height: in the somewhat remote event of a sasquatch/yowie basketball game the Aussies would probably receive a hammering from the Yanks.

While yowie height estimates average out at 7 feet 1 inch [2.16 metres], the 'average' sasquatch tops 7 feet 6 inches [2.29 metres].

Hair length: the bulk of sasquatch witnesses describe them as being covered with usually straight hair which is 'short' to 'medium' in length – perhaps 4 inches [10 centimetres] on average.

Working from our admittedly much

smaller statistical base, we have counted a proportionately larger number of references to creatures being covered with 'long' hair. We therefore tend to the view that the 'average' yowie may be somewhat shaggier than the 'average' sasquatch.

Hands: the few hand prints which have been found, plus Indian carvings and the testimony of a small number of close observers, indicate that the sasquatch's hands are basically human-shaped but with a thumb that is less opposable and not always employed in grasping objects.

Their hands, then, appear to be radically different from the yowie hand prints with the apparently opposable 'second thumb' reported by Jephcott in 1912.

The talon-like nails sometimes referred to in yowie reports are very rarely mentioned in accounts of sasquatch sightings.

Tracks: in North America track finds are almost as common as actual sighting reports. Despite many undeniable hoaxes, hundreds of clear, unambiguous tracks, often found in extremely remote areas over a hundred years and more, have been examined, cast or photographed by competent witnesses: police, anthropologists, professional animal trappers, etc.

In Australia, as we have seen, track finds are very rare and often of dubious value.

The much greater incidence of snow and the much higher rainfall, and hence softer ground, in sasquatch stomping grounds could go some way to explaining this great disparity. It does, however, still seem rather strange.

SIMILARITIES

Build: like the yowie, the sasquatch has almost always been described as being of 'heavy' or 'very heavy' build.

Hair colour: most sasquatches (79 per cent) like most yowies (72 per cent) are said to be black to brown in colour. A minority of both types are white, grey or reddish.

Posture: like the yowie, the sasquatch is almost always said to be bipedal although often somewhat stooped. A small minority of reports mention knuckle-walking.

Tails: as with the yowie, tails are never mentioned.

Arms: like the yowie, the sasquatch is usually said to have arms extending to at least mid-thigh – and often to below the knee.

Legs: both creatures are usually said to have long, straight legs, as against the short, bandy legs of a gorilla.

Neck: the sasquatch's neck, when mentioned, like the neck of Kos Guines' yowie and nearly all others, is said to be very short or non-existent.

Head: like the yowie, the sasquatch is almost always said to have a sloping forehead and a flat face. Ears are seldom mentioned. The skin is usually dark but occasionally light.

Like that of the Kos Guines beast, heads are sometimes described as dome-shaped. As with the yowie, long canine teeth are reported on rare occasions.

Sex: as with gorillas, the sexual organs of male sasquatches are not very prominent and the breasts of females are apparently almost unnoticeable unless they are nursing. In only 25 cases out of 1050 were the creatures identified as females. As in Australia, creatures not obviously females are generally assumed to be males.

Smell: an overpoweringly foul odour is reported in 5.6 per cent of North American cases; almost exactly what our yowie statistics suggest.

Feet: ironically, although we have listed the sheer number of track finds as a point of difference between the North American and Australian legends, both the sasquatch and the yowie have a 'problem' with their feet which could be listed here as a point of similarity.

As previously mentioned, the physical description of the yowie in our hundred or so reports is fairly consistent – but only down to ankle level. Few witnesses have observed the feet, and track finds vary wildly from three to four to five or even more toes.

The great majority of sasquatch tracks are pretty consistent: like huge, flat human feet with five toes and often an extra crease in the ball of the foot. A sizeable minority of track finds, however, sometimes discovered after quite convincing eyewitness reports, consist of weirdly-shaped three and four-toed footprints.

John Green and other veteran sasquatch hunters have always been rather nonplussed by these 'weird' tracks – which are virtually the only blot on the otherwise near-perfect composite sketch of the sasquatch.

Behaviour: like the yowies, nearly all sasquatches are said to shy away from humans, although some approach with apparent curiosity. Signs of aggression are rare, although as in Australia, stone throwing has been reported and people have occasionally gone missing in very strange circumstances in sasquatch hot-spots.

The vast majority of sasquatches appear to be solitary; only 5.4 per cent of reports involve more than one individual, and sightings of more than two at a time are extremely rare – roughly the same as the Australian pattern.

Like the yowies, the sasquatches appear to be omnivorous; they have been seen nibbling on everything from tiny new leaves to fish, garbage and dead deer.

Because their eyes, like those of the yowie, are said to reflect headlight beams, it is often assumed the creatures are largely nocturnal.

Reactions of other animals: one possibly significant element which crops up repeatedly in apeman reports in both North America and Australia is the extreme fear reaction of other animals – particularly dogs.

In both continents there are many stories of normally fierce dogs whining and clawing to get inside houses or tents when the hairy giants appear. There are several stories, also, of horses either driven to hysteria or reduced to a catatonic state by the proximity of the creatures.

Elusiveness and invulnerability: while every other animal in North America has been shot, dissected, stuffed, eaten, studied, farmed or otherwise harassed, the sasquatch shares with the yowie the ability to evade capture year after year, decade after decade.

As in Australia there are several very old, unprovable stories of hairy giants being killed or carcases found. But in the modern era at least, the sasquatch, like the yowie, appears to be bulletproof.

John has recorded over 80 cases of the creatures being blasted by everything from .22s to 30.06s. Some fall down for a moment but don't oblige by staying down. Most, like Kos Guines' yowie, just 'keep on truckin'.

Native American traditions: like the Australian Aborigines, the Indians, particularly those of the Pacific northwest, have strongly believed in the hairy giants since time immemorial.

Kwakiutl Indians of the Canadian west coast carved representations of the ape-like *dsonoqua* on totem poles and ritual masks. Stone carvings which represent ape-like heads and the huge feet of the sasquatch can also be found in the Vancouver City Museum.

Like the Australian Aborigines, the Indians frequently said the giants were maneaters and, as in Australia, there is some tribal lore concerning wholesale warfare with the hairy men in ancient times.

Another curious coincidence: while white Americans generally think of the hairy giants as man-like apes, native Americans, like the Aborigines, almost always refer to them as ape-like men.

Other apeman legends

As well as tallying so closely with the sasquatch phenomenon the yowie has many points in common with apeman legends on other continents.

We don't have space to deal with all of these, but we would like to mention just one. As mentioned earlier some pioneers, such as Alexander Harris, reported Aborigines as sometimes saying the yowies' feet were *turned backwards*. It is a curious fact, which may be of interest to folklorists, that this strange, illogical detail occurs in several other apeman traditions worldwide.

It is not modern witnesses, explorers or colonists who mention this odd detail, but the indigenous inhabitants.

In Nepal, for instance, it is a standard feature of yeti lore, and the Malaysian aborigines, the Orang Asli, told us the same thing about the hairy and super elusive *orang mawas*.

Even on remote Andros Island, in the Bahamas, we were warned by locals that in the event of finding tracks of the fearsome *yay-ho*, we should '... go the way his feet are pointin' – because he goin' the other way; his feet – they turned backwards.'

On Andros, the coincidence extends a little further still. The local villagers usually call the super elusive apemen with the backward-pointing feet *yay-hos*, but sometimes – like the Australian Aborigines – they call them *yahoos*.

As you will have noticed, in writing this chapter we have sometimes used the term 'yowie phenomenon' and at other times referred to the 'yowie legend' or 'yowie tradition'. We have also used the terms 'sighting', 'alleged sighting', 'supposed sighting' or 'reported sighting' pretty well at random. This reflects our unresolved thinking on the mystery – our ambivalent attitude towards our furry friends, whom we have pursued for so long.

On one hand, we acknowledge that in view of the recurring folklore motifs such as the 'reversed feet syndrome' and the worldwide nature of the hairy giant legends – not to mention the continuing absence of a dead or captured yowie – it is hard to accept that the Australian apemen could really exist.

On the other hand, when we talk face to face with obviously sincere, intelligent, rational people – and sometimes groups of people – who describe broad-daylight, short-range encounters with hairy giants; when we note time and again details such as the extreme fear reaction of dogs and when we look again at the consistency of the yowie tradition from antiquity down to the present day, we think again that maybe, just maybe, there *is* something out there in the bush. Some holdover from the Dreamtime, slipping through the night. Watching. Waiting us out.

References

Archer, M., 'Monkeying With the Theory of Evolution', *Australian Natural History*, vol. 20, no. 11, 1982
Australian Town and Country Journal, 4 and 18 November 1876
Canberra Times, 5 April 1976; 12 August 1990
Centralian Advocate, 18 February 1987
Cooma Express, 30 October 1894
Courier Mail, 4 January 1980
Cropper, P., The Yowie: A Catalogue of Cases, 1840–1985, MS Sydney, 1985
Dahinden, R. and Hunter, D., *Sasquatch*, McClelland and Stewart, Toronto, 1973
Daily Telegraph, 5 December 1984
Ellis, N., *Braidwood, Dear Braidwood: A History of Braidwood and District*, self published, Braidwood, 1989
Empire (Sydney), 17 April 1871
Favenc, E., *The History of Australian Exploration From 1788 to 1888*, Turner and Henderson, Sydney, 1888, pp. 188 and 202
Freeman's Journal, 13 April 1878
Gale, J., *An Alpine Excursion*, serialised in the *Queanbeyan Observer*, 13 February to 17 March 1903; *Canberra: History of and Legends relating to the Federal Capital Territory of the Commonwealth of Australia*, A.M.Fallick and Sons, Queanbeyan, 1927
Gillespie, L., *The History of Canberra 1820–1913*, Australian Government Publishing Service, Canberra, 1991
Gold Coast Bulletin, 17 November 1977; 2 February 1978; 7 April 1978; 25 August 1978
Green, J., *Sasquatch: The Apes Among Us*, Hancock House, British Colombia, 1978
Gresser, P., *Manuscripts Relating Principally to the Aborigines of the Bathurst District*, Bathurst, 1964, pp. 167–71, MS 21/2, Australian Institute of Aboriginal Studies Library, Canberra
Harris, A., *Settlers and Convicts or Recollections of Sixteen Years Labour in the Australian Backwoods*, London, 1847, reprinted, Melbourne University Press, 1969
Healy, T., Monster Safari, MS, Canberra 1982
Herald (Melbourne), 27 July 1987
Joyner, G., *The Hairy Man of South Eastern Australia*, Union Offset, Canberra, 1977;
More Historical Evidence For The Yahoo, Hairy Man, Wild Man or Australian 'Gorilla', typescript, Canberra, 1980;
The Meaning of Yahoo and dulugal – European and Aboriginal perspectives on the so-called 'Australian Gorilla', *Canberra Historical Journal*, March 1994
Lismore Northern Star, 17 May 1878, 4, 5 and 7 July 1977; 23 May 1981; 3 June 1981
Macleay Argus, 4 and 18 September 1976
Moruya Independent, 3 August 1978
Mudgee Guardian, 10, 22 and 24 June 1909
Napier, J., *Bigfoot, the Yeti and Sasquatch in Myth and Reality*, Jonathan Cape, London, 1972
Naseby, C., *The Aboriginals of Australia: Stories About the Kamilaroi Tribe*, communicated to John Fraser, Maitland, Mercury Office print 1882
Povah, F., *You Kids Count Your Shadows*, Wollar, NSW, 1990
Queanbeyan Age, 27 July 1871; 12 November 1976; 26 October 1979; 26 June 1981; 14 December 1983
Queanbeyan Observer, 30 November 1894
Reminiscences of a Sojourn in South Australia by 'A Squatter', Kent and Richards, London, 1849
Robertson Advocate, 18 June 1909
Robertson, R., *Black-Feller White-Feller*, Angus and Robertson, Sydney, 1958
Smith, M., 'Analysis of the Australian "Hairy Man" (Yahoo) Data', *Cryptozoology*, vol. 8, 1989
South East Magazine, 25 October 1982
Sun Herald, 20 September 1970; 12 September 1976; 13 March 1977
Sun, 10 November 1912; 1 August 1965; 31 July 1979
Sunday Mail (Brisbane), 9 November 1980
Sunday Press (Melbourne), 20 June 1982
Sydney Mail, 9 October 1912
Sydney Morning Herald, 16 September 1872; 12 October 1877; 1 September 1987
Telfer, W., 'The Early History of the Northern Districts of New South Wales' [c.1898], University of New England Archives A147/V213, pp. 32, 34
Trezise, P., *Dream Road*, Allen and Unwin, Sydney, 1993.
Trezise, P. and Roughsey, D., *Turramulli the Giant Quinkin*, Collins, Sydney, 1982
Tumbarumba Times, 31 August 1977

Chapter Six

THE BUNYIP

THE BUNYIP

Bunyip, beast that lives forever, terror of the outback night, slimy swimmer in many a deep, dark billabong, nemesis of the unwary, is one of Australia's most enduring legends and one of the few Aboriginal traditions which has been embraced and perpetuated – albeit in a slightly modified form – by non-Aboriginal Australians.

Contrary to popular belief, there is more to the bunyip tradition than native myth or the tall tales of drunken bushmen. Oral traditions, pictographs and ground carvings testify to a universal belief by the Aborigines of southeastern Australia in the existence of large, amphibious, man-eating creatures in some freshwater lagoons, rivers and swamps. Scores, if not hundreds, of early European settlers, including sober bankers, surveyors and men of the cloth, also reported seeing such creatures.

Aboriginal beliefs

Because the original Australians had no written language, because so many of the southern tribes have been wiped out, because Aboriginal folklore contained so many other fabulous animals and because many whites in recent times have tended to treat the whole matter as a joke, attempting to summarise Aboriginal bunyip lore is no easy matter.

It seems certain, at least, that at the time of first white settlement, belief in the creatures was almost universal among the Aborigines of southeastern Australia.

Some writers have stated that the bunyip legends covered all of Australia but we don't entirely agree. Coastal Aborigines in the Northern Territory and northern Queensland certainly believed in sea monsters and Western Australian tribes believed in giant winged creatures which spent some time in waterholes, but these are clearly not the same as the 'classic' freshwater bunyip.

To date, our own research indicates that Aboriginal belief in the 'true' bunyip was restricted to Victoria, New South Wales, parts of South Australia and southern Queensland. Since many whites have reported seeing bunyips in Tasmania, it seems likely the Tasmanian Aborigines also believed in such creatures. So far, however, we have been unable to verify this.

Throughout southeastern Australia the bunyip was known by many names: on the Darling Downs as *mochel-mochel*; in South Australia as *moolgewanke*; in NSW as *dongus, bunyup, kianpraty, tunataboh* and *katenpai*; and in Victoria as *kajanprati, tumbata* and *toor-roo-dun*. The word bunyip itself was widely used in Victoria but also in New South Wales. It was first noticed by whites in the Sydney area.

In 1812 the *Sydney Gazette* published a pamphlet by James Ives in which the 'bahnyip' was described as 'a large black animal like a seal, with a terrible voice which creates terror among the blacks'.

The Aborigines seemed to agree the bunyips were large and fierce, given to emerging from the water at nightfall in search of victims and to bellowing in a terrible manner. That the creatures were in some way supernatural, with the power to attract or confuse victims was widely believed, as was the notion that, although evil themselves, they punished evil-doers. It was often said the bunyips preferred eating women and that they lived in burrows with underwater entrances where they laid huge eggs.

During the days of considerable scientific interest in the bunyip many whites were frustrated by the readiness of some Aborigines to identify all manner of nondescript bones as bunyip remains. Brough Smyth remarked that they '... appear to have been in such dread of [the bunyip] as to have been unable to take note of its characteristics', but this comment does not seem to be entirely fair.

Certainly ample evidence exists of their fear. William Buckley, an escaped convict who lived with the Wothowurong people in the Geelong area from 1803 to 1835, stated that their dread of the animals was very great indeed. Some Aborigines would supposedly risk death by bushfire rather than shelter in a bunyip-infested waterhole.

Despite their fear, however, some Aborigines had fairly strong ideas about the creatures' appearance and passed them on to interested Europeans. Although details varied somewhat, and though much was no doubt lost in translation, what emerged was this: the Aborigines appeared to believe in *two different kinds of bunyip*.

One type was said to resemble a very shaggy seal or a large swimming dog. Its eyes were sometimes said to shine. A white pioneer, T. Hall, who himself saw one of the creatures scurry across a sand bar, said the Blucher tribe of the Darling Downs were 'unanimous' in their description of this type. The creatures were '... in shape similar to a low-set sheep dog, the colour of a platypus, head and whiskers resembling an otter'.

The second type was a much stranger animal. It was said to be a quadruped the size of a calf or of a bullock, or even larger. Its body was covered with fur or feathers and it had a long, maned neck with a head roughly resembling that of an emu. Sometimes it was said to have small tusks and a horse-like tail. Both types of creatures were said to be amphibious.

Several native drawings of bunyips were collected by white pioneers but it was said no two were alike. The two which survive are rather disappointing. One, drawn by Kurruk, a native of Victoria's western district, might be meant to depict the long-necked type. It features the large body and emu-like head and neck. Unfortunately, however, it has only two legs and resembles an emu in almost every other way.

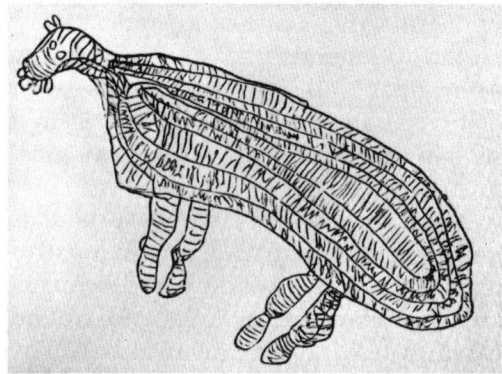

A bunyip as sketched by Kurruk, a native of Victoria's western districts.

It may be foolish, at this late stage, to try to make sense of the drawing. It could be, however, that the artist, though familiar with the back, head and neck of the creatures, used artistic licence to make up for his lack of knowledge about its lower body – which would normally be submerged.

One other point may be worth considering. Although Kurruk's sketch shows only two legs, most Aborigines said this type of bunyip had four legs, each with three toes rather like an emu's.

Archibald Meston, a government official who worked with Queensland Aborigines for many years, said 'hind feet

The bunyip, as drawn by a Murray River Aborigine for J.P. Main in 1848.

like an emu were in all the legends of the bunyip'. He saw inexplicable emu-like tracks himself and was assured they were those of a bunyip.

The second surviving bunyip sketch was drawn in 1848 by a Murray River Aborigine for J.P. Main. It appears to represent a short-necked, tail-less quadruped. The body may be covered with feathers or scales. While this drawing might have been intended to depict the seal-dog/otter-like bunyip it could just as easily be a sketch of a cow or a sheep.

Although the original no longer exists, we have copies of a *third* Aboriginal bunyip drawing – actually, in this case, a ground carving. It is usually referred to as the 'Challicum bunyip'.

It was often said that to attack a bunyip was taboo but the people near Ararat, Victoria, claimed their ancestors speared one to death on the banks of Fiery Creek, presently on Challicum Station.

An outline of the Challicum Station ground carving.

The outline of the beast was supposedly traced on the ground where it lay and the turf removed. In the early days of white settlement the Aborigines still returned to the spot annually to retrace and clear the outline, which was about nine metres long.

A sketch of the ground drawing, made by I.W. Scot in 1867 shows (if we assume the head to be on the right hand side) a seal-like animal.

In an effort to preserve the carving the owners of Challicum Station fenced off the area around it. But year by year the Aborigines dwindled in numbers and eventually there was no one left to tend the site. The fences collapsed, cattle moved in and the Challicum bunyip simply faded away.

Bunyip and the white men

Although there were some rumours of 'marsh monsters' near Sydney in the very early days it seems the first real involvement of non Aborigines in the bunyip mystery occurred at Lake Bathurst, New South Wales.

On 5 April 1818, the day after they discovered the lake (which is 40 kilometres south of the present site of Goulburn), explorers Hamilton Hume and James Meehan found skulls and bone fragments of what they thought were large amphibious animals.

We can find no proof that Hume or Meehan knew of the Australian water monster legend at that time, but it seems certain that Hume, noted for his ability to communicate with the Aborigines, would have been familiar with it. Strange to relate, however, the explorers apparently did not carry the bones back to Sydney, because three years later the Philosophical Society of Australasia offered to pay Hume's expenses if he would return to Lake Bathurst to obtain a skull or skin of the beast.

The earliest actual sighting of a bunyip was claimed by Edward Smith Hall, one of the first settlers at Lake Bathurst. In a letter to the *Sydney Gazette* on 27 March 1823, Hall said that in November 1821 he and others had seen an 'extraordinary creature' in the lake.

Many people in later decades told of closer encounters with bunyips, but since Mr Hall's sighting was apparently the first by a non Aboriginal it seems appropriate to present his story in full:

One fine morning in November 1821, I was walking by the side of the marsh which runs into Lake Bathurst, when my attention was attracted by a creature casting up water and making a noise, in sound resembling a porpoise, but shorter and louder: the head only was out of the water.

At the distance I stood (about 100 yards) it had the appearance of a bulldog's head, but perfectly black; the head floated about as though the animal were recreating itself; it cast up the water behind, but the quantity thrown up evinced neither strength nor bulk; it remained about five minutes, and then disappeared. I saw it at a greater distance afterwards, when it wore the same appearance.

One night my overseer placed a cart in the marsh and in the morning got into it armed with a musket, very heavily charged with pieces of lead. The creature appeared at daylight, and the man fired; he saw the creature rise, and lie at full length on the reeds, about five feet [1.5 metres] long, but his shoulder was in such excruciating pain, from the recoiling of the musket, that he involuntarily shut his eyes from the agony, and, when he opened them, the creature had just turned over and disappeared. Numbers of them have since been seen, but never been shot at.

In December last Mr Forbes and I were bathing at the East-end of the Lake, where an arm runs among the honey-suckles. As I was dressing, a creature, at the distance of about 130 or 150 yards [about 130 metres], suddenly presented itself to my view; it had risen out of the water before I perceived it, and was then gliding on the smooth surface with the rapidity of a whale-boat, as it appeared to me at the time.

Its neck was long, apparently about three feet [one metre] out of the water, and about the thickness of a man's thigh; the colour a jet-black; the head was rather smaller in circumference than the neck, and appeared surrounded with black flaps, which seemed to hang down, and gave it a most novel and striking appearance. The body was not to be seen; but, from the rippling of the water, I judged it to be not longer than the neck. After it had continued its course for about 300 yards [270 metres], I turned round to ascertain if Mr Forbes had also seen it, and, on looking again, it had dived, and was seen no more.

I should have concluded this creature the same as the one before described, but that the head appeared of a different form; for the first animal did not appear to have any flaps about its head; nevertheless, I was never near enough to see, sufficiently distinctly, as to this and other particulars.

One thing is curious – the natives of the Lake, and its neighbourhood, can never be prevailed upon to go near the marsh, and describe this creature as having formerly taken their children into the water. They call it, in our tongue, 'Devil-Devil'.

E.S. Hall was instrumental in the foundation of the Bank of New South Wales, later held the post of Coroner and was quite an eminent man in colonial Australia. Hardly the type of person, one would think, to make up wild stories.

His account does, nevertheless, contain some rather odd elements. Unless he was mistaken, there appear to have been *two* different types of strange creatures in the lake: one resembling the 'seal/dog/otter' type reported by the Aborigines and another which looked a bit like a small version of the long-necked type. But as Mr Hall said, he was never quite close enough to be certain of every detail.

In fact, even *one* type of large aquatic animal would seem too much for Lake Bathurst. It is very shallow, only five kilometres long and four wide, and, like its larger neighbour Lake George, dries up completely in times of drought.

It is just possible Mr Hall and his friends misinterpreted sightings of ordinary animals. This, and the possibility of large,

THE BUNYIP

'The beast was the size of a fully developed sheep-dog, and it appeared to have two small flappers, or wings ...'

normally saltwater creatures reaching the lake via the Wollondilly River will be examined later.

While E.S. Hall is probably the first European to have seen a bunyip it is possible one other white man beat him to it. As previously mentioned, the escaped convict William Buckley told of the great fear the blacks had of bunyips. In his biography, *Life and Adventures of William Buckley* by John Morgan (1852) he also claimed to have seen the creatures himself on numerous occasions:

In this lake [Modewarre], as well as in most of the others inland, and in the deep-water rivers, is a very extraordinary amphibious animal, which the natives call Bun-yip, of which I could never see any part except the back, which appeared to be covered with feathers of a dusky-grey colour. It seemed to be about the size of a full-grown calf, and sometimes larger. The creatures only appear when the weather is very calm and the water smooth. I could never learn from any of the natives that they had seen either the head or tail, so that I could not form a correct idea of their size, or what they were like.

Here [on the Barwon River] the Bun-yips, the extraordinary animals I have already mentioned, were often seen by the natives, who had a great dread of them, believing them to have some supernatural power over human beings, so as to occasion death, sickness, disease, and such like misfortunes.

When alone, I several times attempted to spear a Bun-yip; but had the natives seen me do so it would have caused great displeasure. And again, had I succeeded in killing, or even wounding one, my own life would probably have paid the forfeit; they considering the animal, as I have already said, something supernatural.

While very interesting, Buckley's story does not add much to what we know of

'The animal was about half as long again as a retriever dog, the hair all over its body jet-black and shining ...'

the bunyip's appearance. If there really were two kinds of bunyip it is impossible to tell, from his account, which kind he saw. It seems, in fact, that he thought there was only one type.

As British settlers pushed deeper into Australia, more and more of them began to report encounters with strange aquatic animals. Some reports were obviously practical jokes and some sightings were too fleeting to be of any use.

A close look at the records, however, clearly shows that the bulk of the reports can be sorted into two major categories. These categories tally quite well with the two different types of bunyip described by the Aborigines. About 60 per cent of non Aboriginal eyewitnesses said the creatures resembled seals or large swimming dogs and roughly 20 per cent described large-bodied animals with long maned necks and fairly small heads.

The 'seal-dog' bunyip

Great Lake, Tasmania, 1863

One January morning Charles Headlam, an old and respected Tasmanian, was rowing with a friend when they almost literally bumped into a bunyip.

... my oar nearly came in contact with a large-looking beast about the size of a fully developed sheep dog ... It appeared to have two small flappers, or wings, which it made good use of ... We watched it as far as the eye could reach and it appeared to keep on the face of the water, never appearing to dive. I never remember seeing such an animal before or since.

Midgeon Lagoon, Narrandera New South Wales, 1872

This report appeared in the *Wagga Wagga Advertiser* in April 1872.

What is the bunyip? There really is a bunyip, or Waa-Wee, actually existing not far from us; and others probably nearer than we imagined. The animal has been seen by many persons whose veracity is unimpeachable, and whose intimate acquaintance with the fauna of the Murrumbidgee, coupled with their general intelligence and observation, puts it altogether beyond doubt that in the Midgeon Lagoon, sixteen miles [25.5 kilometres] north of Narrandera, there exists an animal which in every respect tallies with the description of the creature frequently reported as seen in various places. Here is the account of a gentleman who had a quiet half-hour's view of this strange nondescript.

'A few days since, Mr A., who was driving sheep across country to Melbourne, camped on the lagoon. He called at my house and asked what the animal was that we had in our swamp and proceeded to describe something which had alarmed him and the shepherds. I ridiculed his report and he got angry, inviting me to come down and see for myself. I went down early next morning, between six and seven o'clock, accompanied by two other persons, and had not waited long before I heard the sound as of a body rushing rapidly through the water, making a noise as loud as that caused by a North Shore steamer. Looking in the direction of the sound I saw a creature coming through the water with tremendous rapidity, and directing its course immediately towards us.

'We stood still, deeply interested, and watched the approach of the animal, which having, as we presumed, lately risen to the surface, was evidently not aware of our presence. It came on with great swiftness until it was scarcely 30 yards [27 metres] from the edge of the lagoon, when it appeared suddenly to catch sight of us, and stopped instantly.

'It lay on the water then perfectly still, and I had a splendid view of a creature that surprised me more than anything I had ever before seen in my life. The animal was about half as long again as an ordinary retriever dog; the hair all over its body was jet-black and shining, its coat was very long, the hair spreading out on the surface of the water for about five inches [twelve centimetres], and floating loosely as the creature rose and fell by its own motion. I could not detect any tail, and the hair about its head was too long and glossy to admit of my seeing its eyes; the ears were well marked.

It made no noise, but kept its position for half-an-hour, surveying us, no doubt, leisurely, although its visual organs were hidden from us. At length it turned quietly round and swam off easily, without any manifestation of alarm, and we watched [it] moving leisurely along the surface of the lake until it was hidden by the distance. We have been greatly excited by its appearance, and I have offered £20 for its dead body, and £50 if captured alive.'

This statement may be relied upon, and there can be no doubt whatever the gentleman saw all he has described.

Malmsbury, Victoria, early 1870s

In 1876, in *The Aborigines of Victoria*, R. Brough Smyth described an incident which occurred some years earlier. The reservoir in question is on the Coliban River which runs inland to join the Murray–Darling system.

Major Couchman, the Chief Mining Surveyor in the Mining Department, says that he and Mr Lavender saw an animal resembling a water-dog swimming in the reservoir at Malmsbury. It was large, and of a very dark colour. He watched the animal for some time, when it dived and disappeared. He saw it again when it was nearer, and then knew that it was not a dog. Its head resembled that of a seal.

Both Mr Lavender and he watched it for some time, and its form and the period during which it remained under water after it had dived satisfied them that it was not any animal known to them. Are there fresh-water seals in Victoria, and is the Bun-yip a fresh-water seal?

Near Canberra, late 1800s

In 1927, when he was 95 years old, John Gale, the founder of the *Queanbeyan Age* recalled the following:

While dealing with the subject of the fauna of the Federal Capital Territory, I have a word or two to say with respect to certain animals whose presence is more or less a matter of doubt or superstition. The first of these to be dealt with here is the fabled

(?) bunyip. But, is it a fable? Here are evidences to the contrary.

The late Captain Sam Southwell, one of the most truthful of men, told me the following story: He was riding along the banks of the Murrumbidgee River, somewhere above Cusack's Crossing, when he saw a strange animal of proportions akin to those of a three-months'-old calf, basking on a sandbank at the water's edge. The clatter of his horse's hoofs on the stony ground beneath its feet disturbed the creature, which at once wriggled, rather than walked, into the deep water and disappeared.

The rider, dismounting from his steed, descended afoot to the place where this strange animal had been basking, and examined closely its trail. This had the appearance of fins or flappers, and not of feet, visible to the very water's edge, whence the thing had disappeared. Though he tarried, he saw no more of it.

I myself, when duck-shooting along the banks of the Queanbeyan River, saw rise, a hundred yards [90 metres] or so ahead of me, a big dog-like amphibian, which (apparently seeing me) plunged beneath the water and I saw it no more. Other credible persons had seen the like in the same river near town, and reported their observations.

The Darling Downs, Queensland, 1860s or 1870s

In *History of the Blucher Tribe, Queensland*, T. Hall, pioneer and veteran cattleman, wrote the following:

THE BUNYIP OR MOCHEL MOCHEL
I am now touching upon a subject that has always been open to argument and doubt, and for that reason I propose to give my own conclusions, after having investigated the matter as thoroughly as possible on the spot, as it were.

From the first the blackfellows of the 'Blucher' tribe were unanimous in their description of the Mochel Mochel which in a way corresponded with that of an otter, also that it was only to be found in and about deep permanent waterholes; further, that it was a very shy animal which required great cunning and stealth to get a glimpse of, owing to its quickness and alertness. Thus armed, I had my opportunity owing to the surroundings of my bush life to come upon my quarry sooner or later.

I was told that it could both see and hear under water. That was particularly the case as regards anything moving about on the bank, in the vicinity of its home; further, that it could produce sounds under the water.

At last my opportunity came, in this way. With my brother and another white man I was bringing a mob of wild horses down from the head of Swan Creek, and when we came to a place known as the junction of the Gap Creek, being some distance ahead of the horses so as to prevent them breaking away on either side, I heard a piercing kind of a scream similar to that uttered by a female in terrible distress. The noise came from the shallow end of the junction hole, and I at once turned in that direction, my horse also having been startled by the scream.

Much to my surprise I saw an animal in shape similar to a low set sheep dog, the colour of a platypus, head and whiskers resembling an otter, passing from the shallow water over a strip of dry land to the deep water. The back view of this creature's head was exactly like the bald head of a blackfellow, which I found corresponded with the figure drawn on the tree at the Bora ground, also with the Aboriginal description 'Cumi Patoic', meaning bald head.

When my companions arrived on the scene they at once saw the frightened look of my horse and my own excitement, and asked what was the matter. On explaining, they were inclined to treat it as a case of leg-pulling, but were soon convinced when they saw the commotion of the water *in the hole and the muddy appearance of it. Before long they were as excited as the writer, and on my suggesting means of securing the animal they promptly overruled this, saying 'No', our horses are of more importance than the Mochel Mochel, particularly as there were some 3 year old unbranded ones in the mob.*

Under the circumstances there was nothing for it but to abandon the idea of seeing any more of the Bunyip just then but I had made up my mind to do so later on should an opportunity occur. This, however, never came. The impression made upon my mind was that the Mochel Mochel was a kind of otter.

The blacks had a great dread of the Mochel Mochel, and nothing could persuade them to go near or bathe in a waterhole supposed to be the home of this animal, neither would they camp in the vicinity.

Long-necked bunyip

While eyewitness reports of the long-necked type are much rarer than those of the 'seal-dog' there are several fairly interesting ones on record.

The Lachlan River, near Oxley, New South Wales, 1847, and the Murrumbidgee River, 1840s

On 29 June 1847 the *Argus* published the following article (see facsimile opposite).

William Hovell's letter to the *Sydney Morning Herald*, 16 June 1847 contains additional information about the shepherds sighting:

... while he was standing on the bank of the Murrumbidgee, he saw something (similar in appearance to the one mentioned in the accompanied letter) rise suddenly out of the middle of the stream, that it shewed, as he supposes, about half its figure, and that while in the act of shaking itself, it caught sight of him and instantly disappeared, but although the time could not have exceeded a few moments, he saw sufficient to enable him to describe it to me, and which nearly agrees with what I have been told by the Aborigines.

THE BUNYIP.—Mr. Hobler, a settler at Nap Nap, on the Murrumbidgee, gives the following account of a living specimen of the Bunyip, in a letter published in the Sydney Morning Herald. Mr. H. says— The Lachlan when flooded spreads its waters over an immense extent of lowland, covered with reeds, through which the water finds its way to the junction, with the Murrumbidgee. There is on the edge of this large reed bed, about twelve miles from the junction a cattle station, recently settled by a Mr. Tyson: the river has been overflowing these reed beds for some month's past. Well, some few weeks ago, an intelligent lad in Tyson's employ who was in search of the milking cows on the edge, and just inside this reed bed, where there are occasionally patches of good grass, came suddenly, in one of these openings upon an animal grazing, which he thus describes: it was about as big as a six months' old calf, of a dark brown colour, a long neck, and long pointed head; it had large ears, which it pricked up when it perceived him; had a thick main of hair from the head down to the neck, and two large tusks; he turned to run away, and this creature equally alarmed, ran off too, and from the glance he took at it, he describes it as having an awkward shambling gallop; the fore-quarters of the animal were very large in proportion to the hind-quarters, and it had a large tail, but whether he compared it to that of a horse or a bullock I do not recollect; he took two men to the place next morning to look for its track, which they describe as broad and square, somewhat like what the spread hand of a man would make in soft muddy ground. The lad had never heard of the kine pratia, and yet his description in some respects tally with that of the aborigines, who pretend to have seen them, so that I am inclined to think there is one of these extraordinary animals still living within a few miles of me, and I cannot but entertain a hope of being some day fortunate enough to come in contact with one, and if so, I shall do my best to bring him home with me. Captain Hovell, who communicates Mr. Hobler's letter to the Herald, gives a similar description of another live specimen seen by a shepherd in the Murrumbidgee.

Rocky River, South Australia, 1853
This story appeared in the *Argus*, 19 December 1853

'It was as big as a six months old calf, of a dark brown colour with a long neck and a pointed head ...'

A gentleman writing from Rocky River, near Mt Remarkable, under date of the 15th instant, says: 'About four nights ago I was camped close to a large and exceedingly deep waterhole here, and the night being very sultry and the mosquitoes exceeding troublesome I was unable to sleep. My horse was tethered not many yards from my camp fire.

'Whilst I was thus restless, I was startled by hearing a curious noise in the water. I jumped up and looked towards the place from which the noise seemed to proceed, and as the moon was very bright I was enabled to perceive a large blackish substance advancing towards the bank and which, as it approached, raised itself out of the water. I crept towards it, and perceived that it had a large head and a neck something like that of a horse, with thick bristly hair.

'I supposed it must have seen me for it proceeded down the river, keeping a few yards from the bank, towards which it made again nearly abreast of my horse, which no sooner saw it than it made a rush, breaking the tether-rope and bolting. The noise occasioned by the horse running away caused my strange visitor to disappear immediately, in consequence of which I had not an opportunity of examining it more minutely. From what I saw of it, however, I should think its entire length would be from fifteen to eighteen feet [4.5 to 5.5 metres].'

The Murray and Goulburn Rivers, 1857

A naturalist called Stocqueler, who sailed up and down the Murray and Goulburn rivers in a canvas boat, later claimed to have seen extremely odd-looking 'freshwater seals' which he took to be the legendary bunyips. When he showed his sketch of the creatures to local Aborigines, they said the drawing was 'the bunyip's brother' – a duplicate or likeness of the bunyip.

Stocqueler told the *Moreton Bay Free Press* (15 April 1857) that the creatures had 'two small paddles or fins attached to the shoulders, a long, swan-like neck, a head like a dog and a curious bag hanging under the jaw, resembling the pouch of the pelican'. He said the creatures varied in length from five to over fifteen feet [1.5 to over 4.5 metres].

The head of the largest was the size of a bullock's head and was three feet [one metre] out of the water. They were covered in glossy black hair like the platypus and could move against the current at the rate of about seven knots.

He claimed, said the *Free Press*, to have seen 'no less than six of the curious animals at different times; his boat was within thirty feet [nine metres] of one, near McGuire's punt on the Goulburn and he fired ... but did not succeed in capturing him.'

'Mr Stocqueler states that he could have approached close to the specimens he observed, had he not been deterred by the stories of the natives concerning the power and fury of the bunyip and by the fact that his gun had only a single barrel and his boat was of very frail description.'

One of Stocqueler's sketches, examined by the *Free Press* correspondent, showed 'a view of the neck and shoulders of the animal.'

There are, it must be admitted, quite a few discrepancies in these alleged eye-witness accounts. We feel, however, that given the difficulties involved in observing shy aquatic animals, they are uniform enough to suggest there really may have been two different types of large unknown amphibians haunting Australia's river systems.

Bunyip and the scientists

In early days of colonisation it seemed quite logical that the then unexplored continent of Australia should have a marsupial equivalent of, say, the hippopotamus, filling an ecological niche in its river systems. Many scientists were therefore quite amenable to the idea of the bunyip's existence and made diligent efforts during the first half of the nineteenth century, to kill, capture or categorise the beast.

When what appeared to be the thigh bone of 'a huge marine animal' was found near the Great Corangamite Lake in 1845, Dr Hobson, one of Melbourne's leading scientists, undertook a long and arduous journey to the site in the hope of finding further remains – which he supposed to be of the bunyip.

That the subject was taken seriously at all levels of society is attested to by the letters of Governor La Trobe who took quite an interest in the matter. Presumably because most reports by both whites and Aborigines appeared – generally speaking – to break down into the two categories already mentioned above and because he possessed two Aboriginal sketches of

'His boat was within thirty feet of one, and he fired at it, with no success ...'

bunyips (now lost) which he considered to be of some scientific value, he favoured the idea that there were two different types of animal involved. He called these the 'northern' and 'southern' bunyips, although it is unclear, now, which was which.

On 23 January 1847 he wrote to his friend Ronald Gunn:

You have heard probably the constant rumours of the existence of some unknown beast in the rivers and lakes of P. Phillip – under the native name 'Bunyep' or 'Bunyip'. That there is such an one whether round or square, fat or lean – and that of tolerable size – I have been long convinced. At last, Lonsdale writes me word that they have found the head of one in some stream near Murrumbidgee and that it has been brought down to Melbourne. According to description it must be a long snouted animal something of this shape:

a long bill-like snout the forehead rising abruptly the eye placed very low, strong grinders, cavity for brain very large. The end of the snout is broken off but the blacks who have seen it say it ought to have two long tusks projecting downward at the termination.

It appears to be a recent skull as some of the flesh was on it when found – and a search is going to be made for the bones. Now what can this be? They do not give me any dimensions – but state it must be a very large animal.

Serious scientific interest peaked in 1847–48 with the 'bunyip skull' discovery mentioned by La Trobe. The excitement began when William Hovell wrote to the *Sydney Morning Herald* on 19 February, 1847 saying that his friend Atholl Fletcher had found the skull of a bunyip (or *katenpai* as it was known in the area) on the banks of the lower Murrumbidgee. When the skull went to Melbourne for examination by 'those skilful anatomists, Dr Hobson and Mr Greeves' and was put on display, great public interest was aroused, not only in Australia but even in England. In the first flush of excitement several experts declared that the bones were of something unknown to science.

One naturalist, W.S. Macleay, said the skull differed from those of all known mammals and might have been that of a huge bird, but later decided it was possibly that of a young camel, or 'a misshapen foal'. Finally, though he never set eyes on the relic, the great sage Professor Owen declared, from London, that it was merely the skull of a calf. In an age where the 'cultural cringe' was much more pronounced than it is today, that was the final word on the matter and the skull was hidden away in the Australian Museum, where, in true bunyip style, it vanished.

The embarrassed scientific establishment rapidly lost interest in bunyips and the newspapers and public quickly adopted a more cynical, frivolous attitude than had previously been the norm. The Melbourne *Argus* propagated a hoax concerning a bunyip supposedly haunting a pond in the Botanic Gardens and the word 'bunyip' entered the colloquial language as a synonym for imposter or humbug.

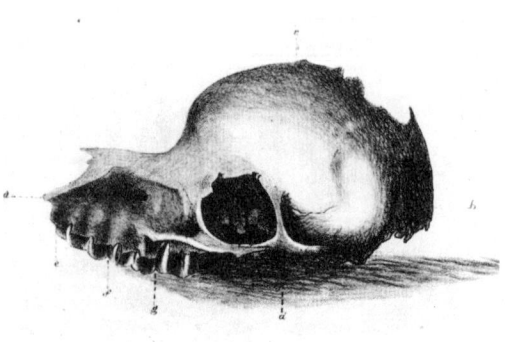

The 1847 'bunyip skull'.

THE BUNYIP

'Its neck was long, about three feet out of the water and about the thickness of a man's thigh ...' (see page 164)

The bunyip, however, was a hardy beast; it may have been officially declared dead, but it was reluctant to lie down: as we have already seen, reports of sightings continued to come in year after year.

Scientific interest continued to flicker in some quarters. When a nine-metre long creature quaintly described as having a head like a bull dog, a tail as thick as a man's thigh and a body 'as thick as Mr Barr's belltopper' was allegedly seen in a swamp near Euroa in 1890, a Mr Meekin of the Melbourne Zoological Gardens combed the area with a team of forty men.

In Tasmania – where, unless we are mistaken, only the dog/otter/seal-like bunyip appears to have been reported – the government geologist, Charles Gould, presented a case for the existence of the animals, based on many reports he gathered at first hand, to the Royal Society of Tasmania in 1872. The animals were allegedly seen in the Great Lake, Lake Tiberius, Echo Lakes and deep pools along the Jordan River. Clive Lord, the curator of Hobart Museum, was also convinced the creatures were real.

Bunyip reports tapered off quite sharply at about the turn of the century and although sightings continued to be reported intermittently through the early 1900s they finally became so rare that, it might be fair to say, people who now believe in bunyips are almost as scarce as the animals themselves.

The bunyip 'explained'

After the Murrumbidgee skull episode many colonial scientists, no longer willing to believe in the physical reality of the bunyip, cast around for logical explanations for the phenomenon and in a few years a consensus view emerged. The sightings, they said, were merely those of seals which had occasionally strayed far inland via the river systems, where they supposedly terrified the inland Aborigines and ignorant white shepherds who were not familiar with such animals. The associated roaring was made by the swamp-living bittern, whose booming cry caused bushmen to name it the 'bull bird', the 'swamp bull' or, significantly perhaps, the 'bunyip bird'.

If we ignore the minority of reports which speak of long-necked bunyips, quite a good case can be made for the seal theory. In the colonial era several inland sightings of what were quite unambiguously stated to be seals were made by apparently reliable observers. Mr R.E. Day saw and identified one 400 kilometres up the Murray and in 1850 E.J. Dunn – one time director of the Geological Survey of Victoria – and several other people watched a large herd of them swimming up the flooded Murrumbidgee near Gundagai, approximately 1200 kilometres from the sea.

Even more conclusively, seals have actually been captured or killed far inland. According to Troughton a fur seal was captured about 48 kilometres up the Shoalhaven River and in 1870 a three-metre leopard seal (whose stomach was found to contain a platypus) was killed in the same river. Perhaps significantly, Burrier, near the mouth of the Shoalhaven, had a strong bunyip tradition. In 1850 a seal was killed, stuffed and displayed in a hotel at Conargo on the Moulamein River, 900 kilometres from the sea.

Since freshwater seals exist in the Caspian Sea and in Lake Baikal, over 3000 kilometres from the sea, it is reasonable to suggest that in earlier times herds of seals may have occasionally penetrated the Murray–Darling system, particularly in times of flood. When the floodwaters receded, individual animals, perhaps large old bulls defeated by younger rivals, could have become stranded in isolated swamps or billabongs.

In the early nineteenth century fur seals and elephant seals were plentiful in Bass Strait and they often visited the beaches and estuaries of southern Victoria. Their near-annihilation by hunters throughout the 1800s could partly explain the steady decline in bunyip reports towards the end of the century. It has also been suggested that the appearance of paddle steamers on the Murray–Darling system may have frightened the seals away.

Another factor could have been that as dams and weirs began to be built along the Australian river systems increasingly large areas of the inland would have become off-limits to wayward seals, thus explaining the scarcity of recent bunyip reports.

The ground carving at Challicum can also be seen to support the seal theory. If we assume the right-hand end of the carving represents the head we can see that the outline is a fairly good representation of a seal. While the length of the ground drawing – 'eleven paces' – is too great for even the elephant seal (which grows to 6.5 metres) it is possible that as the outline was cleared and recut, annually for perhaps hundreds of years, it slowly grew until it reached its final size.

The seal theory might even account for the bones found by Hume and Meehan and the 'monster' sightings by E.S. Hall and others at Lake Bathurst.

In 1947 four seals were reported to be 'inhabiting' the Mulwaree River within five kilometres of Goulburn. This creek originates just southwest of Lake Bathurst and at one point is separated from the lake by only 700 metres of boggy ground, which would be no barrier to a determined seal. In seasons of very high rainfall the lake, normally landlocked, probably connects with the river. It is possible also that the years 1818–21 were exceptionally wet because in 1823 the waters of neighbouring Lake George were at the highest level ever recorded.

Mulwaree River drains into the Wollondilly which, via the Nepean and Hawkesbury, reaches the sea at Broken

THE BUNYIP

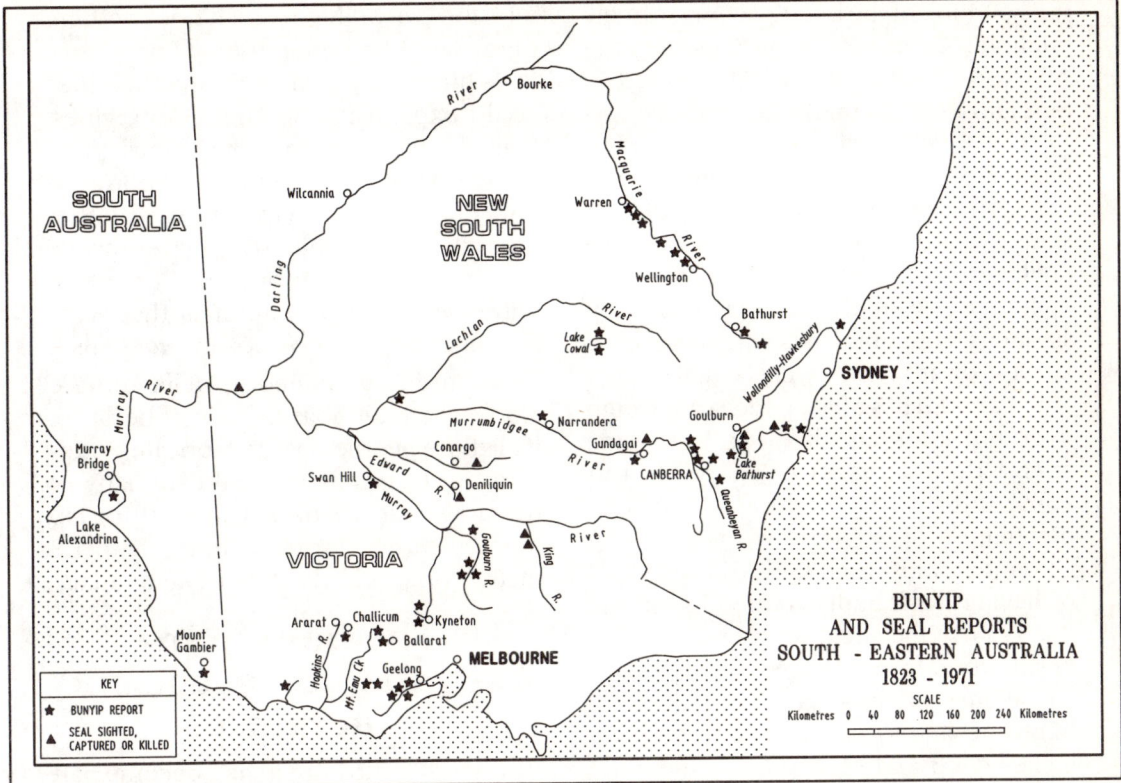

Bay. It may be worth noting that Wingecarribee Swamp near Moss Vale, which also drains into the Wollondilly, was, for many years, reported to be the home of a fearsome bunyip. If the Lake Bathurst 'monster' and the Wingecarribee bunyip were nothing more than seals, the fact that neither has been reported in recent times could be explained by the fact that the Wollondilly is now blocked by the massive Warragamba Dam.

Although there seems little doubt that seals caused many bunyip reports, there are several major problems with the theory. First, many of the same Victorian Aboriginal groups which so feared the bunyip were perfectly familiar with seals and in fact routinely killed and ate them. Second, Buckley, who saw bunyips and was familiar with seals, thought them to be different animals. Third, some other European witnesses made a point of mentioning that although the creatures appeared *seal-like*, they were not any known species of seal. Finally, most species of seal, far from being shy and elusive, were remarkably easy for both non Aborigines and Aborigines to stalk and kill.

We find it difficult to believe that sightings of seals could explain all bunyip reports. We must admit, however, that the pattern which emerged when we plotted all the known locations of seal and bunyip sightings on the map does provide a strong argument for the bunyip=seal theory.

It is, of course, just possible that in earlier days Australia, like Russia, possessed a type of purely freshwater seal, that those seals were much fewer in number than their saltwater cousins, hairier and perhaps nocturnal.

With regard to the bunyip's famous roar, the notion that generations of Aborigines could have been deceived by the booming of the bittern seems scarcely credible. As Barrett acknowledges: the Aborigines '... knew more about the bittern and its ways than our ornithologists ...' The Rev George Taplin, who often heard booming noises attributed to the Lake Alexandrina bunyips said that 'It cannot be the peculiar sound of the Murray bittern, as I have heard that too ...'

It is quite likely that some bunyip sightings – but only ones which occurred at dusk or at night – were actually large Murray cod. These fish, which can weigh over 100 kilos and live for 100 years, spend their days in deep pools but sometimes feed in the shallows at nightfall.

Canberra historian Lyall Gillespie tells of having been badly startled by one in the 1930s. One night as he was fishing beside the Murrumbidgee, a huge dark shape burst out of a marshy pool behind him, tore across an area of water only inches deep and plunged into the main body of the river. 'It was certainly big enough to have been a seal,' says Mr Gillespie – who has quite an interest in the bunyip mystery – 'but I finally decided it was a very big cod.'

The only other animal which could have a strong bearing on the bunyip legend is the saltwater crocodile. According to most anthropologists all Aboriginal groups entered the continent through the crocodile-infested northern regions and there is very strong evidence, including rock carvings and teeth, to suggest that saltwater crocodiles coexisted with early Aborigines in parts of southern Australia.

Obviously, folk memories of these daunting beasts could have been handed down to recent generations. Like bunyips, crocodiles sometimes roar loudly and often come right out of the water to attack their prey. Another strength of the theory is that, as far as we can tell, bunyip traditions are restricted to areas which in modern times are *not* frequented by crocodiles. There is, of course, one big problem with the crocodile theory: it does nothing to explain bunyip reports by Europeans.

While folk memories of crocodiles could explain the southern Aborigines' fear of large river-dwelling animals, and while seals can explain many Aboriginal and European bunyip reports, neither theory can fully explain the mystery away. A significant number of European witnesses described animals that were seal-like, but fairly obviously *not* seals.

We are not inclined to believe these stories were all hoaxes, simply because, if all those people were to fabricate stories of water beasts, why would so many of them choose to invent something so mundane as a four to six foot [1.2 to 1.8 metre] long, seal/dog/otter-like animal?

The bunyip in Australian language and literature

By the 1840s the bunyip had become part of the consciousness of most white Australians and its abandonment by the scientific establishment in 1848 did nothing to diminish this. If anything, the Murrumbidgee skull episode, with its embarrassed 'experts', added a humorous dimension to the bunyip saga which seemed to appeal to the colonials and which strengthened its hold on the Australian imagination. As a direct result of the skull episode, a new and strong word was adopted into the Australian vocabulary. 'Bunyip' became and remains a synonym for imposter, pretender, humbug and the like.

A couple of years later, when W.C. Wentworth and other wealthy conservatives proposed the establishment of a colonial peerage, D.H. Deniehy, in an immortal speech, made them the laughing stock of the country by mocking them as 'Botany Bay magnificos', 'Australian mandarins' and – most tellingly – as a 'bunyip aristocracy'. Since then the bunyip has thoroughly immersed itself in the Australian political lexicon and surfaces regularly to attack any similar attempts to imitate British institutions.

In 1976, for instance, the attempt by the Fraser government to have knighthoods added to the Order of Australia was labelled 'bunyip snobbery' and in 1984 it was suggested that Bob Hawke's presidential style of leadership might result in a 'bunyip monarchy'.

Any form of pretension is in danger of earning the 'bunyip' label, hence the 'old families' of Adelaide have been labelled 'bunyip aristocrats'. The determinedly egalitarian Xavier Herbert used the contemptuous term 'bunyip lords' to refer to any Australian who accepted an imperial title of any kind.

During the latter half of the nineteenth century the bunyip worked its way into the Australian vocabulary in many other ways. It remained a synonym for imposter (as in J.R. Houlding's 1867 *Australian Capers*, where a conman is described as 'a regular old bunyip') but also came to be used as a term for wild, unbranded cattle and even for extremely unpleasant weather. A type of improvised surveying instrument was christened a 'bunyip level'; any muddy depression a 'bunyip hole' and a brand new word 'bunyipian' was used as a synonym for fantastic.

Further evidence that the bunyip had taken hold of the Australian imagination by the mid-nineteenth century can be found in Australian literature. In H. Kingsley's *Geoffrey Hamlyn* (1859) dire warnings of a bunyip are used to prevent a child swimming in a dangerous river; the heroine of *Chowla* (1867) nobly declares: '... rather would I take the baleful bunyip to my bosom ... than give my hand to a man I loathe' and many other references to the beast appear in novels right up to the present day. In 1956 A.D. Hope made the amusing observation that 'the bunyip of literature is the mythical great Australian novel': the monster that has never been revealed.

Several poems have been written about the beast including John Manifold's 'The Bunyip and the Whistling Kettle' in which (in a continuation of the Aboriginal tradition of the bunyip as the nemesis of wrongdoers) an arrogant litterbug gets his just deserts at the hands of the local water monster.

Interestingly, a similar ecological message (along with many others such as the virtues of temperance, charity, obedience, etc.) is also contained in the first children's book about a bunyip: J.R. Lockyear's charming tale *Old Bunyip, the Australian River Monster* (1871).

In 1935 the noted artist Mary Cecil Allen advocated a national search for the best representation of the bunyip on the grounds that '... it might nourish the sense of fantasy in which Australians are deficient'. No doubt Ms Allen would be gratified by the massive numbers of children's fantasy books now in print and by the fact that the bunyip is playing an increasingly large role in such literature.

The bunyip, in fact, has really come into his own in this type of literature. After loaning his name to Bunyip Bluegum in Norman Lindsay's *The Magic Pudding* he has appeared, in some shape or form, in dozens of other children's books. One author alone, Judith Whitlock, has written five books about bunyips and Patricia Wrightson at least two.

The beast lives on

Although the heyday of the creatures was over by the turn of the century, we are happy to note that occasional bunyip sightings are still reported every few years from isolated corners of the country. It seems, however, that none of the reports refer to the long-necked kind. Sadly, that type – assuming it really did once exist – seems to have gone the way of the diprotodon and flared trousers.

All the modern reports seem to fit, more or less, into the 'seal-dog' category, although sometimes, we admit, a fair amount of pushing and shoving is required to *make* them fit. At least half of them seem to contain some decidedly odd elements. Take the following story, from the *Argus*, 19 September 1947. It was headlined 'It Swims, Whistles and Spouts. What Is It?'

A mysterious black creature which spouted water, swam against a strong current and emitted ear-piercing whistles had supposedly been haunting the Swan Hill district for several weeks – only three men, C.L. and J.S. Moser and A. Rice claimed to have seen it – in the Little Murray River about six kilometres outside town.

They first saw it lying on the bank. It seemed to be black and about three to three and a half feet [about a metre] long. Thinking it might be a pig, they paid it little attention. A month later, however, they heard heavy splashing at the same spot and saw the object swimming upstream, at walking pace, against a powerful current. Mr C. Moser said the head and neck were about nine inches [22 centimetres] thick and about one foot [30 centimetres] out of the water. He swore it was spouting water about five feet [1.5 metres] into the air – apparently from its neck.

The party turned a spotlight onto the creature and followed it 'for about two chains' [40 metres]. It then swam to the opposite bank where it 'lay in shelter and emitted a loud, shrill whistle that could be heard half a mile away'. The men could have shot it but 'disliked the idea of destroying something they knew nothing about'. They could see it 'had two very bright eyes, but no visible ears, though its ears might have been lying close to its head'. By the time they left, the whistle had 'reached staggering proportions'.

Mr Moser said that J.H. Maher, who owns the adjoining property, told them he had heard whistling in the vicinity for many weeks and that local children feared to venture out at night.

Although we know of no seals that whistle or spout, it may be worth mentioning that Swan Hill is only 150 kilometres from Conargo, where what was definitely a seal was killed in 1850. According to John Turnbull, a Canberra fishing writer, another seal was shot dead near Deniliquin, even closer to Swan Hill, in 1951.

A whistling, spouting bunyip is bad enough, but the following story, from the *Sydney Morning Herald*, 9 September 1949, is even more bizarre.

Weird Animal "Uses Ears As Paddles"

MELBOURNE, Thursday. —Kyneton has joined in the open season for bunyips. Mr. and Mrs. L. Keegan reported to-day that several times in the past fortnight they had been astounded by what they described as an animal at least four feet long, with long shaggy ears, in the new Lauristor reservoir, adjoining their property.

While it is tempting to throw this story straight into the 'too weird' basket, it is worth noting that Lauriston Reservoir is only two kilometres upstream from Malmsbury Reservoir – the site of a good nineteenth century bunyip sighting which was discussed earlier.

A report twenty years later from northeastern New South Wales fits more easily into the nineteenth century 'seal-dog' category.

'Swan-Devouring Monster Lurks in the Lagoon' trumpeted the *Australian* on 27 September 1971. 'Hunt for Lagoon's Whining Monster' blared the Sydney *Daily Mirror* on 3 October, but the story itself sounded fairly straight.

In the preceding twelve months, in a

lagoon near Lismore, there had supposedly been six sightings of an animal which none of the witnesses could identify. It was furry, with a head like a dog and sometimes whined like a dingo. Up to six feet [1.8 metres] in length, it had the girth of a 12-gallon oil drum (the *Mirror* upgraded that to a 44-gallon drum). The creature apparently possessed a hearty appetite: several wild fowl, ducks and at least two swans had disappeared into the murky waters with – as the *Daily Mirror* put it – '... a flurry of feathers and agonised squarks'.

Jack Evans, owner of the Tweed Heads Pet Porpoise Pool, was attempting to recruit university zoologists for a full-fledged examination of the site. Although the boffins appear to have been sceptical, Mr Evans seems to have really believed he was onto something big. Statements made by his daughter, Mrs Toni Cameron, have a ring of sincerity to them:

The monster is neither a hoax nor a publicity gimmick. My father has been gathering data on it for at least two years. He has learned, for instance, that about 70 years ago two Aboriginal stockmen who camped by the lagoon one night disappeared. Other Aboriginals with them said they went into the water and were 'eaten by a big fish'. Since then, particularly over the past twelve months, it has been reported that the monster – or whatever it is – is again active.

There are no crocodile tracks around the lagoon and how would a seal ever get there? He believes it is something from another era. The sightings have not been made by ratbags. They all come from reliable, astute bushmen. And they all say the animal is something out of this world.'

The exact location was being kept secret for two reasons:

The farmer ... doesn't want people ... killing the creature. And my father doesn't want anybody to get under his neck if it turns out to be of great scientific interest.

One of the keenest bunyip hunters of recent years was Jack Mitchell of Wellington, New South Wales. If Mr Mitchell was correct, the greatest bunyip hot-spot of modern times is the Macquarie River between Wellington and Warren.

He became interested in the subject after he left the RAAF at the end of the Second World War, and took up a river-frontage property at Dubbo. Several of his neighbours claimed to have seen bunyips and although he never saw one himself he gathered many stories from the district. Later, when he ran a garage in Wellington, he advertised for information and received 'scores' of reports from Aborigines, graziers and tourists.

All the sightings took place on a 200-kilometres stretch of the Macquarie River between Wellington and Warren. Some were seen while sunning themselves on banks, others while swimming against the current or while thrashing about in the water.

Mr Mitchell's claims should give hope to all aspiring bunyip busters, but unfortunately he is now deceased and his records and maps have been difficult to track down.

From the scanty details contained in the secondary material it seems Jack Mitchell's bunyips may have been of the 'seal-dog' variety – but fairly muscular examples of the type.

'In every case the animal is the same,' he was quoted as saying. 'It swims in the river, makes a fearful noise, has a head like a calf and tremendous strength. Aborigines have told me it flails the water to foam and easily bursts through their fishing nets.'

Although out-of-place seals could certainly explain many sightings, we have never been convinced that the seal theory – or the crocodile theory, or the cod theory – explains away the entire bunyip mystery. But whether the creature has or has ever had a physical reality, is in a way irrelevant, because it has now become so embedded in the Australian consciousness, language and literature, that it has attained effective immortality – just as it possessed in earlier days, in the folklore of the Aborigines.

Because the bunyip legend is one of the few Aboriginal traditions which has been embraced by non-Aboriginal Australians and because it can be seen as one of the few links between the two cultures, it is interesting to note that in 1984, with the bicentennial approaching, it was used in a speech by Donald Horne to symbolise another elusive concept which has been the object of similar long and painful searches: the Australian national identity itself.

References

Argus, 18 July 1848; 21 November 1848; 19 December 1853; 28 February 1890; 1 March 1890; 19 September 1947

Australian, 27 September 1971; 14 June 1976

Baker, S., *The Australian Language*, Sun Books, Melbourne, 1966

Barrett, C., *The Bunyip*, The Mail Newspapers Ltd, Adelaide, 1946

Beatty, W.A., *Treasury of Australian Folktales*, Ure Smith Pty Ltd, Sydney, 1960

Blake, L.J. (e.), *Letters of Charles Joseph La Trobe*, Victorian Government Printer, 1975

Brough Smyth, R., *The Aborigines of Victoria*, John Curry, O'Neill, Melbourne, 1876 and 1972

Bulletin, 4 February 1899; 9 August 1975

Canberra Times, 12 June 1981

Costello, P., *In Search of Lake Monsters*, Garnstone Press Ltd, London, 1974

Daily Mirror (Sydney), 3 October 1971

Fearn-Wannan, W., *Australian Folklore*, Landsdown Press, Melbourne, 1970

Fishing News, Melbourne, August 1987

Gale, J., *Canberra: History of and Legends Relating to the Federal Capital Territory of the Commonwealth of Australia*, A.M. Fallick and Sons, Queanbeyan, 1927

Gillespie, L., *Aborigines of the Canberra Region*, Canberra Publishing and Printing, Canberra, 1984; *Canberra, 1820–1913*, Australian Government Publishing Service, Canberra, 1991

Hall, T., *The History of the Blucher Tribe, Queensland* (no bibliographic details available, book held in the John Oxley Library, Brisbane)

Heuvelmans, B., *In the Wake of the Sea Serpents*, Rupert Hart-Davis, London 1968

Massola, A., 'The Callicum Bunyip', *The Victorian Naturalist*, vol. 74, October 1957

Meehan, J., Field Book, quoted in R. Webster, *Currency Lad*, pp.20–21, 35

Moreton Bay Free Press, 15 April 1857

Morey, E., *The Morey Papers: Reminiscences of Edmund Morey, Esq*, unpublished MS, John Oxley Library, Brisbane

Morgan, J., *The Life and Adventures of William Buckley*, Hobart, 1852, reprinted by Australian National University Press, Canberra, 1980

Morris, E. (ed.), *A Dictionary of Austral English*, Sydney University Press, 1972

Mundy, Lt Col. G., *Our Antipodes*, vol. 2, Richard Bentley, London, 1852

Northern Territory News, 20 February 1980

Ramson, W. (ed.), *The Australian National Dictionary*, Oxford University Press, 1988

Robinson, R., *Black-Feller, White-Feller*, Angus and Robertson, Sydney 1958

Sunday Telegraph (Sydney), 6 March 1972

Swain, D., 'The Bunyip', *The Etruscan Magazine*, March 1965

Sydney Gazette, 20 and 27 March 1823

Sydney Morning Herald, 12 July 1845; 16 June 1847; 9 February 1849; 25 October 1849; 16 January 1853; 24 June 1868; 5 March 1870; 24 August 1872; 25 October 1876; 9 September 1949; 20 April 1973; 31 March 1984

Sydney Sun, 7 October 1977

Troughton, E., *Furred Animals of Australia*, Angus and Robertson, Sydney, 1946

Webster, R., *Currency Lad*, Leisure Magazine Pty Ltd, Avalon Beach, NSW, 1982

Wignell, E., *A Boggle of Bunyips*, Hodder and Stoughton, Sydney, 1981; 'Beware the Bunyip of the Deep', *Sydney Sun*, 29 December 1982

'The Mystery of the Bunyip', *This Australia*, vol. 2, no. 3, Winter, 1983

Wild Life, no. 4, April 1947

Wilkes, G.A., *Dictionary of Australian Colloquialisms*, Sydney University Press, 1978

Yass Post, 28 July 1982

Chapter Seven

A GLIMPSE INTO THE SHADOWS

A GLIMPSE INTO THE SHADOWS

As we said in the introduction, we see ourselves primarily as researchers and chroniclers of the mystery animal saga. In the preceding chapters we have laid out Aboriginal tradition, archival material, modern sighting reports and other data in as coherent a form as we possibly could.

In work of this scale there are bound to be some errors and for those we apologise. We have made every effort, however, to verify those things which are verifiable. In this final chapter, we run through a few ideas and theories, some of which might throw additional light on the subject.

Given the large number of multi-witness, broad daylight, extremely close-range sightings which have occurred over so many decades, often involving police, surveyors, rangers and other trained observers, we believe the majority of Australian mystery animal reports cannot be explained away as hoaxes or as cases of mistaken identity.

So, does that mean the creatures really exist?

Perhaps so. But as suggested in the introduction, some of them seem a lot more likely to exist than others.

The bunyip: Aboriginal bunyip lore, nineteenth century bunyip reports and recent eyewitness accounts are quite tantalising, and it would be nice to think the creatures are still lurking out there somewhere. No matter how hard we look, however, we can find nothing other than folklore and testimonial evidence to support the case for the bunyip's existence.

The yowie: while Aboriginal tradition and European testimony relating to the Yowie is a great deal more detailed and uniform than that concerning the bunyip, concrete evidence of its reality is almost as hard to find.

The Queensland marsupial tiger: because it had, in the prehistoric *Thylacoleo*, a 'tailor-made' ancestor and because it seemed to be a marsupial filling an appropriate ecological niche, we have always felt that the Queensland marsupial 'tiger' probably is or was a real animal.

Aboriginal *yarri* lore seems to lend strong support to the idea, as does the testimony of white bushmen. While concrete evidence is completely lacking we have a strong feeling the creatures really did exist until very recent times – and quite possibly still do.

The Tasmanian tiger: as we have seen, many experts such as Dr Eric Guiler think it very likely thylacines still roam the Tasmanian bush. No doubt all Australians sincerely hope they are right. However, apart from the excellent eyewitness testimony, often from highly qualified observers, there is almost no real evidence to suggest the creatures still survive.

Mainland thylacines: ironically, there may be more evidence to support the existence of *mainland* thylacines than the Tasmanian variety. If the thylacine bone found in the Kimberleys in 1970 is confirmed as being less than 80 years old, and if Athol Douglas is correct in saying that the Mundrabilla thylacine carcase may have been only months old when found in 1966, then the existence of living, breathing thylacines on the Australian mainland is all but proven.

Alien big cats: eyewitness reports of Australian 'big cats' far outnumber all other kinds of strange animal reports.

Crystal-clear tracks which perfectly match those of foreign big cats have been found and cast on many occasions. In addition to this, two or three photographs exist which may be of the animals. Ample evidence exists, too, of massive predation of stock in 'big cat' areas.

Despite the strange fact that no one has ever succeeded in capturing one, dead or alive, the existence of the creatures seems, to many people, to be virtually proven.

To us, however, the Australian big cats represent a conundrum. Looked at one way, the footprint casts, the killings of stock and the fact that so many reliable people have described them so consistently means the creatures surely *must* exist. On the other hand, if even half the reports are correct the country would be practically overrun with huge cats. They are reported *too* often in *too many* different areas. Like all normal Australian animals they should be killed by cars, trains, shooters and poison baits on a regular basis. Looked at in this way, the creatures *can't possibly exist*.

There is a way of explaining this conundrum but it is an explanation which raises almost as many questions as it answers. Some readers will find it infuriating. They will see it as merely a clumsy attempt to solve one mystery by creating another.

This theory suggests that the 'big cats', and perhaps some other Australian mystery animals, are not at all what they seem, but are part of a much deeper mystery. It suggests that the 'cats' though real enough, sometimes, to be seen, to leave tracks and to kill animals, are not entirely 'real' in the usual sense of the word.

According to this theory the 'alien big cats' are very alien indeed: they are some kind of psychic phenomenon.

When we first became aware of the 'paranormal theory' we thought it too bizarre for serious consideration. Gradually, however, we had to admit there were certain aspects of the mystery – such as the extreme fear exhibited by dogs when the 'big cats' were around – which did appear to hint at the paranormal.

Although the 'paranormal theory' – like all the other apparently more rational explanations – contains many flaws, we don't reject it out of hand. We see it as one of several possible explanations for at least some of the phenomena discussed in this book. Consider the following points: between 1885, when they were first mentioned in the newspapers, and about 1940, it seemed that most of Australia's mystery big cats were said to resemble either lions or tigers. For some strange reason, however, since the 1940s the 'lions' and 'tigers' have virtually disappeared and the great majority of modern big cats are said to be either puma-like or panther-like.

Just as strangely, the brown 'pumas' and the 'black panthers' have been reported in close proximity to each other in all major big cat 'hot-spots'. As pointed out earlier, since real pumas are never black and since leopards are never sandy-brown and spotless, the Australian 'big cats' seem to be some animal unknown to science. Their habit of strolling across the road in front of cars is also, as pointed out earlier, not typical of any known big cat, apart from the African lion.

Because their footprints show no similarity to the feet of the marsupial 'lion' of ancient times, because they are rarely reported in trees and because, unlike the *yarri*, they were apparently unknown to the Aborigines, it seems highly unlikely they are descendants of *Thylacoleo*.

The next point lends a whole new dimension to the mystery. The brown/black 'puma/panthers' are not restricted to Australia – they are regularly reported in several countries including, of all places, the United Kingdom!

'Big cats' have been reported from all

over Great Britain but, as in Australia, the sightings often seem to be concentrated in fairly well-defined hot-spots and, as in Australia, these hot-spots have given rise to local nicknames for the beasts. Since the early 1960s hundreds of people have reported big cat encounters in wooded areas of Surrey and the bordering areas of neighbouring Sussex, Hampshire and Berkshire.

The most intense outbreak occurred between 1964 and 1966 when the Godalming Police Department collected 362 reports – some made by their own officers, including a police inspector. Although the 'Surrey puma' was usually said to be brown in colour and to closely resemble an American mountain lion, some witnesses said it looked like – you guessed it – a big black panther.

The same pattern was repeated in 1979–80 during the 'Inverness lioness' flap: an outbreak of big cat sightings and stock deaths which occurred mainly between Inverness and the Black Isle. During the more recent 'Exmoor beast' outbreak – in which Royal Marine snipers were deployed for six weeks in an attempt to shoot the creatures – the colour pattern was reversed: black 'panthers' predominated and brown 'pumas' were in the minority.

The British cryptozoologist Bob Rickard, editor of *Fortean Times*, a journal which chronicles such matters, has remarked: 'The alien big cat phenomenon is one of Britain's biggest contemporary unsolved mysteries.'

While it is just conceivable that large numbers of imported big cats could exist in Australia, with its large flocks of sheep and huge areas of wilderness, he points out that the existence of so many big cats in Britain is an 'ecological impossibility'. Janet and Colin Bord, who have also investigated the British 'big cat' phenomenon for many years, believe the creatures, though 'real' to a point, are not normal animals. The big cats are, they suggest, phantoms which can occasionally put in real, physical appearances.

Big cats do, of course, really exist in North America: pumas once roamed all over the continent. During the European invasion, however, the cats were hunted, trapped and poisoned to the point that they are now – apart from a very small colony in Florida's Everglades – officially considered extinct east of the Rocky Mountains.

Despite this, pumas are regularly reported in almost all of the eastern states of the USA and the eastern provinces of Canada. If all the reported 'eastern pumas' were of the normal sandy brown colour this phenomenon would, perhaps, seem not so very strange. What strikes American and Canadian investigators as odd is this: a considerable proportion of the 'eastern pumas' are said to be *jet-black*.

Stranger still is the fact that the black 'pumas' are often reported in areas which are also notorious for bigfoot/sasquatch sightings. While visiting reputed bigfoot locales in many parts of North America, we noticed very tight groupings of bigfoot and black 'puma' reports in six different hot-spots in the US and Canada. Many North American researchers told us they had noticed the same pattern. The correlation of 'black panther' and bigfoot reports was so pronounced in parts of the Florida Everglades that one State Game

Logo of the New England Bigfoot and Black Panther Research Alliance, Brandon, Vermont, USA.

Officer, 'Doc' Medlin, believed the creatures *travelled together*.

It is simply beyond reason that the bigfoot and the black 'pumas' – two totally different types of large, uncatchable, supposedly rarer-than-rare animals – should crop up time and again in such close proximity to each other in so many different parts of North America. Because of this and for other reasons many American researchers have reluctantly decided that while the creatures are 'real' to a point, they are essentially a paranormal phenomenon.

This theory, crazy as it may sound, gathers strength when we shift our attention back to Australia. On this continent, as in North America, sightings of alien big cats – usually black 'panthers' – are often reported in exactly the same areas which produce a lot of hairy apeman reports.

Some Australian hot-spots where yowies and big cats have been reported practically hand in glove are the Brindabella Mountains (Namadgi), the Kangaroo Valley area, the Araluen Valley and Lamington National Park.

The suggestion that some of Australia's mystery animals are in some way uncanny is not entirely new. Our conversations with Aborigines have convinced us that while they really believe the yowies exist, many of them don't believe they are 'real' in the full, 'western' sense of the word. They are real enough to leave footprints and to kill animals and even men, but they are, at the same time, partly of the spirit world and virtually uncatchable.

Interestingly enough, some sherpas told us the same thing about the yeti and some American Indians said the same about the bigfoot.

At the Miccosukee Indian village, in the heart of Florida's Everglades, a policeman, Don Osceola, told us that his people believed the creatures could 'appear and disappear'.

'They're solid enough when they're here,' he said, 'they make tracks, kill animals – you could probably even photograph them, I don't know – but then they can disappear totally.'

The Miccosukee term for the creatures, he said, was *yati wasagi*. '*Yati* means "man", *wasagi* means "lost", "separated", "different" – something like that. What my people are saying, really, is that these things are from another dimension.'

Confronted with such mind-boggling concepts, some cryptozoologists speculate about 'window areas' linking us to parallel universes or make jokes about a 'cosmic prankster' who must surely be using the disappearing animals to tease and bamboozle we hapless humans.

In the field of cryptozoology, where uncertainty is the name of the game, we feel it would be foolish to dismiss any theory as being too absurd. By the same token it would be equally foolish to hold too firmly to any single explanation. In this strange business the most important thing – next to having a good sense of humour – is to keep an open mind.

Ninety per cent of yowie reports contain nothing which indicates the creatures are anything other than flesh and blood animals, and we are sure that most of the witnesses to whom we have spoken genuinely believe the hairy giants they encountered were living, breathing entities. It can't be denied, however, that a minority of reports do contain some distinctly weird elements.

Readers will have already noticed a number of references to dogs – often large hunting dogs – displaying abject fear in the presence of the apemen. This same detail occurs constantly in North American bigfoot/sasquatch reports. Humans, also, sometimes react strangely. No doubt a close encounter with a shambling, three metre tall apeman would give anyone a bit of a jolt, but during our time in North America we noticed that some bigfoot witnesses appeared to have been a little *too* scared by their experience – or, at least, more frightened than one would expect.

In central Manitoba, for instance, one man who viewed a sasquatch at close range from the safety of a car fainted dead away and stayed unconscious for several hours. The same thing has happened in Australia. Readers will recall that one of Mr Harper's companions reacted in exactly the same way during their 1912 yowie encounter.

Perhaps 10–15 per cent of yowie stories have a weird element in them. We have some fairly strange reports in our files, including one from, of all unlikely places, Wilcannia, which reads almost like a ghost or poltergeist story.

A little less far-out, and more typical of the slightly weird yowie reports to which we are referring, is a story which appeared in the *Australian Town and Country Journal* of November 1876.

According to the *Journal*, two yowie encounters occurred within a single week at a spot on the Lachlan River, near the present site of Wyangala Dam. Significantly, perhaps, the events occurred in a deep, dismal gorge which local Aborigines avoided like the plague.

The first witness was a lad by the name of Porter who, while tending a flock of sheep, saw 'an inhuman, unearthly-looking being', a 'hairy man', climbing down the steep, rocky cliffs towards him. His dogs reacted in the now-familiar way: they '... would not attack, became timid, and crouched around the lad's legs ...' Young Porter was himself 'horror-struck with fear'. He left the sheep to their fate and ran, with his dogs, for home.

The second incident occurred a few days later when a party of young men and women went to the nearby Rocky Bridge waterholes for an evening's fishing. A large fire was made and two hours before sundown most of the party went to set their lines, leaving one young woman to boil the billy and prepare supper:

While engaged, the young woman was suddenly startled by observing a man, as she naturally imagined at first sight, was one of their own party coming towards the fire, but on walking closer, discovered the appearance to be unsightly and inhuman, bearing in every way the shape of a man with a big red face, hands and legs covered over with long, shaggy hair – from fright became almost spell-bound, screamed and screeched – but unable to run. The men, on hearing such unearthly cries, left their fishing lines and ran with all speed towards their comrade. On reaching the fire, the monster of alarm was only distant some fifty yards [4.5 metres]. On their appearing it stood for a minute or two and turned away and made for the rocks.

Two of the men armed themselves with a tomahawk and cudgel and followed this extraordinary phenomenon of nature for a short distance up the rocky and rugged mountain; when suddenly it turned round, and stood viewing the men as they were approaching. They also halted, being about sixty yards [54 metres] from the object of terror, commanding a full view of his whole shape and make, resembling that of a big slovenly man. The head was covered with dark grissly hair, the face with shaggy darkish hair, the back and belly and down the legs covered with hair of a lighter colour. This devil-devil – whatever it may be called – doubled round, and hurriedly made back towards the fire and women again. On seeing him coming, a fearful commotion amongst the females and a kind of supernatural terror amongst the men took place. In the meantime, before reaching the camp, it sidled away towards the inaccessible rocky mount.

The names of two of the men who witnessed and took part in the scene are Porter and Dunn, well-known settlers on the Abercrombie and Lachlan River ... Whether this be the black's veritable Yahoo devil-devil or the white man's hairy man of the wood, time, it is hoped, will now shortly tell.

As already mentioned in 'A century of sightings', a slightly weird element also occurred in two much more recent reports from the Taree area.

When Alwyn Richards and his sister approached the yowie near Killawarra in 1974, they noticed 'a terrible burning smell'. Geoff Nelson, who encountered a yowie near Scott's Creek, Oxley Island in 1977, reported the same strange phenomenon: the yowie left a strong acrid smell at the spot, like burned electrical wiring or scorched bakelite.

Although the 1981 Dunoon incident (see 'A century of sightings') appeared to be quite straightforward at the time, there was a rather strange aftermath to that encounter also.

Recently the mother of the oldest witness told us that her son, who had been the only one of the three boys to actually make eye contact with the yowies, had suffered health problems for months afterwards.

Not only did he suffer recurring nightmares, but his eyes were constantly sore and inflamed. After trying conventional treatments to no avail, the woman asked a visiting faith healer to look at her son. To her great relief the 'laying on of hands' was immediately effective and the boy recovered completely.

As far back as the mid-1930s, R.W. McKay, the pioneer Australian cryptozoologist, noticed the apparent yowie–'big cat' connection and decided both animals were paranormal entities.

'Perhaps these animals come in waves,' he wrote to Rod Estoppey, 'first a wave of lions or tigers, then a wave of panthers and lionesses. I'm sure that before long you will hear of a big gorilla-like animal somewhere in Gippsland.'

As early as 1934 Mr McKay was referring to the 'big cats' and yowies as 'appearing animals' and he talked about them 'arriving' in certain locales as if he meant they were somehow teleported there. He mentioned their apparent invulnerability to bullets and traps. ('Whatever these animals are they seem to have something protecting them ...') and like some modern researchers, he felt the extreme terror exhibited by dogs was a clear indication the mystery animals were 'something supernatural'.

Keith Zeinert, who investigated the 'Emmaville panther' outbreak and many other reports of strange animals during the 1950s and 1960s, also concluded, reluctantly, that there was something quite uncanny about the seemingly uncatchable creatures.

Although the great majority of eyewitnesses do not believe they have seen anything other than a normal flesh and blood animal, some graziers who have had considerable experience with the 'big cats' have independently come to the same conclusion as McKay and Zeinert. One such grazier was Clive Berry of Uralla, NSW, who lost 340 sheep to the 'Kingstown killer'/'Emmaville panther' in 1956–57. After pursuing the infuriatingly elusive creature(s) for a long time he developed the conviction that he was hunting 'something intangible'.

At the risk of thrashing the paranormal theory completely to death, we could point out that many mainland thylacine sightings have also occurred in very close proximity to the scene of 'big cat' and yowie reports.

As most readers will have already noticed, the area where thylacines are most often reported in southwest Western Australia is the very same area allegedly prowled by the 'Cordering cougar'. In western Victoria, the hunting grounds of the thylacines (the 'Ozenkadnook tiger') overlap the supposed range of the 'Grampians puma'. Thylacines, therefore,

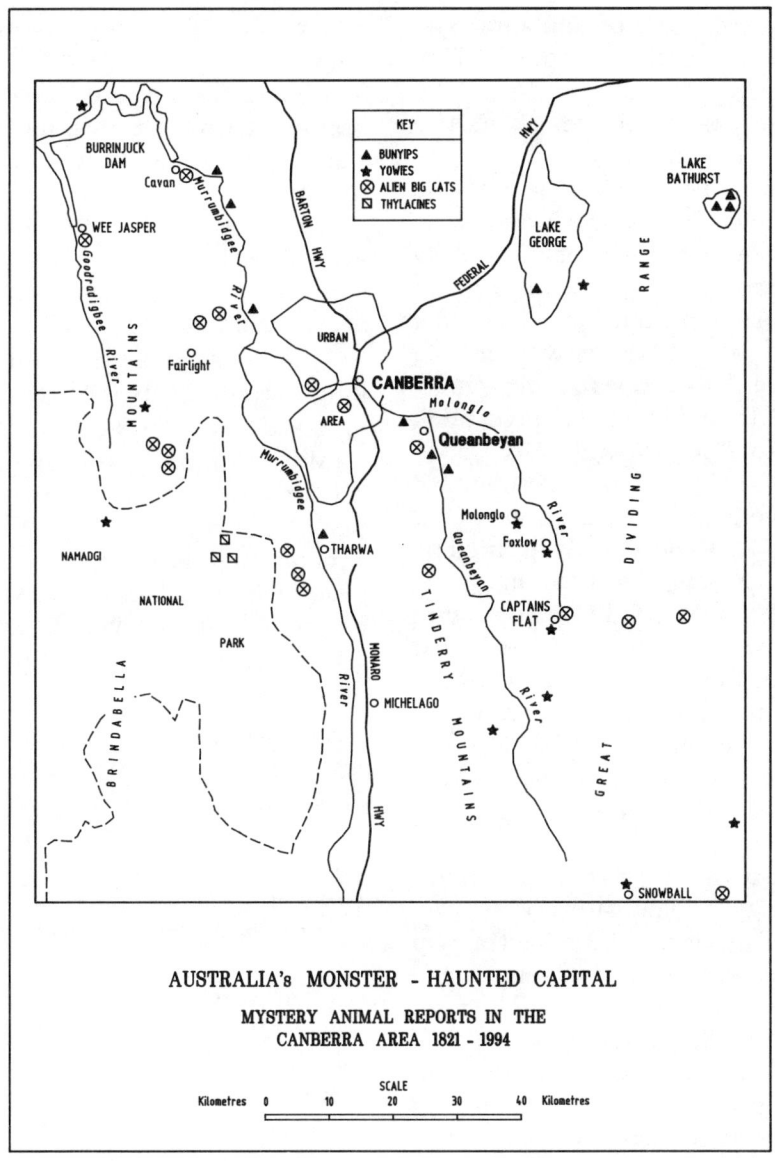

AUSTRALIA's MONSTER - HAUNTED CAPITAL

MYSTERY ANIMAL REPORTS IN THE
CANBERRA AREA 1821 - 1994

have often been reported actually *in* the Grampians mountains, and 'big cats' have been reported west of Ozenkadnook.

One area where yowies, 'big cats' and thylacines have all been reported in close proximity is between Pambula and Bombala in southeast New South Wales. As mentioned earlier, a wave of yowie sightings occurred there in 1912 and sixty-four years later Kos Guines shot a yowie in the same area. During the 1930s and 1940s the area was notorious as the haunt of a 'big cat' known locally as the 'Tantawanglo tiger' and black panthers have been reported there more recently. In 1984, as discussed earlier, John Chevalier and his sister had a close encounter with a thylacine in the same area and in 1990 another thylacine was seen several times near the Pambula cemetery.

Other areas where all three types of creature have been reported close together are the Brindabella Mountains (near the present site of Canberra) and the Dandenongs, virtually on the outskirts of Melbourne.

Because, as we have seen, the thylacine humerus found in the Kimberleys in 1970 *might* be only 80 years old, and because the Mundrabilla carcase *might* have been dead for only one year, it may seem foolish to try to force the mainland tiger into the same paranormal 'bag' as the yowie and big cats. It nevertheless does seem strange, to say the least, that they have been reported so frequently in such close proximity to the other mystery animals.

The several instances where fierce dogs were said to be abjectly terrified by the thylacines also seems to hint at the paranormal. So does Sid Slee's assertion in *The Haunt of the Marsupial Wolf* that 'a prickly feeling' in the hairs on the back of his neck tells him when thylacines are in the area. Perhaps when he used the word 'haunt' in the title of his booklet, Mr Slee was closer to the mark than he realised.

The map of the Canberra region (previous page) illustrates how yowie, alien big cat, thylacine, and indeed bunyip reports frequently occur in remarkably close proximity to each other (although sometimes several decades apart in time). This unlikely clustering of several different types of reports seems to hint strongly that the mystery animals are not strictly a zoological problem.

Much more could be said about the paranormal theory – the several ways, for instance, in which the bunyip legend resembles the lake monster traditions of Britain, Canada and many other places and the way in which strange, floating 'min min' lights and other eerie phenomena are sometimes reported in close proximity to mystery animal sightings – but an examination of every aspect of the theory would soon become tiresome.

Before leaving it altogether, however, it is worth looking at two more pieces of data.

Among the Puyallup Indians of the northwest United States, the bigfoot, or 'forest people' as they call them, are thought to be not entirely of this world. A woman of the tribe told a friend of ours, Ronald Beck, that 'If we really saw them as they really are, our senses cannot accept what we see'.

In view of that belief, a letter we have long thought of as the weirdest in our files begins to make an eerie sort of sense.

Mr F. Homburg's encounter with the 'Grampians puma' began like many others when, one night in 1989, he caught an apparently puma-like animal in his car headlights near Moyston. As he left the car and stepped towards the creature, however, affairs took a distinctly weird turn:

I soon realised that I was not looking at a fox, a puma or any animal I had previous knowledge of ... It looked me full in the eye and its stare seemed to penetrate my very soul. A feeling of some strangeness came over me ... I feared for my life. The hair on the back of my neck rose sharply.

This animal ... is not a puma or a leopard or a tiger. It has a strange effect which tended to leave one in a state of mental confusion. I conclude that this animal is ... something nature never designed ... I issue a warning – if sighted do not leave your car ... it has extraordinary powers.

Strongly resist all temptations to look directly at it otherwise a mysterious trance-like condition will surely occur, which will lead an observer to wrongly believe they have been looking at a puma.

Although it is possible the paranormal theory is correct, we hope it is not. It would be nice to think all the mystery animals discussed in this book are flesh and blood and that they really *are* out there somewhere, running around in the bush.

It goes without saying that if the paranormal theory *is* correct the world is a much stranger place than it appears to be. To express his feelings on the matter R.W. McKay once quoted Shakespeare: 'There are more things in heaven and earth Horatio, than are dreamt of in your philosophy.'

John Keel, an American veteran of 40 years of yeti, bigfoot and alien big cat hunting, said the same thing, but in his own earthy way: 'Let's face it – our little planet is haunted'.

The authors do not necessarily subscribe to the paranormal theory. We have had a lot of fun over the years, bouncing different ideas around and, as fortean researchers, are wary of engraving any one theory in stone.

It may seem unreasonable that after twenty years of mystery animal research we are not prepared to come to any firm conclusions. As we have seen, however, the mystery animals phenomenon is a complex, many faceted puzzle. While the thylacine and Queensland marsupial 'tiger' mysteries appear reasonably straight-forward, we have not as yet found any single theory which can adequately account for every aspect of the yowie, bunyip and alien big cat mysteries.

Actually, much of what we have said about the paranormal theory could just as easily be used to argue that all or most of Australia's mystery animal reports are a result, not of psychic phenomena, but of mass hallucination. If one conveniently ignores the scores of crystal clear casts of unambiguous big cat tracks and also ignores the thousands of sheep which have been devoured in big cat hot-spots, a fairly good case *can* be made for the mystery animals as hallucination.

This series of mass hallucinations would, of course, be in itself a major phenomenon worthy of great attention by the head-shrinking fraternity. These remarkably uniform hallucinations would have to have affected many thousands of Australians of every age, sex, race and background in every part of the country, day and night, in all seasons, from the present day back to antiquity.

One aspect of the mystery animals phenomenon which could be used to support either the paranormal theory or the hallucination theory is what we call the 'overlap' effect. Although the mainland thylacine and alien big cat phenomena are essentially separate, self-contained mysteries, there is, on the edges of each, a 'blurry' area where one mystery seems to overlap into the other.

Admittedly, if two different types of large predator were roaming the same area, it would not be surprising if some confusion occurred in the minds of observers or journalists. In some cases, however, well qualified witnesses are quite adamant that what they saw was not a thylacine or a cat but something which had some of the qualities of *both*.

In September 1982 Tony and Julie Brindley of Donvale, Victoria, reported seeing a strange creature in Kalbarri National Park, Western Australia. Mr Brindley, then 42, is a member of the Marsupial Society and a keen wildlife observer. He said the creature was on the edge of the road '... lying on its belly, eating the whole skull of a kangaroo'.

When they stopped the car it ran into the scrub. It was the size of a German shepherd, 'but it moved cat-like, not dog-like. The intriguing thing is that it had markings like a Tasmanian tiger ... but ... the tail looked like a panther or puma tail. It's either an escaped caged animal from a circus or something, or the pictures I have seen of Tasmanian tigers are wrong.'

Strangely enough, there is also a slight 'overlap' between the seemingly very different yowie and bunyip.

The Melbourne *Herald* reported on 29 October 1849 that:

The veritable Bunyip has been seen at last! We are informed by Mr Edwards, the managing clerk at the office of Messrs Moore and Chambers, that during his late trip, and making the circuit of Phillip Island, he and his party were astonished at observing an animal sitting on a bank in a lake. The animal is described as being from six to seven feet [about 2 metres] long and, in general appearance, half man and half baboon. Five shots were fired, and the last discharge was replied to by a spring into the air, and a contemptuous fling out of the hind legs, and a final disappearance in the placid waters of the lake. A somewhat long neck, feathered like an emu, was the peculiar characteristic of this animal.

In isolation this bizarre report could easily be dismissed as what it sounds like: a tall story. Oddly enough, however, yowie/bunyip 'hybrids' have been reported on a few other occasions.

On 24 August 1872 the *Sydney Morning Herald* reported that 'a party of surveyors, whose account can be relied upon' were boating on Cowal Lake when they saw a bunyip about 150 yards [135 metres] off:

They describe it as having a head something resembling a human being, or, in their own words 'like an old man blackfellow with long, dark-coloured hair'. When seen it appeared to be going in a straight direction, rising out of the water so that they could see its shoulders, and then diving as if in the chase of fish ...

On 18 July 1848 the *Argus* told an odd story of a huge humanoid seen swimming in the Eumeralla one day and a classic long-necked bunyip in the same stretch of water the following day.

Interestingly enough, the yowie and bunyip traditions 'blur' into each other even in the tribal lore of some Aboriginal groups.

In 1973, when the Murray Bridge town council erected a statue of a rather reptilian-looking bunyip as a tourist attraction, the local Aboriginal community reacted angrily. They said the statue was a completely inaccurate representation of the *mooluwonk*, as the bunyip was known locally. According to tribal elders, the local bunyip was an ape-like man; '... he was more than ten feet [three metres] tall, had long black hair, dark red eyes, large teeth and webbed feet and hands'.

Under the direction of eight elders, including 62-year old Mrs P. Lindsay who saw the animal in 1925, an Aboriginal student, Brian Vercoe, produced a sketch of the creature – which could be viewed as a yowie/bunyip composite.

The most recent yowie/bunyip 'hybrid' comes from Tasmania and represents the one and only yowie report we have from that state.

On 2 January 1987 Stella Donahue and Bill Johnstone of Kew, Victoria, were camped on the shores of Lake Dulverton, near Oatlands. At 2 am Ms Donahue looked out of the tent and was shocked to see an enormous creature standing waist deep in the still, moonlit waters, only eighteen metres from shore. It was making a strange noise.

She and Mr Johnstone said it was approximately 2.5 metres tall, with a huge, hairy, ape-like body. It looked silvery in the moonlight.

Suddenly the hulking apeman began wading out of the water, heading straight for the terrified couple, who fled the camp site, leaving all their belongings behind. Several newspapers carried the story and rumours of previous encounters soon emerged. Lake Dulverton is only ten kilometres from Lake Tiberius, once notorious for more conventional ('seal/dog') bunyips, and it drains into the once bunyip-infested Jordan River.

Curiously, while in North America, we heard one report of a sasquatch standing chest-deep in a part of the Klamath River which is also noted for Loch Ness-style water monster reports. Similarly, at water monster-haunted Lake Winnipegosis we were told of a sasquatch wading ashore.

Depending on how deeply one wants to go into it (or, as sceptics might say, depending on one's capacity for fuzzy thinking), the Australian mystery animal phenomenon raises many questions about zoology, mythology, folklore, psychology, parapsychology, life, the universe and everything.

As we said before, however, we see ourselves primarily as collectors of data and as chroniclers of the mystery animals saga. Obviously, we would like to see it proven that the creatures discussed in this book really *are* out there somewhere, lurking in the bush. Certainly some of them, like the thylacine and the Queensland marsupial 'tiger', seem more likely to really exist than others.

At any rate, we hope that the evidence presented in this book is strong enough to convince you, the reader, that the existence of some of these creatures is at least a possibility. We suspect, however, that no matter how good the footprint casts or testimonial evidence may be, you, like ourselves, will never *fully* believe in any of these creatures until you see one yourself.

But who knows? Perhaps next time you're driving down a dark and lonely country road you'll turn a corner and there, right in front of you, *something* – some looming, hairy nightmare – will step

... out of the shadows.

References

Australasian Post, 21 September 1991
Beck, R., letter to T. Healy, 22 July 1981
Bord, J. and C., *Alien Animals*, Granada Publishing, London, 1980
Clark, J. and Coleman, L., *Creatures of the Outer Edge*, Warner Books, New York, 1978
Fishing News (Melbourne), August 1987
Fortean Times, issue nos. 20, 25, 32, 35, 39, 40, 44, 45 and 52

Healy, T., Monster Safari, MS, Canberra, 1982
Herald (Melbourne), 6 January 1987
Keel, J., *Strange Creatures From Time and Space*, Fawcett Publications, Greenwich, Conn., 1970
McAdoo, M., *If Only I'd Listened to Grandpa: Recollections of the Old Days in the Australian Bush*, Lansdowne Press, Sydney, 1980
McKay, R., letter to R. Estoppey, 22 April 1940
Strange Magazine, Special Edition, no. 5

Index

A

Abel, Charles 12
Aboriginal Black Theatre Arts and Cultural Centre 116
Adams, Barbara 37
Addinsall, Irene 83
Agricultural Protection Board (APB) 45, 90, 91, 93
Alcock, Kath 37
Alice Springs 150
Allen, Mary Cecil 177
almasti 153
Anderson, Dawn 36, 37, 49, 53
Anderson, Iris & Archie 52
Anderson, Les 76, 78, 84
Andros Island 152, 156
Anger, Olive & Neville 26
Araluen Valley 115, 186
Ararat 71, 163
Archer, Dr Michael 41, 47-48, 53
Armidale 60
Arnhem Land 23, 52
Arrawatta Creek 63
Arthur River 17
Atherton Tableland 105
Atkinson, Peter 28
Australian Conservation Foundation 13
Australian Museum (Sydney) 25, 172
Australian National University 16, 146
Avoca 81
Avondale 120

B

Badingarra 92
Bald, David 39
Balfour 12
Barrengarra 65, 66
Barwon River 165
Basta, Peter 50
Batemans Bay 116, 126
Bathurst 116
Batty, Wilf 7
Beck, Ronald 190
Bega 115, 116, 126
Bemboka 114
Bendeela 70
Bendigo 81, 82
'Benjamin' 7
Bergin, Jim 63
Berry, Clive 59, 188
'Best of All' lookout 135, 137
Beulah 13, 14
Bicton 51
Bidwell 108
bigfoot ix, 19, 34, 113, 153, 186
Binalong Bay 14
BIOCLIM 16
Birch, George 126
Birthday Bay 12
bittern 174, 176
Blinman, Doris 67
Bloomfield, Karen & Henry 151
Blucher tribe 162
Blue Mountains 116, 143
Blythe, Pat & David 42, 43
Bokal 90
Bolman, Jenny & John 138
Bombala 114, 189
Bord, Janet & Colin 185
Bordertown 31
Bourke 24
Bowen 101, 102
Bowral 126
Braidwood 146, 148, 149
Branch Creek 81
Brazil 152
Briagolong 145
'Briagolong tiger' 71
Bridgetown 42
Brighton, Peter 91
Brimpaen 35, 52, 79
Brindabella Mountains 121, 186, 189
Brindley, Julie & Tony 191
Brisbane 107, 150, 151
Brisbane River 107
Bristow, Rose 30
Brooks, Kevin 132
'Brookton tiger' 91
Brown, Dr Bob 7, 13
brown Jacks 117
Brown Mountain 115
Bruem, Janice 69
Bruem, Peter 70
Brumley, John 82
Brunner, Hans 16, 80
Buchanan, Gary 124, 131, 138
Buckley, William 162, 165-166, 175
Budgong 67
Bull Hill 113
Bunyip Bluegum 177
bunyup 161
Burakin 69, 92
Burbridge, Dr Anthony 46
Burns, Frank 150, 151
Burns, V. 32
Burrell 105
Burrier 174
Burrinjuck Dam 117
Busselton 42, 45, 93
Butler, Harry 65, 91
Byaduk 72

C

Cairns 106
Caldwell, J. 28
Cambewarra Mountain 64, 65, 66
Cameron, Kevin 45, 46-47, 48, 49
Cameron, Shane 45
Cameron, Toni 179
Canberra 25
Cape Liptrap 27
Cape Nelson 39, 40
Cape Patterson 27
Cape York 105, 116
Captain's Flat 148, 152
Cardigan River 12
Cardwell 101, 102
Carmichael, Ian 79
Carmody, Freda & Joe 42-43
Carnarvon 51
Caspian Sea 174
cassowary 101
Casterton 35
cat, feral domestic 15, 86-87
Caucasus mountains 153
Cavendish 78
Challicum bunyip 163, 174
Challicum Station 163
Chapple, Peter 84
Cherrypool 79
Chevalier, John & Sharon

INDEX

26, 189
Chiltern 71
Christensen, Warren 138
Churchill, Elias 7
Clark, Julie 138-139, 145
Clifford, Donald 59
Clyde River 122
Coliban River 167
Collins, Casey 89
Colombia 152
Comaum 38
Conargo 174, 178
Cooktown 26
Cooma 139, 148
Cooma Creek 139
Cooper, Shaun 137
Coorong 37
Corangamite Lake 171
Cordering
   85, 88, 90, 91, 93, 94
'Cordering cougar'
   82, 84-96, 101, 188
Corin Dam 25
cougar, *see puma*
Cowal Lake 192
Cowan's Lane 129
Cradle Mountain 14
Creewah 113
Crewe, Thelma 130
crocodile, saltwater 176
Crown Lands and Survey Department 75
Cryptozoology   viii
Cullendulla 126
Cultivation Creek 78
Cumming, J. 93
Cunningham, J.R. 106-107
Cunningham's Creek 120
Currickbilly Range 122
Cusack's Crossing 168
cuscus 101

D

Dahinden, Rene 150
Daisy Hill 75, 77, 81
Dandenongs 190
Danjera Creek 68
Darkan 88
Darling Downs 162
Dasyurops maculatus
   103, 108
Davis, Professor 115
Day, R.E. 174
De Tournouer, G. 103

Deakin University
   78-79, 82, 83
Dendrolagus lumholtzi 103
Deniehy, D.H. 176
Deniliquin 178
Denison River 12
Dereel 53
Derwent Bridge 15
'Devil-Devil' 164
Dimboola 35
dingo 23, 24, 48
Dix, John 76
Doak, Les 29
Donahue, Stella 192
Donald, Will 123, 124
dongus 161
Donovan, Tom 'Foss' 38, 39
Donvale 191
doolagard 115
doolagarl 115, 118
Douglas, Athol
   46, 48-49, 183
Douglas, G.W. 75
Drew, E. 63
Drew, Mike 88, 92, 93
Drinkwater, Rosemary 65, 66
dsonoqua 155
Dubbo 179
dulagarl 144
Dunn, E.J. 174
Dunoon 137, 138, 188

E

Ealey, E.H.M. 49-50
Earnshaw, Dennis
   84-85, 87, 89, 91, 93
Earnshaw, Ross 84-85, 89
Echo Lakes 173
Echuca 146
Edenhope 32
Edmondson, Robert 39
Egan Peak 115
Emery's Plateau 67
Emmaville 59, 63, 71, 84
'Emmaville panther'
   59-63, 101, 188
emu 162
Eora tribe 116, 119
Estoppey, Rod 71, 145, 188
Eucla 23, 25, 53
Eumeralla 192
Eungella 107

Euroa 173
Evans, Jack 179
'Exmoor beast' 185

F

Farrell, Dick 60, 62
Farthing, Les 74-75
Featherstone, Ern 28
Ferguson, Jim 12
Field, Arthur 60, 62, 63
Fiery Creek 163
Finch, Janet 25
Fish River 142
Flea Creek 121
Fleay, David 8, 11-12, 14
Fleming, Trooper Arthur 7, 14
Fletcher, Atholl 172
Florentine Valley 7
Fort, Charles   x
Foskett, Alan 75-76, 78-79
Foster 27
Frances 37
Frankland River 19

G

Gale, John
   121, 122, 144, 167-168
Gannon, Tom 27, 29
Gap Creek 168
Garry, Ian 29, 32
Gee, Betty 127, 129
Geelong 78, 79, 162
George, Patricia & Leo 137, 140
Geranium Springs 79, 80
Gibraltar Creek 25, 26
Gigantopithecus
   143-144, 145-146
Gilberton 102
Gilette, Don 37, 51
Gillespie, Lyall
   122, 145, 176
Gilroy, Rex 25, 116, 119, 143-144, 152
Glen Innes 60, 63
Glenn, Gordon 50
Gooding, Des 90
Goodwin, Shane 139
gooligah 115
Gootchie 107
Gordon River 12
Gordonvale 106
Gorey, Arron 151

Goroke 33, 35
Goulburn 148, 163, 171, 174
Goulburn River 170
Gould, Charles 173
Grabowsky, I. 12, 14
Grampians mountains 35, 72
'Grampians puma' 71-84, 101, 188
Grantville 30
Gray, George 126
Great Lake 166, 173
Green, Dr Bob 14
Green, John 153, 155
Greenes Creek 12
Gresser, P.J. 116
Griffith, Jeremy 9, 13, 14
Guatemala 152
Guiler, Dr Eric 6, 7, 12, 13, 14, 15, 16, 52, 183
Guines, Kos 113, 115, 116, 149, 154, 155, 189
Gulliver's Travels (Swift) 115
Gundagai 174
Gunn, Ronald 172
Gunnedah 147
Gurdies, The 29, 30
Gwydir River 60

Gympie 109, 144

H

Hade, Ernie 29
'hairy man' 144
Hall, Edward Smith 163-165, 174
Hall, T. 162, 168-169
Halls Gap 72, 83
Hallstrom, Sir Edward 15, 59, 60
Hamilton 31, 71, 83
Hamilton, David 77-78
Hampson, Frank 135
Hancock, Lyn 89
Hansen, Clarrie 64, 67
Harcourt 53
Harper, Charles 122-124, 141, 187
Harris, Alex 46
Harris, Alexander 149, 156
Harris, Samela 36

Hart's Creek 26
Hawkesbury River 174
Haylock, Kath 25
Haylock, Philomena 25
Headlam, Charles 166
Heathcote National Park 151
Heidelberg Man 146
Hemery, N.F. 44
Henderson, Barry 75
Henry, Dr John 79, 80
Herbert River 103
Herbert, Xavier 177
Herbertson, Bob 40
Heyfield 71
Hiatt, Bob 78
Higgins, John 80-81, 82
Himalayas ix, 113
Hinch, Howard 33
Hobart 40
Hobart Museum 173
Hobart Zoo 7, 19
Holland, Garry 45
Holland, Slim 29
Holyman, Max 12
Homburg, F. 190
Homo erectus 118, 146, 147
Hooper, Ken 32, 33
Hope, A.D. 177
Horne, Donald 180
Horne, Rob 20
Horsham 31, 32, 71
Hotspur 83
Houghton, Des 137
Houlding, J.R. 177
Hovell, William 169, 172
How, Gavin 16-17
Hower, Bill 79
Hull, Mr 103, 105, 107
Hume, Hamilton 163
Hunt, Graham 75
Hunter 149
Huon Valley 12
Huonville 12
hyena 28

I

Idriess, Ion 105
Inverloch 27
Inverell 23, 24, 62, 63
'Inverness lioness' 185
Ives, James 161

J

Jackson, Craig 132, 133, 134
jaguar 60
'Jamberoo tiger' 71
James, Estin 89
Java Man 118, 146, 147
Jephcott, Sydney Wheeler 113-115, 141, 142, 145
jimbra 115
Jinden 122
jingera 115
Jingera, the 115
Johnson, Ian 81-82
Johnson, Mark 81-82
Johnston, Gary 73-74
Johnstone, Bill 192
Johnstone, Robert 103
Jordan, Adye 8-9, 15
Jordan River 173, 192
Jowalbinna 26, 27
Joyner, Graham 115-116, 145, 152
junjadee 117
Jurcevic, Franjo 151

K

kajanprati 161
Kalbarri National Park 191
Kalgoorlie 95
Kangaroo Island 86
Kangaroo Valley 64, 71, 81, 84, 186
'Kangaroo Valley panther' 63-71, 82, 86, 87, 144
Katanning 96
katenpai 161
Katoomba 144
Kedron State High School 138
Keel, John 191
Keith Turnbull Research Institute 16, 80
Kelly, Viv 16
Kempsey 126, 143
Kennedy, Gail 147
Kenny, Daniel 151
Kenny, Phyllis 150-151
kianpraty 161
Kilcoy 138, 149
Killawarra 126, 127, 188
Kimberleys 41, 48, 53, 183, 190

INDEX

Kingsley, H. 177
Kingston 31
Kingstown 59
'Kingstown Killer' 59, 188
Kitchener, Des 46
Klamath River 192
Knight, Peter 38
Kookaburra 126
'Koonjewarre' 132, 137
Kow Swamp 146, 147
Kow Swamp people 146, 147
Krambach 139
Kuranda 104
Kurruk 162
Kwakiutl Indians 155

L

La Trobe, Governor 171-172
Lachlan 16
Lachlan River 169, 187
Lah-Arum 72
Lake Alexandrina 176
Lake Baikal 174
Lake Bathurst 163, 164, 174
Lake Bonney 39
Lake Carey 94
Lake Dulverton 192
Lake George 164, 174
Lake King William 15
Lake Pambula 26
Lake Taupo 144
Lake Tiberius 173, 192
Lamington National Park 131, 186
Lang Lang 29, 30, 32
Launceston 9, 11, 14
Lauriston Reservoir 178
Lavis, Bill 42
Lawrence, Alan 94-96
Le Souef 105
Lea-Scarlett, Errol 145
Leader, Charlie 60-62
Leigh, C.R. 63
Leongatha 27, 31
Leongatha Star 31
leopard 60, 64-65
Lewis, Wallace E. 60
Lightburn, Lee 32
Lilley, Maurice 92
Lilydale 71
Lindsay, Norman 177

Lindsay, P. 192
Lismore 124, 137, 179
Little Laura River 26
Little Murray River 178
Loch Ness ix, 18, 19, 34
Lockyear, J.R. 177
Longbottom, Tom 42, 44
Lonsdale 172
Lord, Clive 173
Lowcock, Bob 78
Lowry, Jacoba & David 48
Lucindale 35, 36, 37, 39
Lumholtz, Carl 103-104

M

Mace, Bernie 83
Mackay 107
Mackay River 103
Macleay, W.S. 172
Macquarie Harbour 4
Macquarie Island 86
Macquarie River 179
Maffra 71
Maher, Bert 15-16
Main, J.P. 163
Majorca 81
Malaysia 152
Malley, James 13, 14
Malmsbury 167
Malmsbury Reservoir 178
Manifold, John 177
Manjimup 42
Manning River 127
Marion, Adam 139
Marion, Peter 139
Marlow, Irene & John 72-73
Maroonah Station 94
Marra, Des 35
Marrin, Arthur 148-149, 150, 152
Martin, Geoff 89
Martin, Graham 50
Martin, Rilla 33, 34, 37, 40, 49, 52
'Marulan tiger' 63
Mary River 107
Maryborough (Qld) 108
Maryborough (Vic) 71, 77, 81, 82, 83
Maughan, June 44
Mawbanna 7
McDonald, Alexander Joseph 122
McDonald, Eric 122

McDonald, John 122
McKay, R.W. 71, 145, 188, 191
McMahon, Harold 64
McPherson Range 130
McWilliams, Johnnie 122, 141
Medlin, 'Doc' 186
Meehan, James 163
Melbourne Museum 79
Melbourne Zoo 78, 79, 173
Merrilees, Duncan 51
Meryla Valley 64
Meston, Archibald 162-163
Mibus, Graham 40
Middleton, John 75
Midgeon Lagoon 166
Milbury Creek 142
Millicent 37
Mitchell, Bob 124
Mitchell, Jack 179
mochel-mochel 161, 168
Moir, George 92-93
Mole Creek 14, 16
Mole Creek Wildlife Park 17
Monash University 50
Monk Farm 113
mono grande 153
moolgewanke 161
moomega 115
Mooney, Nick 14, 16, 18, 19
Moree 59
Moreton National Park 64
Morgan, John 165
Morris, Alec 94
Morris, Barry 94, 96
Morris, Desmond 11
Morris, John 81-82
Morrison, Bill 10
Morwell 71
Moss Vale 175
Moulamein River 174
Mount Pritchard 23
Moyston 78
Mt Arapiles 35
Mt Barrow 11
Mt Bealiba 75
Mt Bepcha 77, 78, 80
Mt Gambier 82, 83, 146
Mt Naman 25
Mt Remarkable 170
Mt Salt 38

Mt Scott 16
Mt Stanley 107
Mt William National Park 11
Mt York 143, 144
Mulgrave River 106
Mullins, Pat 139
Mulwaree River 174
Mundrabilla 48, 49, 53, 183, 190
Mundrabilla Station 23, 49
Munna Creek 103
Munster 94
Murray cod 176
Murray River 163, 170, 174
Murrell, Dora & Andrew 40
Murrumbidgee 117, 166, 168, 169, 172, 173, 174, 176
Myalup 45

N

Naarding, Hans 17-18, 32
Namadgi National Park 25
Nambung 92
Nannup 42, 44, 45
'Nannup tiger' 42
Napier, John 144
Naracoorte 35, 36, 37
Narrandera 166
National Museum (Vic) 33
Natureland Zoo 134
Neale, Robyn 66, 69
Nelson, Geoff 128-129, 145, 188
Nepal 152, 156
Nepean 174
Nerang 137
Neuman, Bob 89, 90, 91, 93
New Guinea 23, 146, 153
New Zealand 153
Ngunnawal 117
nimbunj 117
Nix, Dr Henry 16
Noakes, Raymond 64-67
Noble, Don 93
Nollamara 94
noocoonah 115
North America 152, 155
North Balwyn 29
Nowra 126
Nullarbor Plain 23, 24

O

Oatlands 192
O'Brien, Nancy 106
O'Chee, Bill 131, 132, 133, 134, 136, 137
Offer, Ian 51, 93, 96
Opit, Gary 79, 84
Orang Asli 156
orang mawa 152, 156
orang pendek 153
O'Reilly, David 89, 96
Osborne, George 120, 140, 141, 150
Osceola, Don 186
Owen, Professor Richard 57, 172
Oxley 169
Oxley Island 127, 129, 188
Ozenkadnook 32, 33, 35, 36, 39, 50
'Ozenkadnook tiger' 31-35, 36, 37, 50, 51, 188

P

Packer's Swamp 113, 115, 144
Palen Creek 124, 137
Pambula 26, 113, 189
Pamir mountains 153
Paramanov, S.J. 24-25
Parker, Dorothy 37
Parker's Gap 149
Pascoe, J.B. 39
Passfield, A. 91
Patyah 33, 35
Pearce, H. 15
Perth 40, 42, 92
Perth Zoo 90
Peter's Hill 78
Phillip Island 192
Pilbara 23
Pinker, Bert 89
Piper's Creek 71
Pitt, Jim 73
platypus 162, 174
Plunkett, Janeice (Kay) 105-110
Pocock, John 37
Pontague, Fred 94-95
Port Arthur 4
Port Davey 17
Port Hacking 116
Port MacDonnell 39
Port Phillip 116

Portland 40
Povah, Frank 118
Pretty Gully 59
Promontorys National Park 29
puma 68-69
Putland, Jim 87-88, 92, 93
Pyrenees Range 81

Q

Queanbeyan 121, 167
Queanbeyan River 168
Queen Victoria Museum 14
quinkin 115, 116, 118

R

Radford, John 82
Ramage, Jim 23-24
Rare Fauna Research 26, 31, 49, 79, 84
Read, Jillian 73-74
Reitsma, Sjoerd 31
Rendlesham 37
Rentsch, Les 72
Rethus, Wendy & Bob 35
Richards, Alwyn 126-127, 129, 139, 145, 188
Rickard, Bob 185
Ringarooma River 11
Robertson, Keith 50
Robinson, Dr Tony 38
Robinson, Roland 118, 145
Rockingham Bay 102
Rockingham Range 103
Rocklands Reservoir 77, 78
Rocky Bridge 187
Rocky River 170
Rodgers, D.G. & D.E. 109
Rogers, Peter 134
Roughsey, Dick 118
Royal Society of Tasmania 173

S

Saligari, Dick 82, 83
Salmon River 18
Sandy Cape 10, 12
Sandy Creek 138
Sarcophilus harrisi 9
sasquatch 19, 113, 152, 153-155, 186
Schmedje, T.J. 28
Scot, I.W. 163
Scott, W.T. 102

INDEX

Scott's Creek 128, 129, 188
Scougall, P.B. 103
seal 174-175
seal, elephant 174
seal, leopard 174
Sega, Roman 68
Seglen, Dr Per 92
Sharland, Michael 8, 14
Sharp, Albert 29, 31
Sharp, George 105, 110
Sheridan, Brinsley 102
shiru 152
Shoalhaven River 174
Shuker, Karl 110
Simmons, John 14
Simon, Peter 25
Simpson desert 86
sisemite 152
Sissens, David 66, 67
Slater, George 28
Slee, Sid 43-44, 45, 52, 190
Smith, Dr Steven 9, 11, 12, 15
Smith, Howard 134
Smith, Malcolm 107, 150-152
Smith, Ron 67
Smith, Wally 77
Smyth, Brough 161-162, 167
Snowball 122
Solano, Tony 138
South Australian Museum 36
South Lismore 124
Southport School 131
Southwell, Captain Sam 168
Springbrook 131, 136, 137, 152
St Arnaud 71, 81, 84
St Mary's Pass 15
Staggy Creek 23, 62
Staub, R. 29
Stocqueler 170-171
Stratford 106
Sumatra 146, 153
Summerell, George 114-115, 142
Sumner, Charlie 86-87
Sumner, George 96
'Surrey puma' 185
Sutton Forest 121

Swan Creek 168
Swan Hill 146, 178
Swift, Jonathan 115
Swimcart Beach 14

T

Talbot, Jack 17
Tallong 64
'Tallong tiger' 63, 71
Tamworth 59
Tangey, Chris 15
'Tanjil Terror' 71
Tantanoola 38, 39
'Tantanoola tiger' 31, 38-39, 40
Tantau, Ian 53
'Tantawanglo tiger' 189
Taplin, Rev. George 176
Taradale 71
Taree 126, 127, 139, 145
Taronga Park Zoo 15, 146
Tasmanian devil 9, 13, 15, 53
Tasmanian Fauna Board 15
Tasmanian Museum and Art Gallery 7
Tasmanian Wildlife Park 14
Taylor, Trevor 36
Tenterfield 59
Terry, Ned 13
Thompson, Laurie 10-11
thoolagal 115
Thorne, Dr Alan 146, 147
Thorpe, B. 12
Thorpe, Charlie 29
Thylacine Hole 23, 40, 49
Thylacoleo ix, 57, 59-60, 96, 102, 107, 110, 183, 184
Tiaro 103
Tidbinbilla 26
Tiger Hotel 38, 39
tiger quoll 108
tjangara 115
Togari 17
Tooborac 53
toor-roo-dun 161
Top Bore 150
Trafalgar 71
Traralgon 71
tree kangaroo 101
Trezise, Percy 26-27, 118
Triffin, Mick 12
Troughton, Ellis 105, 174
Trowutta 13

Tucker, Cyril 32, 50
Tucker, Stewart 32
tumbata 161
tunataboh 161
John Turnbull 178
Turramulli 116, 118
Tutt, Charles 107
Tutt, Nigel 107
Tweed Heads Pet Porpoise Pool 179

U

ucumar 152
Uhr, Reginald 103, 110
Uralla 59, 188

V

Van Diemen's Land 4
Van Diemen's Land Company 7
Vercoe, Brian 192
Vermin and Noxious Weeds Destruction Board 75
Victoria Point 81
Victorian Fauna Protection Council 29
Victory, Jack 37

W

waaki 117
Wagga Wagga 166
Waller, Bruce 68
Waller, Julie 68
Wallis, Rob 72, 78
Walsh's Pyramid 106
Walter, Bryan 87
Wanaaring 24
Wannan, Bill 27
Ward, Ian 50
'Warialda cougar' 63
Warman, Alf 39
Warragamba Dam 175
Warrego River 24
Warren 179
Warrumbungle Mountains 25
Watts, David 13, 14-15
Webb, Joseph 121
Webb, Peter 16
Webb Range 121
Webb, William 121
Wedderburn 76, 84
Weldborough 11
Wellesley Road Wildlife

199

Park 93
Wellington 179
Wentworth Falls 137
Wentworth, W.C. 176
West Pingelly 44, 52
West, Sharon 93
Western Australian Museum 46, 48, 51
Western Australian Wildlife Research Centre 46
Whayman, D. 52
Wheeler, George 86
Whyte River 16
Widgee Mountain 124
Wilcannia 187
Willey, Dennis 76-77
Williams, Harry 117
Wilsons Promontory 27
Wimmera 32
winambuu 117
Wingecarribee Swamp 175
Woess, Geoff 77
Wollondilly River 165, 174-175
Wollongong 68
Wongan Hills 93
Wonthaggi 27, 28, 32
'Wonthaggi monster' 27-31
Woodenbong 130, 137, 152
Woolley, A. 12
Woolmai 30
Woolnorth 12, 14
World Wildlife Fund 13
Wothowurong 162
Wright, Peter 14
Wring, Pat 141
Wyangala Dam 187

Y

yahoo 115, 121, 144, 147, 150, 152, 156
Yahoo Peak 115
Yahoo Valley 115
Yalanji people 116, 118
Yalwal 64
Yambah Station 150
yaroma 115
yarri 103, 183, 184
Yass River 117
yati wasagi 186
yay-ho 152, 156
'Yednia tiger' 107
yeren 153
yeti ix, 113, 152
Yoongarillup 43, 46
Younghusband Peninsula 37
yourie 116
yowrie 116
Yowrie River 116
yowroo 116
yuuri 118

Z

Zeinert, Keith 50, 188